Innovations in Lifelong Learning

This book opens up ways to engage critically with what counts as innovatory practice in lifelong learning today, locating its discussion of innovations in lifelong learning within an international and comparative framework.

Innovations in Lifelong Learning engages first-hand with issues and concerns from around the globe, offering an international perspective on current trends through its range of contributions from across the UK, Australia, New Zealand and the US. The broad focus allows for diverse information on the nature of these changes to come together under an assortment of empirical, theoretical and methodological approaches.

The book takes three key elements of lifelong learning:

- learning communities;
- participation and non-participation; and
- work-based learning and learning through work.

It links these with themes on diversity, social justice and economic and global development so as to negotiate and re-negotiate the constant importance of innovation with employers, learners and educational institutions.

All those working in the broad arena of lifelong learning will benefit from this comprehensive examination of current debates in the field, including policy-makers, researchers, teachers, lecturers, educational managers and employers engaged with work-based learning.

Sue Jackson is a Professor of Lifelong Learning and Gender and Director of Birkbeck Institute for Lifelong Learning at Birkbeck, University of London, UK.

Innovations in Lifelong Learning

Critical perspectives on diversity, participation and vocational learning

Edited by
Sue Jackson

LONDON AND NEW YORK

First edition published 2011
by Routledge
2 Park Square, Milton Park, Abingdon, Oxon, OX14 4RN

Simultaneously published in the USA and Canada
by Routledge
711 Third Avenue, New York, NY 10017

Routledge is an imprint of the Taylor & Francis Group, an informa business

Typeset in Galliard & Gil Sans
by Swales & Willis Ltd, Exeter, Devon

British Library Cataloguing in Publication Data
A catalogue record for this book is available from the British Library

Library of Congress Cataloging-in-Publication Data
A catalog record has been requested for this book

ISBN13: 978–0–415–54878–6 (hbk)
ISBN13: 978–0–415–54879–3 (pbk)
ISBN13: 978–0–203–83395–7 (ebk)

Contents

Acknowledgements

This book derived from a conference on *Innovations in Lifelong Learning* at Birkbeck Institute for Lifelong Learning, Birkbeck, University of London, although it contains contributions from several authors who were not at the conference, as well as from others who were. However, my thinking about the book, its structure and its key themes began in preparation for that conference, developed during the conference itself, and evolved in the work that took place in preparing this volume. I am, then, very grateful to all those who contributed to the original conference – whether as presenters or as delegates, as academic or as administrative colleagues – who helped me in my early work on this book. My deep thanks too, of course, to all the contributors to this book, who have participated in critically exploring innovative practices in lifelong learning from a range of international perspectives. It has been a pleasure to work with them in the production of this book. I am very grateful to Routledge, and especially to Philip Mudd, for making this book possible, and for the continued support from conception to completion. Finally, and as always, my thanks and love to my family, who support me unwaveringly in all I do.

Contributors

Mary V. Alfred is Associate Professor of Adult Education and Associate Dean for Faculty Affairs in the College of Education and Human Development at Texas A&M University. Her research interests include learning and development among women of the African Diaspora, sociocultural contexts of migration, welfare reform and economic disparities among low-income adults and issues of equity and social justice in higher education and in the workplace. Her most recent book (edited with Carmela Nanton) is *Social Capital and Women's Support Systems: Networking, Learning, and Surviving* (2009). Other recent work has appeared in *Adult Education Quarterly*, *International Journal of Training and Development* and *International Journal of Lifelong Education*.

Mejai B. M. Avoseh is currently an Associate Professor of Adult and Higher Education at the University of South Dakota. He received his PhD in Adult Education and an MA in Philosophy from the University of Ibadan. He also holds an MSc in Educational Leadership from the College of Saint Rose and K-12 teaching and administrative licences. He was a founding faculty member and Senior Lecturer in the Department of Adult and Non-Formal Education at the University of Namibia. His research interests include indigenous and comparative education, critical pedagogy, culture, empowerment and social justice issues in adult and higher education.

Lisa M. Baumgartner is an associate professor of Adult Education at Northern Illinois University, DeKalb, IL. In 2007, she received the Cyril O. Houle Award for Outstanding Literature in Adult Education for her book *Learning in Adulthood: A Comprehensive Guide* (third edition) co-authored with Sharan B. Merriam and Rosemary S. Caffarella. Baumgartner was awarded the Cyril O. Houle Scholars Research Grant for Emerging Scholars in Adult Education and completed a study on Septima Clark's lifelong contributions to social justice adult education. Lisa Baumgartner's research and writing focus on adult learning and development, chronic illness, and White privilege in adult education.

Jan Etienne teaches Sociology at Birkbeck and is a graduate of the University of Bristol. She began her career as a Women's Officer for the London Borough of Hackney before becoming Head of Equalities in Hammersmith and Fulham. She has conducted research for the Centre for Excellence; Learning from Experience Trust; Institute for Policy Studies in Education and for Birkbeck's Institute for Lifelong Learning where she explored lifelong learning and the Women's Institute. She is co-author of 'Black Managers in FE' – a study exploring the career challenges of the minority ethnic manager, for which she received the 2006 BELMAS prize.

Fiona Frank is Senior Development Officer at Lancaster University Department of Continuing Education. She worked for many years in research, teaching and development in workplace language, literacy and numeracy, and more recently has been involved in developing partnerships between universities and older adults. She is completing a part time PhD at the University of Strathclyde Centre for Oral History, looking at transmission of Jewish culture through five generations of one extended Scottish Jewish family.

Barry Golding is an Associate Professer and Vocational, Adult and Community Education Researcher in the School of Education at University of Ballarat, Victoria, Australia. Barry has extensive teaching and research experience in school, vocational education and training, adult and community education and university sectors. His Australian adult learning research in the past 15 years has focused mainly on community and adult education. A recent emphasis in Barry's research has been men's learning, particularly the learning experienced beyond work in community contexts. He is facilitating a major, ongoing international study of men's learning and wellbeing through community participation.

Patricia A. Gouthro is Professor in the Graduate Studies in Lifelong Learning program in the Faculty of Education at Mount Saint Vincent University in Halifax, Nova Scotia, Canada. Her research interests include critical and feminist theory, citizenship, fiction writing, cross-cultural research, women's learning experiences and learning in the home. She has been published in the *International Journal of Lifelong Education*, *Canadian Journal for the Study of Adult Education*, *Convergence*, *Studies in Continuing Education*, *Teaching in Higher Education* and *Journal of Education Thought*. Patricia is currently conducting research on connections between lifelong learning, citizenship, and fiction writing.

Shibao Guo is an Associate Professor in the Faculty of Education, University of Calgary. He is an affiliated researcher with the Prairie Metropolis Centre of Excellence for Research on Immigration, Integration, and Diversity. His research interests include citizenship and immigration, Chinese immigrants, social justice and equity in education, adult education and community development, lifelong education, comparative and international education. Shibao's recent works include publications in the *Journal of International Migration and Integration*, *International Journal of Lifelong Education*, *Canadian Journal for the Study of Adult Education* and *Frontiers of Education in China*. Currently he is the Co-President of the Canadian Association for the Study of Adult Education.

Yvonne Hillier is Professor of Education in the Education Research Centre, University of Brighton. She is currently Chair of the Society for Research in Higher Education (SRHE) and a founder member of the Learning and Skills Research Network. She has researched issues of teaching and learning in post-compulsory education including basic skills practice, national vocational qualifications, initial teacher training, work-based learning including foundation degrees and educational regeneration. She undertook an ESRC funded project with Professor Mary Hamilton on the history of basic skills policy. She has published widely, including on FE policy, adult basic skills and adult literacy, numeracy and language.

Sue Jackson is Professor of Lifelong Learning and Gender and Pro-Vice-Master for Learning and Teaching at Birkbeck University of London. Although she loves the role, in which innovations in lifelong learning are central, she continues to find the title 'Pro-Vice-Master' at odds with her feminist identity! Sue is Director of Birkbeck Institute for Lifelong Learning, from where this book originated. Sue's research focuses on the intersections of multiple learner identities, including gender, age and social class. Her recent books include *Reconceptualising Lifelong Learning: Feminist Perspectives* (with Penny Burke) and *Gendered Choices: Learning, Work, Identities in Lifelong Learning* (forthcoming, with Irene Malcolm and Kate Thomas).

Zenobia Jamal has a special interest in issues of difference, diversity and anti-racism in learning environments and workplaces. She has a Master's degree in Education, with a specialisation in Adult Education from the University of Alberta. Zenobia has worked in a variety of settings to increase awareness of the many kinds of difference encountered in educational settings and workplaces, and to provide effective strategies to respond to the ongoing challenge of creating equitable learning and working opportunities. Zenobia teaches as a sessional instructor at the University of Alberta and has authored a number of publications in her areas of expertise.

Juanita Johnson-Bailey is a faculty member at the University of Georgia, where she holds the title Josiah Meigs Distinguished Teaching Professorship. She teaches in the Program in Adult Education and is Director of the Institute for Women's Studies. Her book, *Sistahs in College: Making a Way Out of No Way*, received the 2001 Phillip E. Frandson Award for Literature in Continuing Higher Education. Juanita has made significant contributions to the literature in adult education and women's studies through her extensive list of publications on issues relating to race and gender in educational and workplace settings.

Jacqueline McManus is Senior Lecturer in the School of Education at the University of New South Wales and Director of the Masters of Philosophy (Higher Education) Program. Her area of research predominantly focuses on the development of an holistic approach to learning, particularly in relation to learning for and at work. This research has led to a better understanding of how the development of capacity in workers supports and enhances career progression. Jacqui's professional experience as a Chartered Accountant and tax consultant prior to entering academia contributes to her research and ability to apply it effectively.

Keith Percy is Emeritus Professor at Lancaster University, where he was Head of the Department of Continuing Education for thirty years until his retirement in 2009, and Director of the School of Lifelong Learning and Widening Participation from 2005–9. Keith's research interests include learning in later life, widening participation in higher education and lifelong learning, self-directed learning among adults, work-based learning, innovations in on-line learning, and comparisons between provision of and participation in lifelong learning in the UK and overseas. In particular, he has published widely on education for older adults. Keith is Editor of the *International Journal of Education and Ageing*.

Gemma Piercy teaches in the Labour Studies and Social Policy programmes at the University of Waikato. She is also a researcher with the Centre for Labour and Trade Union Studies. In 1999 Gemma completed her Master's thesis comparing reforms to Apprenticeship in New Zealand and Australia from 1987 to 1992. From 2001 she continued this research and traced the broader changes to tertiary education as well as the more specific changes to Apprenticeship in New Zealand during the third way Labour-led Governments from 1999 to 2008. She is currently working on her PhD examining work-based and workplace learning in cafés.

Jon Talbot works with the Centre for Work Related Studies at the University of Chester, one of the largest centres for work-based learning in Europe. He is currently lead tutor for the Professional Doctorate programme but contributes to a variety of learning pathways on the University's work-based learning programme. Jon has taught in Higher Education for a number of years but has a professional background in town planning and is still in practice. His research interests are in the nature of and delivery of innovative learning as well as the institutional challenges they present to established universities.

Introduction

Innovations in lifelong learning: politics, power and pedagogic practices[1]

Sue Jackson

It is the best of times, it is the worst of times; it is the age of wisdom, it is the age of foolishness; it is the epoch of belief, it is the epoch of incredulity; it is the season of light, it is the season of darkness, it is the spring of hope; we have everything before us, we have nothing before us; we are all going directly to Heaven, we are all going the other way.[2] It is the age of lifelong learning.

As you may have guessed from those opening words, I am in a mood for storytelling. So are you sitting comfortably? Then I'll begin . . .

Once upon a time a girl-child was born to a working-class, Jewish family living in the East End of London. There was much rejoicing and celebrating at the birth of this, the first child of the family. The child was loved, grew up and went to school, doing the things that girl children do. Through her family and through her friends, through her school and through her community, through her reading and through her playing, she learned what was expected of girls and how to become a young lady. She learned that her place in the home, at work and in the community would be different from that of boys. She left school at fifteen to do a secretarial course at a local college, and went on to become practised at being an office wife before she became a real one. And of course she fell in love with a nice Jewish boy. Reader, she married him,[3] and had two children of her own.

It should have been enough for a happily ever after. But the girl became a woman who was sometimes restless, dissatisfied, bored and frustrated, despite loving her family dearly. She began studying at her local college, enrolled with the Open University and completed her degree; did voluntary work; became a batmitzvah; did an MA, teacher training, a PhD; started lecturing; read, wrote, built a career. She learned that she could do all of these things if she did them part-time, whilst continuing to be a full-time wife, mother, daughter.

In addition to her formal and continuing education, she learned in many ways: whilst bringing up children, learning with them and from them (and sometimes in spite of them). She learned through women's groups and with her friends, and later through her grandchildren. Now she learns as a professor of lifelong learning and gender and pro-vice-Master[4] for learning and teaching at Birkbeck University of London. A textbook case to illustrate the benefits of lifelong learning? Perhaps I am.

But despite my 'success', my story is embedded within structures and organisations that are gendered, racialised and classed. My 'lifelong' engagement with learning took the path it did both because of and in spite of the fact that I was a young mother of two from a working-class background. I count my meaningful educational experiences as beginning with that first step into college when I was 26, soon after the birth of my first child. Had I been someone else in a different place and maybe a different time, I would have been starting my career as an academic at that point, not just beginning as a student. However, I also learned that although I had thought education was not for the likes of me, I was, and continue to be, a lifelong learner, although, as many of the contributors to this book show, that in itself is a problematic term.

This book is concerned with lifelong learning, and with its innovations and innovative practices, although it views 'innovation' critically. In this introductory chapter, I shall begin by exploring some of the meanings and politics of lifelong learning, arguing that lifelong learning in its current form is far from innovative, increasingly likely to enhance exclusion rather than inclusion. Secondly I shall consider power, including where it is located, with whom, and why; but also how power might be resisted or reclaimed. Finally I shall outline what I see as the pedagogic challenges, arguing that real innovations in lifelong learning demand a return to some of the radicalism of earlier incarnations of lifelong learning, continuing education, and social action. Embedded within this discussion are issues central to the book's three Parts on learning communities, participation (and 'non-participation'), and vocational learning.

Politics

Lifelong learning is a highly fluid and contestable concept with multiple overlapping and differing meanings. Meaning is elusive and, despite the myriad of definitions available, the phrase escapes definition. Definitions are fluid and imprecise, loosely used with vague but hegemonic understandings (Burke and Jackson, 2007).

Nevertheless, lifelong learning has been high on the political agenda in much of the developed world, constructed as an unconditional good – for individuals, nation states and globally. It is described as though it is apolitical, ahistorical and uncontestable, with little understanding of the ways in which learning is differently experienced by different groups and individuals constructed through gendered and other inequalities; and, as the contributors to this book demonstrate, little account given of a wide range of different histories and experiences. Nor is account taken of the personal and political learning that may challenge the structures and politics of neighbourhoods and nations.

In a world that, at the time of writing, is in the depth of a global recession, lifelong learning – increasingly constructed within a skills agenda – has been seen as an answer to unemployment, political stability, and social inclusion. Individuals are expected to develop their own lifelong learning to get themselves out of unemployment, fill employment gaps, and help move countries out of recession. Across the developed world lifelong learning is increasingly taken as synonymous with formal post-compulsory and, more and more, vocational learning. The discourses and policies of lifelong learning have become ever more firmly linked to economic participation through the employment market and the development of skills and training, with a policy focus on skills development for the workplace, and greater participation from employers in determining learning opportunities and directions. The development of human capital becomes the responsibility of individuals, on whom it is incumbent to find, recognise and develop the learning opportunities that will enable them to take their place in a working society, although the types of opportunities are selective and hierarchical. There is a call for apparently economically valuable skills to be delivered through a demand-led approach, facilitated by a new culture of learning, and an appetite for improved skills amongst individuals and employers.

Yet in a gendered, classed and racialised labour market, the acquisition of economically valuable skills is no guarantee of an economically valuable job. In addition, 'economically valuable skills' are narrowly defined. It seems to mean the development of specific skills for specific markets, without recognition of the value of different types of skills for the economy, including the key transferable skills that are developed through lifelong learning. Neither is there an understanding that the economy is sustained by much of the caring and voluntary work that takes place outside the labour market. The workplace, education, training, and interpretations of 'skills' are all highly gendered, as well as being determined by social class and socio-economic backgrounds.

As the contributors to this book show, there are increasing demands that lifelong learning should enable the development, up-skilling and retention of the current workforce, leading to more flexible employees. Clearly flexibility will be of some benefit to the workforce, giving greater opportunities for employment in changing markets. But to stay continually flexible also means having to accept short-term contracts and less job security, as well as having to be prepared to continually up-skill – meaning that existing skills are eternally in deficit. Yet for many of us, the employment available to us is determined by factors that have nothing to do with acquisition of 'skills', including our gender, 'race', socio-economic background and age (Hughes et al., 2006). And for many people in employment, the work they do is poorly paid, unrewarding and exploitative. Working-class men are still disproportionately affected by long-term unemployment. Although not so affected by unemployment, women still earn less than men, are more likely to be in part-time non-secure and hourly paid work, are less likely to have work-related pensions or other benefits and are less likely to reach senior management positions.

Furthermore, the economy is conceptualised purely with regard to paid work. A concentration on employment and training excludes those whose contribution to the labour market is unrecognised or whose skills remain devalued, including homeworkers and carers, volunteer workers, unemployed people or older people. The excluded are those who are defined as not economically active.

As this book shows, what is emerging is a gendered and class-based skills-driven agenda for lifelong learning, which is more about learning to take our places as neo-liberal subjects than about radicalisation as empowered members of local, national and global communities. There is little or no recognition of alternative ways of developing and enhancing learning opportunities, including part-time and flexible study, and informal as well as formal learning. Without more innovative practices, the most disadvantaged continue to be excluded from a range of learning opportunities.

Power

In considering ways in which innovations in lifelong learning become including in dominant discourses and policies, and others are dismissed out of hand, I move on to consider power and power relations. Discussions of power occur in many places throughout this book. For example, the chapters in Part I on learning communities are concerned with the complexities of social relations and cultural diversities embedded within learning communities; Part II considers ways in which power relations play into understandings of 'participation' and 'non-participation'; and Part III is concerned with power in the workplace. Like several of the other contributors to this book, in exploring power I argue that gender, class and other inequalities still matter, although this is little recognised by some of the practices named as innovative in lifelong learning.

As Michel Foucault has shown, power and knowledge are inextricably linked:

> Power produces knowledge. Power and knowledge directly imply one another. There is no power relation without the correlative constitution of a field of knowledge, nor any knowledge that does not presuppose and constitute at the same time power relations.
>
> (Foucault, 1980: 93)

Legitimated knowledge is persistently constructed as neutral, objective, apolitical and value-free. However, what counts as knowledge is always intricately bound to the power relations of class, gender and race. The lack of recognition that knowledge is socially constructed and contextualised exacerbates cultural, material and discursive inequalities, which remain embedded in lifelong learning policies and practices.

Discourses of lifelong learning, for example, institutionalise and regulate gendered and normalised understandings about what learning is and who counts as a learner.

I point, as way of example, to current discourse about lifelong learning and the development of social capital, which is shown as a universal good. Discourses of lifelong learning highlight ways in which learning helps interweave diverse sets of relationships and develop the capacity for reciprocal trust, co-operation and active citizenship: in other words, the development of social capital. However, social capital can be used to exclude as well as include. I have written elsewhere about definitions of social capital, and the lack of value that is placed on the social capital that is developed, for example, by women working in the home or community (Jackson, 2004). Being included or excluded from any particular network can be partly determined by a sense of personal identity, including constructions of gender and social class.

Identities and sense of self are formed through social practice and are tied both to social inequalities and discursive and cultural recognitions and misrecognitions. Theories of identity are important for examining how identifications are understood and performed discursively as well as in practice, and feminist post-structuralism sheds light on understandings of self that are multiple, contradictory and shifting. Constructions of identity – including working-class identities – remain central to how learning opportunities are negotiated. We all have to recognise something of ourselves in current or future possibilities and a sense of who we are (or are not) can further exclude us from places where we perceive ourselves to be already excluded (see Reay et al., 2001). Universities and other institutions of learning continue to be seen as 'not for the likes of us', and working-class identities are not associated with academic success.

The discourses that surround issues of tackling social exclusion are often linked not to poverty but to raising or changing working-class aspirations or attitudes (see Archer et al., 2003). It may well be that some working-class people view themselves as 'not good enough', and believe that they 'know their limits' in relation to post-compulsory educational routes. However, these views are constructed and compounded by complex social, structural and institutional factors. Located within discourses of personal choice and agency, structural inequalities and exclusions are often ignored. Although there may well appear to be a lack of appetite for improved skills, this is located in the material realities of people's lives. All too often, working-class identities are seen as in deficit, although 'deficit' itself is of course constructed.

Foucault demonstrates that power can be productive as well as coercive, and I am not arguing that we do not positively exercise agency in the choices that we make and the decisions we reach. However, agency does not exist outside of our unconscious or subconscious subjectivities, nor does it exist outside of the material conditions of our lives. Whilst lifelong learning can open up possibilities, for some the possibilities are greater than for others. As I have indicated, socio-economic and other factors lead to a narrowing down or even absence of possibilities, whilst the more privileged are able to claim greater access to limited resources. There are, for example, very many talented and qualified working-class people who are denied places at 'elite' universities, which remain dominated by largely middle-class groups, ensuring the reproduction of privilege.

Women are now taking their places in universities and colleges in equal (or above equal) numbers to men, although this is expressed as a problem rather than a celebration of a redressing of balance for women, and has led to questions being asked about whether women are taking over the academy (Quinn, 2003). The growing dominance of female students in British universities has been described as 'one of the biggest problems facing higher education', and 'a success story that has gone . . . wrong' (Henry, 2007). Women, though, are still more likely than men to be studying part-time, are still primarily located in specific subjects and disciplines, and less likely to be represented at higher levels. However, explanations are likely to be located in the lack of ambition of individuals rather than within structural and discursive inequalities.

Neo-liberalism states that the rights of individual freedoms supersede state intervention, and that governments should not therefore inhibit free trade and free enterprise. For lifelong learning, this results in an emphasis both on market forces and on individualism. However, apparent non-intervention is an ideological position that in fact stems from political decisions and interventions, and results in hierarchies of learning. For example, the hierarchies of learning that currently exist have seen cuts in funding for community, adult and continuing education, and now for lifelong learning in its broadest sense, with resources being directed instead to learning that focuses on those supposedly economically valuable skills. States foster conditions where active engagement in lifelong learning is narrowly defined, with the flexible worker/learner located in a work ethics of neo-liberalism.

Paulo Freire describes neo-liberalism as the transference of knowledge for industrial productivity (Freire, 2004: 77). He argues that education has come to be about technical knowledge, training learners in skills that enable them to adapt to economic globalisation, but leaving little space for utopian dreams.

> The more education becomes empty of dreams to fight for, the more the emptiness left by those *dreams* becomes filled with technique, until the moment comes when education becomes reduced to that. Then education becomes pure training, it becomes pure transfer of content, it is almost like the training of animals, it is a mere exercise in adaptation to the world.
>
> (Freire, 2004: 84, original italics)

When education and knowledge are described purely in terms of technology and training, then, as Freire has shown, 'in a postmodernity touched at every moment by technological advances' 'new pedagogical proposals become necessary, indispensable, and urgent' (Freire, 2004: 107; see also Jackson, 2007).

Although governments may introduce policies and funding councils implement them, it is in part through pedagogic challenges that innovations can be developed, resistances can be played out, and power exercised, and it is to those pedagogic proposals to which I now turn in this final of the introductory chapter.

Pedagogic challenges

In moving towards ways in which innovations can be developed and pedagogic challenges made, I turn from Freirian utopian dreams to the notion of diaspora.

Far from utopia, diaspora is about being exiled, scattered, dispersed, forced to leave one's homeland, but goes beyond that, deep into one's psyche. As Ann Phoenix and Avtar Brah have shown, the concept of diaspora intersperses with theories of borders and feminist politics. They argue that the intersection of diaspora, borders and feminist politics can be understood through the concept of 'diaspora space'. Difference then becomes conceptualised as 'social relation; experience; subjectivity; and, identity' (Brah and Phoenix, 2004: 83).

In considering diaspora and cultural identity, Stuart Hall (1990), describes

> the traumatic character of the 'colonial experience'. The ways in which black people, black experiences, were positioned and subjected in the dominant regimes of representation were the effects of a critical exercise of cultural power and normalisation. Not only . . . were we constructed as different and other within the categories of knowledge of the West by those regimes. They had the power to make us see and experience ourselves as 'Other' . . . [I]t is one thing to position a subject or set of peoples as the Other of a dominant discourse. It is quite another to subject them to that knowledge.
>
> (Hall, 1990: 223–4)

It is a diasporan identity that too many learners currently bring to their learning experiences. They are subjected to the knowledge that they are Other, and that they have been admitted under sufferance as long as they conform to dominant constructions of what it means to be a learner, and what counts as knowledge. The construction of 'knowledge' as an ungendered, apolitical and universally shared goal is highly problematic and raises particular issues about who has access to different kinds of learning and knowledge, and who is understood as a 'knower'. Hegemonic knowledge is legitimised through constructions of objectivity, rationality and neutrality, although knowledge is always tied to wider power relations and its production operates in the interests of certain groups (Burke and Jackson, 2007). It is not just that some forms of knowledge count and others do not: rather it is that some forms of knowledge count *because* others do not. Learning can and does empower: however, what we learn about ourselves and our place in the world can also lead to exclusion. Lifelong learning as currently conceptualised may well result in maintaining and legitimising structural barriers of gender, class and 'race'.

However, whilst diaspora is about loss, it is also about new beginnings, finding different ways of belonging, developing alternative ways of being. The pedagogic challenge for innovations in lifelong learning is to develop new cultures of learning, finding ways not only to recognise the power relations embedded in constructions of knowledge and of learning, but also in finding ways for teachers and learners to resist and reclaim them. When I started my teaching career, as a portfolio worker taking whatever part-time work I could find, I taught sociology on an access course in that same further education college where I began my educational journey. There I used to talk about the development of a sociological imagination

(Mills, 1959). What I am arguing for here is for those of us who are teachers, as well as those of us who are learners, and policy makers, and researchers, to develop our pedagogical imaginations, recognising that knowledge is constructed, that teachers also learn, and that learners also teach, and that – as bell hooks (1994) has shown – we sometimes need to learn and teach to transgress, rather than learn and teach to conform. Disaporan spaces need to be found which are about the creation of new opportunities, new ways of knowing, new ways of being, for all of us. Drawing on the work of Freire, bell hooks states that one sentence of Freire's became a revolutionary mantra for her: 'We cannot enter the struggle as objects in order later to become subjects' (hooks, 1994: 46).

An innovative pedagogy for lifelong learning which locates us all – learners and teachers – as subjects means that the current mantra about learning for active citizenship must change from learning how to become a citizen who embodies and enacts neo-liberal values to learning about citizenship for social action and social justice. At its best lifelong learning can be a route for personal development *and* economic growth; it can enable personal fulfilment; the development of an active and inclusive society; and political engagement. Clear links have been made between community learning and social and political change, and between informal learning and the development of citizenship (Coare and Johnston, 2003). However, as is apparent from some of the chapters in this book, lifelong learning can also be a mechanism for exclusion and social control, upholding and generating deep-rooted inequalities. Negotiations into and through education are complex and mediated not only by social class but by other factors, including gender and 'race'. It is the best of times; it is the worst of times.

So will we all live happily ever after? Some of us – of a particular age, social class, gender, educational background – will; others of us will not. Within the current neo-liberal ideology so apparent across the developed world, lifelong learning is a subset of a broader agenda that is to do with vocationalism, entrepreneurship, competitiveness, economic well-being. I do not argue that this is, of itself, a bad thing. However, it can never be *all* that lifelong learning is, or can be. The instrumentalism now apparent in lifelong learning does little to bring about social change or challenge inequalities of social exclusion, and it certainly does not lead to innovations in lifelong learning. Nevertheless, as the chapters in this book show, there are many innovative practices that can and do challenge the status quo.

The contributors to this book bring with them a wealth of different experiences, backgrounds, bodies of knowledge, theoretical and international perspectives and contexts that add to the richness of this book. They come from America, Australia, Canada, New Zealand and the United Kingdom. They draw on empirical research, personal stories, life histories, research circles and theoretical analyses to consider a range of perspectives to consider innovations in lifelong learning within a climate of neo-liberalism, globalisation and internationalisation. The explore power and privilege; constructions of knowledge; definitions of 'skills'; and alternative frameworks to make sense of the values that shape our worldviews.

The book consists of three Parts – learning communities; participation and non-participation; and work-based learning and learning through work. They should not, however, be read as discrete. Each of the Parts is concerned with the themes raised in this introduction, including issues of diversity, patterns of equality and inequality, and of course with innovative practices.

The conclusion to the book returns to some of the key themes of the chapters, and considers the implications for innovations in lifelong learning.

Notes

1 This chapter draws substantially on my inaugural professorial lecture, given at Birkbeck University of London on 7 November 2007 (see Jackson, 2007).
2 See Charles Dickens, *A Tale of Two Cities*.
3 See Charlotte Bronte, *Jane Eyre*.
4 Equivalent to Pro-Vice-Chancellor in other UK HEIs, and Vice-Provost or similar overseas, and a highly problematic term for a feminist.

References

Archer, Louse, Hutchings, Merryn, and Ross, Alistair (2003) *Higher Education and Social Class: Issues of exclusion and inclusion*, London: RoutledgeFalmer.

Brah, Avtar and Phoenix, Ann (2004) 'Ain't I a woman? Revisiting intersectionality', *Journal of International Women's Studies*, 5: 3, pp. 75–86.

Burke, Penny and Jackson, Sue (2007) *Reconceptualising Lifelong Learning: Feminist interventions*, London: RoutledgeFalmer.

Coare, Pam and Johnston, Rennie (eds) (2003) *Adult Learning, Citizenship and Community Voices: Exploring and learning from community-based practice*, Leicester: NIACE.

Foucault, M. (1980) 'Two lectures', in Gordon C. (ed.), *Michel Foucault: Power/knowledge*, London: Harvester Wheatsheaf.

Freire, P. (2004) *Pedagogy of Indignation*, Boulder, CO: Paradigm.

Hall, Stuart (1990) 'Cultural identity and diaspora', in Rutherford, J. (ed.) *Identity, Community, Culture, Difference*, London: Lawrence & Wishart

Henry, Julie (2007) 'Worry over girls' dominance at university', *Sunday Telegraph*, 7 July.

hooks, bell (1994) *Teaching to Trangress: Education as the practice of freedom*, London: Routledge.

Hughes, Christina, Blaxter, Lorraine, Brine, Jacky and Jackson, Sue (2006) 'Gender, class and "race" in lifelong learning: policy and practice in the UK and EU', *British Educational Research Journal*, 32: 5, October, pp. 643–8.

Jackson, Sue (2004) 'Widening participation for women in lifelong learning and citizenship', *Widening Participation and Lifelong Learning*, 4: 1, pp. 5–13.

Jackson, Sue (2007) 'Freire re-viewed', *Educational Theory*, 57: 2, pp. 199–213.

Mills, C. Wright (1959) *The Sociological Imagination*, Oxford: Oxford University Press.

Quinn, Jocey (2003) *Powerful Subjects: Are women really taking over the university?*, Stoke-on-Trent: Trentham.

Reay, Diane, Davies, Jacqueline, David, Miriam and Ball, Stephen (2001) 'Choices of degree or degrees of choice? Class, "race" and the Higher Education choice process', *Sociology*, 35: 855–74.

Part I

Learning communities

Introduction

Sue Jackson

In this first Part, and therefore also as an introduction to later themes and issues in the book, the authors explore questions relating to 'learning communities' in their diverse forms. Whilst effective learning communities can be – and often are – part of formal learning environments in classrooms both for children and for adults, as well as in the workplace, in this Part the interest is in the ways in which learning communities become established outside of formal institutions, including the formal institutions of work (see Part III). The chapters in this Part also move beyond much existing work on community education or learning, although they do engage in discussions of learning in the community and of community networks (Coare and Johnston, 2003). Rather they are interested in developing wider understandings of how people engage in learning in and through the communities in which they live and through which they try to make liveable lives (Butler, 2004).

In considering ways in which learning communities develop and are valued (or not), all four chapters are interested in critiques of lifelong learning which are taken as a common good, too often linked to a discourse of inclusion which leaves no spaces for critical discussion (Burke and Jackson, 2007). In the opening chapter, Shibao Guo and Zenobia Jamal begin a discussion that will weave throughout the book, asking how inclusive educational environments can be built that will help to achieve social justice and equity in lifelong learning when the acts of learning and teaching are too often separated from issues of social justice, democracy and citizenship.

The chapters by Guo and Jamal and by Avoseh develop the theme of cultural and other diversities, which will continue throughout the book. Guo and Jamal are interested in ways in which educational environments can be built that help achieve equity and social justice. They argue that lifelong learning is currently at a crossroads or intersection where debates about cultural diversity and inclusive education are shaped within global economic, social and cultural contexts. Such debates are exemplified in Mejai B. M. Avoseh's chapter on community learning in Africa, where he challenges readers to confront the dominance of Western thought in constructions of lifelong learning, arguing that there are unique differences between Western and traditional African value systems and thought patterns, the latter of which is imbued with holistic understandings of community learning.

Throughout Part I, authors raise key issues that will appear and reappear throughout the book, including constructions of knowledge and of power. These themes run through the chapters by Jan Etienne and Sue Jackson and by Barry Golding, both of which develop the debate through empirical research carried out in the UK and in Australia, examining gendered understandings of lifelong learning. They argue that the informal learning that takes place in communal but gender-specific spaces can enhance the ability to resist power relations elsewhere. Nevertheless, they also note the ways in which hierarchies of power are played out, as do Guo and Jamal. Avoseh, on the other hand, is interested in ways in which (inter)-generational hierarchies of privilege and knowledge can enhance community learning. Thus the opening Part of the book clearly sets a critical discussion of innovations in lifelong learning within an international and global framework that spans four continents: Africa, Australia, Europe and North America.

Whilst supporters of lifelong learning argue that it is or can be holistic and visionary (Delors, 1996), its critics are concerned that it has lost any radical edge it may have had, and has become profoundly conformist (Field, 2000). The authors of the opening chapter, Shibao Guo and Zenobia Jamal, explore ways in which an inclusive education can be built when lifelong learning is, as they argue, at a crossroads. As countries and their education systems become increasingly ethno-culturally diverse, social and demographic changes create both opportunities and challenges for lifelong learning. As the authors show, many nations are becoming increasingly ethno-culturally diverse with evolving patterns of mass migrations. Partly as a result, classrooms are becoming increasingly diverse, although cultural diversity is both opportunity and challenge. The aim of this opening chapter is to explore an innovative framework that can be used to provide a broader perspective that incorporates issues of democracy, citizenship and social justice for diverse communities of learners. The chapter concludes that to embrace cultural diversity in a context where teaching is a political act, an anti-racist model of education is the most appropriate for implementing change in lifelong learning.

In Chapter 2, Mejai Avoseh continues some of the issues raised in the opening chapter. He explores ways in which understanding the informal and lifelong dimensions of community learning in Africa may contribute to debates and developments of lifelong learning more broadly, arguing that the dividends of lifelong learning must first accrue to the individual before it is possible to re-invest into the community. Drawing in part on personal experiences, Avoseh outlines and deconstructs some of the institutions of community adult education in Africa, which include acquisition of knowledge regarding community culture and history, as well as the development of skills for professional practice. He argues that community learning includes developing the art of communal living broadly conceptualised, something that is missing from much dominant discourse on lifelong learning (Burke and Jackson, 2007).

Chapters 3 and 4 move on to extend the discussion to explore issues of gender in communities of learning, exploring gendered informal learning which is also constructed through differences of social class (Jackson, 2003; Reay et al., 2005), age (Finsden, 2005), and intersectionality (Brah and Phoenix, 2004). Whilst Jan Etienne and Sue Jackson, in Chapter 3, are interested in women-only spaces of informal learning, Barry Golding (Chapter 4) is concerned with social inclusion and well being for men, who are often excluded from lifelong learning. Both chapters are concerned with the project of becoming and the impact of developing community participation. Older people are often rendered invisible in a society that values youth over age, and one way to claim back an identity is through community participation and through the learning that takes place in informal and safe gender-specific social spaces, which involves the re/construction of identities (Jackson et al., 2010 forthcoming).

In Chapter 3 the authors draw on empirical research developed in the UK through a research project on lifelong learning, community and the Women's Institutes (WI), funded by the UK's Economic and Social Research Council. Traditional images of the WI involve the construction of older women as homemakers, with the most dominant images being ones of jam and cake making, flower arranging, and the development of other homecraft skills. However, in the chapter the authors demonstrate that older women are still active citizens, with a strong political voice in their local communities and nationally. They explore ways in which the WI enables women to fully participate in communities of (informal) learning and community practice into old(er) age.

The concern of the final chapter in this Part is about the informal learning that men might seek and undertake when not in the paid workforce, and the potential benefits of that learning to men's wellbeing. Golding argues that men's disengagement from formal adult learning is particularly acute for men not in paid work. Drawing on empirical research, he uses the case of community men's sheds in Australia as illustrative of how educational innovation need not start from the top down, but can instead emanate from a loose network of community-based grassroots organisations. Golding concludes that this sort of informal learning may be able to break intergenerational cycles of unemployment for men through community involvement and identify opportunities for marginalised men to develop more positive masculine identities.

References

Brah, A. and Phoenix, A. (2004) 'Ain't I a woman? Revisiting intersectionality', *Journal of International Women's Studies*, 5: 3, pp. 75–86.

Burke, J. and Jackson, S. (2007) *Reconceptualising Lifelong Learning: Feminist interventions*, London: Routledge.

Butler, J. (2004) *Undoing Gender*, London: Routledge.

Coare, P. and Johnston, R. (eds) (2003) *Adult Learning, Citizenship and Community Voices: Exploring community-based practice*, Leicester: NIACE.

Delors, J. (1996) *Learning: The treasure within*, Paris: UNESCO.
Field, J. (2000) *Lifelong Learning and the New Educational Order*, Stoke-on-Trent: Trentham Books.
Findsen, B. (2005) *Learning Later*, Malabar, FL: Krieger.
Jackson, S., Malcolm, J. and Thomas, K. (eds) (2010 forthcoming) *Gendered Choices: Learning, work, identities in lifelong learning*, Dordrecht: Springer Academic Press.

Chapter 1

Toward inclusive education

Embracing cultural diversity in lifelong learning

Shibao Guo and Zenobia Jamal

Introduction

Many countries in the world are becoming increasingly ethno-culturally diverse as a result of mass migrations between states. Among major immigrant receiving countries in the West, Australia has the highest proportion of foreign-born population at 22.2 per cent, followed by Canada at 19.8 per cent and the United States at 12.5 per cent (Statistics Canada, 2007). Even among countries that provided emigration in the past, such as Greece and Ireland, their foreign-born population has also surged well above 10 per cent. When immigrants arrive in a new society, they bring with them their values, language and culture, contributing significantly to the diversity of their host countries. Without a doubt, the resulting demographic, social and cultural changes create new opportunities for development as well as new challenges in acknowledging and responding to this diversity. Although inclusion 'is a favourite keyword of those engaged in discussing lifelong learning' (Rogers, 2006, p. 127), this language often masks the realities of how lifelong learning is conceptualised and implemented. One of the challenges of addressing issues of inclusion is the fear of diversity (Palmer, 1998), partially resulting from a lack of knowledge and readiness to respond to cultural diversity. Furthermore, despite the claim that lifelong learning is a holistic, visionary, normative and value-laden concept in the same way as ideas about democracy or equality (Tuijnman and Boström, 2002), many critics point out that lifelong learning has lost sight of the radical dimension of education and has become 'profoundly conformist' (Rogers, 2006, p. 128). As a consequence, democratic processes are being stifled and active citizenship downplayed (Crowther, 2004; Jarvis, 2006).

To foster diversity and inclusive education in lifelong learning, a central question we need to ask is: How can we build inclusive educational environments that will help achieve the goals of social justice and equity in lifelong learning? Related to this are questions such as: Is the field of lifelong learning ready for these changes? Are lifelong educators equipped to respond to the challenges? Similarly, do our curricula and teaching approaches reflect this diversity? The purpose of this chapter is to explore issues of cultural diversity and to suggest frameworks that can be used to provide broader perspectives on lifelong learning that incorporate notions of equitable participation, democracy, citizenship and social justice. Some common approaches used to nurture cultural diversity in lifelong learning, particularly for the purpose of enhancing teaching and learning, are critically examined, with the hope that these endeavours will have global relevance for adult educators in responding to the challenges of cultural diversity and lifelong learning.

The chapter is organised into four parts. It begins with a definition of cultural diversity, followed by an examination of the politics of teaching. The third section reviews three models that can be used to address cultural diversity in lifelong learning, including an intercultural education model, a multicultural education model and an anti-racist education model. The chapter ends with an evaluation of these three models, their application in a variety of settings and contexts and a discussion of their pedagogical applications. A critical review of the models concludes with the suggestion that an anti-racist education model that takes into account issues of social justice in lifelong learning is the most appropriate model for embracing cultural diversity, for ensuring equitable participation and for implementing change.

Defining cultural diversity

To understand the impact of diversity in educational settings, it is first necessary to define some key terms, including culture and cultural diversity. Culture can be defined as a dynamic system of values, beliefs and behaviours that influence how people experience and respond to the world around them. Cultural diversity can be referred to as 'distinctions in the lived experiences, and the related perception of and reactions to those experiences that serve to differentiate collective populations from one another' (Marshall, 2002, p. 7). Although cultural groups share commonalties in perspectives, behaviours and ways of being in the world, they are rarely homogeneous. Within cultural groups, there are differences that affect the way individual members in the group relate to one another and to the group as a whole. Although aspects of culture such as race and ethnicity are generally more visible, as is gender, differences within groups such as class, 'race' and gender intersect and affect other aspects of individual identity and group membership. Members of one cultural group may simultaneously belong to several groups, and these multiple group memberships result in aspects of identity that respond to, conflict with, and contradict each other. Culture, therefore, cannot be viewed as an organising principle that creates static borders based on race or ethnicity, but as constantly changing, dynamic and fluid (Ghosh and Abdi, 2004).

Culture and education are inextricably intertwined, and learners' perspectives and worldviews influence their experiences in educational environments (Gay, 2000; Jones, 2004; Wlodkowski and Ginsberg, 1995). Culture plays an integral part in shaping the ways in which learners learn and communicate, how they relate to other learners and instructors, their motivation levels and their sense of what is worth learning. The degree to which learners feel comfortable in the learning environment will depend on the congruence between their cultural background and the dominant culture of the educational institution. There is evidence to suggest that increased diversity in institutions of lifelong education can benefit learners from all backgrounds both from majority as well as from minority groups (Castañeda, 2004). These benefits include an improvement in intergroup relations and campus climate, increased opportunities for accessing support and mentoring systems, opportunities for acquiring broader perspectives and viewpoints, and participating in complex discussions, all of which can contribute to increased learning. There is a growing number of empirical studies that provide support for these benefits. In a study designed to examine the relationship between the diversity of the student body and interactions among students, Gary Pike and George D. Kuh (2006) found that a diverse student population is related to increased interaction among diverse groups of students, and that the more diverse the student population, the greater the exposure to diverse perspectives and view points. In another study, Patricia Gurin (1999) found that students acquire a very broad range of skills, motivations, values and cognitive capacities from diverse peers when provided with the appropriate opportunities to do so. In addition, campus communities that are more racially diverse tend to create more richly varied educational experiences that prepare them better for participation in a democratic society (Chang et al., 2006). Furthermore, learning environments that are supportive of diversity can lead to more openness to diversity, critical thinking skills and greater personal development (Hu and Kuh, 2003). These studies provide evidence that environments that support cultural diversity can contribute towards an empowering environment for all learners.

Studies also suggest that traditional classroom culture can exclude and marginalise learners in many subtle ways through either the content of the curriculum or instructional practices. For example, in a study with South-Asian learners in a predominantly white Canadian university, Samuel and Burney (2003) report that their respondents felt that a perceived Eurocentric emphasis with a penchant towards Anglo-Saxon assumptions and premises made them feel excluded and marginalised in classroom situations. One learner noted, 'When examples are used with western connotations, then the minority students are left out and minority students don't understand and find it difficult to pick up' (p. 103). Instructional strategies that are based on values such as competitiveness and maximising individual achievement may alienate students from cultures where group achievement is valued over individual achievement (Morey, 2000). It is important, therefore, that educators 'become aware of the ways in which the traditional classroom culture excludes or constrains learning for some students, and learn how to create environments that acknowledge the cultural diversity that new students bring' (Adams, 1992, p. 7).

Lifelong learning: the politics of teaching

The increased diversity of students involved in lifelong learning requires us to pay close attention to the socio-political context within which we view cultural diversity. The development of pedagogical strategies for creating enabling environments that embrace cultural diversity must keep this context in mind. There are numerous frameworks and models of teaching and learning that have been developed over the years to shed light on how teaching and lifelong learning can be envisioned, conceptualised and implemented. We now briefly examine some of these frameworks and models, including andragogy, scholarship of teaching and learning, and the politics of teaching.

The attempt to understand how adults learn, and the best ways to promote this learning, has been widely discussed with a number of models of adult and lifelong learning emerging over the years. A model that has been discussed extensively is the model of andragogy (Knowles, 1980; Merriam and Cafarella, 1999). The term was popularised by Malcolm Knowles and has been used as a basis for developing teaching practices in adult and lifelong learning environments. Knowles suggested that teaching in these environments should take adult learners' needs into account and be based on a framework of assumptions about adult learners. Adults need to know why they need to learn something, can be self-directed in their learning, will be motivated to learn what they perceive will help them deal with their life situation, and have varied backgrounds and experiences which can contribute to their learning. These assumptions about learners can be used to design, implement and evaluate appropriate teaching strategies and create effective learning environments.

However, this model has been critiqued for its limited focus. As Michael Collins (1999) points out, andragogy is 'narrowly pre-occupied with methodology' (p. 53), rather than with the wider concerns of adult education which should move us away from the view of learner as an individual activity and account for the social context of learning within the broader processes of social change. According to Michael Newman (1993), andragogy is essentially a conformist model designed for an American, middle-class and culturally homogeneous clientele. It can be employed to mould people, to manipulate them and to bring them into line. Hence, Newman reminds us, we need to approach andragogy with caution.

In post-compulsory and higher education institutions where formal lifelong learning for adults takes place, there has been an increased focus on improving the quality of teaching by creating a body of knowledge that focuses on effective teaching, and the scholarship of teaching and learning. The insights and knowledge gained from this field have been used to understand the link between student learning and best practices for teaching students, and many models have been proposed to assist in this endeavour. Randall G. Bowden (2007) selects and summarises four key models. The first is Kreber's reflection-based model of scholarship of teaching, which uses transformative learning theory to understand the process of gaining knowledge about teaching. The second model, proposed by Trigwell et al., encompasses knowledge of teaching and learning and its application to a discipline, reflection on this knowledge, selecting appropriate teaching approaches and sharing knowledge about teaching. The third one described by Bowden is Middendorf and Pace's model, which focuses on the problems students encounter in a subject matter. The last model, developed by Richlin, tries to strengthen the relationship between teaching and learning. Although models from the field of scholarship of teaching and learning can be useful in deriving best practices, Carolin Kreber (2006) suggests that there may be a tendency to see best practices as being merely instrumental in addressing outcomes related to the efficiency and effectiveness of teaching and learning. The scholarship of teaching and learning should also be concerned with the broader goals of higher education that address the moral and civic purposes of education, with notions of citizenship and with educating students for participation in a democratic society. These goals should be considered within the context of the social, political and cultural challenges that we are currently faced with.

One fatal flaw inherent in andragogy and various models from the field of scholarship of teaching and learning lies in the separation of the acts of teaching and learning from issues of social justice, democracy and citizenship. As an alternative we adopt critical pedagogy as the underpinning theory for this analysis. Critical pedagogical frameworks are based on the notion that education is politically contested, and that teaching itself is a political act (Freire, 1995; hooks, 1994; Kincheloe, 2008; McLaren, 2003; Ng, 2003). Educational practices are influenced by a variety of historical and social factors, and an unconscious and depoliticised understanding of these factors can lead to oppressive practices. The politics of teaching involves the exercise of critical consciousness in a decision-making process regarding what to teach and how to teach. The current curriculum in lifelong education in many Western countries – characterised by its Eurocentric perspectives, standards and values – does not reflect the knowledge and experiences of a culturally diverse student population (Dei, 1996; Kitano, 1997; Tisdell, 1995). Paulo Freire (1995) illustrates how the banking model of pedagogy, in which knowledge selected by the teacher is uncritically deposited into the learner, perpetuates the oppression of the learner. According to Peter McLaren (2003), oppression is legitimised through both standardised learning situations and unintended outcomes of the educational process – or 'hidden curriculum'. As McLaren notes, the hidden curriculum refers to 'the non-subject-related sets of behaviours produced in students', and it deals with 'the tacit ways in which knowledge and behaviour get constructed, outside the usual course materials and formally scheduled lessons' (p. 212). It includes pedagogical styles, teaching and learning environments, governance structures, teacher expectations and grading procedures.

In the Canadian context of education, for example, the hidden curriculum has become a strong social practice that influences educators' perceptions regarding diversity and issues of knowledge construction and validation. The perception of diversity is often linked to the way in which difference is viewed. There are sufficient studies (e.g. Cummins, 2003; Dei, 1996; Ghosh and Abdi, 2004) to suggest that the perspectives and practices of 'whiteness as the norm' and 'colour blindness' have become the dominant hidden curriculum in Canada that constructs difference as deficit. Rather than seeing difference and diversity as an opportunity to enhance learning by using the diverse strengths, experiences, knowledge and perspectives of learners from various cultural groups, the 'difference as deficit' model sees diversity ignored, minimised, or as a hindrance and obstacle to the learning process. The colour-blind perspective is a point of view that sees cultural, racial and ethnic background as irrelevant, and assumes that treating all individuals the same will erase issues of inequity and injustice (Solomon and Levine-Rasky, 2003). Although this view is superficially appealing because it seems to value all individuals equally, it negates the histories, backgrounds and experiences of diverse cultural groups and ignores the ways in which these affect their experiences in the learning environment. Colour-blind policies that endeavour to treat all learners the same may end up contributing to the perpetuation of injustices (Ghosh and Abdi, 2004).

Embracing cultural diversity: a critical analysis of selected models

The literature on responding to diversity within educational settings provides a rich array of frameworks and models that can be used to explore and understand the different elements to consider when teaching for cultural diversity in lifelong learning environments. Three types of models will be reviewed and compared: the intercultural education model, the multicultural education model and the anti-racist education model. These three models are presented here because each of them can be used to build inclusive educational environments and create change at different levels and spheres of influence, including the self, classroom, institution and community (Kitano, 1997).

The first model is based on intercultural education for the development of individual diversity that can be used by faculty members to reflect on their own attitudes towards diversity and to promote and influence the diversity development of their students (Chávez et al., 2003). The second model is one of multicultural education (Banks, 2010a, 2010b) that provides a framework for curriculum change and reform and can be applied at the level of the self and the classroom. Third, a model based on an anti-racist approach to education is included (Dei et al., 2002).

Although all three models provide valuable insights into the task of addressing issues of cultural diversity, we suggest that the anti-racist model is the most appropriate one for implementing changes required in lifelong education institutions because it provides a critical integrative framework and will help develop the innovations in lifelong learning. It operates at all four levels of influence: the self, classroom, institution and the community. The anti-racist model addresses issues of difference and diversity at the level of the individual, provides strategies for both curriculum and pedagogical change, and addresses issues of inequity in educational institutions.

This section presents a brief overview of each model, followed by a discussion on the applications of each model in the context of lifelong education.

An intercultural education model

The goal of the intercultural education movement of the 1920s and 1930s was to promote tolerance and understanding among different cultural and ethnic groups within the educational system and the community (Banks, 2005). This movement was based on the assumption that similarities among groups were more important than differences, and acquiring information about cultural groups could avoid prejudice and bias and promote respect and acceptance. Efforts were made to implement programs that would help increase knowledge of other cultures, develop positive attitudes towards difference, and teach the skills of interacting and communicating across difference.

The impact of the intercultural education movement in educational environments has been an increased focus on creating changes in attitudes that will lead to more equitable teaching and learning environments. Faculty members and students both come to the teaching environment with varied experiences and social and cultural backgrounds, and may carry with them unexamined assumptions about the characteristics of various cultural groups with whom they are unfamiliar (Marchesani and Adams, 1992). These assumptions are often part of mainstream cultural knowledge, and unless questioned and challenged, can become the basis from which to interact with minority cultural groups. In addition, information about general group characteristics is often applied, sometimes incorrectly, to individuals. Reflecting on and challenging assumptions requires change at the individual level.

The Individual Diversity Development Framework, a model proposed by Chávez et al. (2003) for use in the higher education setting, can be extended for use in lifelong learning that provide post-compulsory education. The model provides a holistic approach for individual knowledge, attitudes and behaviours towards diversity and can be used to suggest a process for faculty to reflect on their own development, as well as encourage and assist the development of their students. To deal with the complexity of people's identities, individuals often use an essentialist approach to understand members of a different group by using their experience (or lack of it) with the group to ascribe to them a set of characteristics. These characteristics are then extended, sometimes incorrectly, to describe individuals in the group. Individuals, however, have complex and sometimes contradictory identities and can be members of many different groups, making it difficult to understand them through one set of characteristics. The individual diversity development framework demonstrates how individuals can gain a deeper understanding of the complexity of identities, and can move towards valuing and validating difference.

The diversity framework has five dimensions, and the process of learning to value a certain kind of difference can occur by moving through some or all of these dimensions. These dimensions include (1) unawareness, (2) dualistic awareness, (3) questioning and self-exploration, (4) risk-taking, and (5) integration.

Individuals who are operating in the first dimension of this framework are unaware that a certain kind of difference exists and would therefore exhibit no feeling about this difference nor respond to the difference in their behaviour. For example, if an individual has had little or no exposure to a different culture, this individual may not be aware of how behaviours that seem different are based on different ways of knowing and being in the world. Individuals at this level can be encouraged to reflect on differences with which they are familiar, to move them towards a consideration of other more unfamiliar kinds of differences such as cultural diversity.

Individuals at the next dimension of dualistic awareness see difference in a dualistic way, as either good if familiar or bad if unfamiliar. They may choose to ignore or avoid contact with difference, or try to minimise the differences they encounter. In an educational setting, there may be behaviours that are considered the norm, such as acceptable ways of interacting with other students or norms for participating in classrooms. When students deviate from these norms, their behaviour may be unfamiliar, and therefore viewed as negative and inappropriate. Individuals at this dimension may not have had their beliefs questioned or challenged and can benefit from being exposed to alternative perspectives on issues and being asked to carefully consider these perspectives.

In the third dimension of questioning and self-exploration, individuals begin to move away from dualistic modes of thinking, and start to see the validity of other perspectives. Initially, this process may be accompanied by fear of losing long-held beliefs, particularly if they are associated with membership of a specific group, for example, a religious group. This growth could be achieved by providing learners with dilemmas or problems that require critical assessment of new perspectives and encouraging self-reflection and dialogue with others to share ideas within an environment of relative safety and support. As individuals become more comfortable with evaluating and accepting different perspectives, being in this dimension can feel more comfortable and even exciting for both teachers and learners.

In the next dimension of risk taking and exploration of otherness, individuals have decided to challenge themselves to understand the worldviews of others, either internally through self-reflection and a search for new ways of thinking, or externally through engaging in situations in which they are compelled to alternative viewpoints. One activity that would benefit individuals in this dimension is participation in a service learning programme in which students are involved with a community or organisation that they are unfamiliar with. This would facilitate exposure to perspectives, values and beliefs that are different and unfamiliar and can encourage students to move out of their zones of comfort.

Individuals using the integration/validation dimension recognise that others have multiple and complex identities, and are able to recognise and validate the differences that arise from these identities. They are able to interact comfortably with people who have different perspectives, values and beliefs and in a variety of settings and contexts. Teachers and learners who are at this dimension can engage in a learning environment that is open and accepting and that affirms and acknowledges the ideas and contributions of many different groups. They have managed to integrate their sense of self with their perception of the other, and continue to strive towards valuing and validating difference wherever they encounter it.

The increased cultural diversity in institutions of lifelong learning requires the creation of inclusive learning environments in which faculty members and learners from different backgrounds and perspectives can interact and respond with understanding and sensitivity to multiple perspectives. The development of such awareness helps to promote acceptance and validation of difference and to ensure movement towards achieving the broader goals of educational equity for learners from all backgrounds. However, creating an inclusive education environment requires more substantive changes than merely encouraging self-reflection and raising awareness about difference. The risk of this approach is that difference within educational environments would be addressed only at the individual level, without attention to the need for change at a broader level. It is essential to examine how curricula, pedagogical practices and policies contribute to inequities in lifelong learning environments, and models of multicultural education go a step beyond intercultural models by addressing these issues.

A multicultural education model

The field of multicultural education emerged in the 1960s as a response to issues of social justice and equity in the education system and was based on principles of cultural pluralism and the elimination of prejudice and discrimination in the education system. The principle of cultural pluralism asserts the right of different ethnic and cultural groups to retain their language and cultural traditions within a climate of respect for the traditions and values of different groups. In the education system, these principles can be realised by affirming the importance of culture in the teaching and learning process, and by providing opportunities for equity and academic excellence for all students, regardless of their racial, ethnic and cultural backgrounds (Bennet, 2001). This goal of equity is achieved, not through equality or sameness for all students, but by acknowledging that students come to the learning environment with diverse backgrounds and needs, and that curriculum and teaching practices should respond to this diversity. The goals of multicultural education focus on change at the individual and classroom level and can be achieved by transforming pedagogical practices, reforming the curriculum and encouraging multicultural attitudes (Bennet, 2003).

A model that can be used to implement change to respond to cultural diversity is Banks' model of multicultural education (Banks, 2010a, 2010b). Although this model is often viewed as a way integrating content about minority groups into the curriculum, the model has broadened over time to encompass five dimensions: (1) content integration, (2) knowledge construction, (3) prejudice reduction, (4) an equity pedagogy, and (5) an empowering learning culture.

The first dimension, content integration, is a response to a predominantly Eurocentric curriculum and refers to the need for inclusion of knowledge and perspectives from a variety of cultures into the subject areas of every discipline. Content integration can be achieved by modifying existing curricula to include information about specific cultural groups or by going a step further to incorporate new course materials and content. A more transformative approach to content integration recognises that knowledge construction is not neutral but is value laden, and that in order to include knowledge from multiple perspectives, it is necessary to make structural changes in the curriculum that provide additional and alternative perspectives in all disciplines. As Kincheloe (2008) has suggested, 'knowledge production and curriculum development are always and forever historically embedded and culturally inscribed processes' (p. 108), making it critical to present differing perspectives within a curriculum.

The process of knowledge construction is the second dimension of the model. This process is based on the frames of reference, perspectives and assumptions that are used when constructing and validating the knowledge that is produced in each discipline. The goal for teachers is to help learners become more aware of these processes of knowledge production so that the perspectives and biases that have influenced the production of certain kinds of knowledge can be revealed and made explicit. For example, how is the creation of knowledge influenced by race, gender ethnic background or class position? Students can be encouraged to think about how their own positions, assumptions and experiences influence the way they engage with and understand curriculum content. The knowledge construction process encourages students to take a more critical approach, to ask complex questions about the content they encounter and to enhance and improve their critical thinking skills and abilities.

The objective of the prejudice reduction dimension of the multicultural model is to shift preconceived attitudes and beliefs that are based on incorrect information about individuals or groups. Prejudice leads to racism, sexism and other forms of discrimination and a learning environment that dispels incorrect beliefs and promotes positive attitudes can encourage students to respect and value difference. The process of prejudice reduction can be facilitated by creating a positive classroom, in which learners of different backgrounds have opportunities to work cooperatively and respect the multiple perspectives within culturally diverse groups.

The concept of equity pedagogy is the fourth dimension of the model, and is based on the assumption that learners have diverse ways of learning influenced by their backgrounds, unique perspectives and worldviews. Teachers can use a variety of strategies to meet the needs of learners from diverse backgrounds and provide content that is relevant and meaningful to them. Teachers also have to be able to relate to and understand learners' histories, backgrounds and the social and cultural influences that have shaped their experiences, and make a concerted effort to adjust the learning environment to respond to these differences.

The fifth and last dimension of the model addresses the need for an empowering learning culture in which learners from diverse cultural backgrounds have access to equitable and empowering learning environments. Barriers to equitable learning environments can include entrance requirements for participation in programs, standardised assessment and testing procedures, a hidden curriculum that is based on dominant modes of knowledge and an implicit school culture that is based on the attitudes and beliefs of the dominant groups. These barriers can be removed by assessing normative processes and practices that are embedded within learning environments, and then working to reduce or remove these barriers.

Banks' model of multicultural education provides a useful framework to contribute to more inclusive and equitable learning environments and addressing cultural diversity in lifelong learning. The framework can be used to transform course materials and to adjust instructional strategies and practices. However, the conceptualisation of a multicultural frameworks and 'its definition in terms of an apolitical, ahistorical cultural pluralism' need to be challenged (Mohanty, 1990, p. 197). Efforts in the multicultural realm tend to focus on initiatives to shift attitudes towards minority groups, promote cross-cultural understanding and encourage dialogue across difference. However, these efforts are often pursued without a contextual understanding of the impact of hierarchies of power and privilege, and the impact of multiple oppressions on marginalised groups. This focus on recognising and celebrating cultural difference may serve to further exacerbate issues of exclusion by reifying and essentialising minority groups. Furthermore, the focus of the multicultural education model on curricular and pedagogical change disguises the need to examine how societal inequities faced by minority groups are reproduced in educational environments. The multicultural model also fails to acknowledge that the process of knowledge production is directly linked to the power exercised by dominant groups. These shortcomings require the pursuit of broader frameworks that encompass the goals of intercultural and multicultural education, but broaden these goals to include recognition of issues of systemic inequity and the need for institutional transformation.

An anti-racist education model

One response to the critique of multicultural education has been to move to a more critical conceptualisation of inclusive education that addresses broader structural issues and confronts the impact of racism on the lives and educational experiences of students. In contrast to models of multicultural education, anti-racist education models highlight issues of difference, power and privilege. They are based on the assumption that improved cross-cultural understanding, co-operation and respect for difference do not address the structural causes of inequity, and that meaningful change can only occur when barriers to inclusive education are challenged and addressed at all levels where they occur (Dei et al., 2000).

George Sefa Dei et al. (2000) propose a critical integrative approach to inclusive education, a model for change based on an anti-racist approach. This model views education 'as a racially, culturally and politically mediated experience' (Dei et al., 2002, p. 8). The model encompasses four learning objectives for both faculty members and learners: (1) integrating multiple centres of knowledge, (2) recognition and respect for difference, (3) effecting social and educational change: equity, access and social justice, and (4) teaching for community empowerment.

The first objective of integrating multiple centres of knowledge involves adding diverse sources of knowledge to the current emphasis on Eurocentric sources so that traditionally marginalised sources can be affirmed and validated. Rather than being an add-on, these centres of knowledge would be integrated into the curriculum at all levels, and would provide alternative centres of knowledge to add to and enrich the learning experiences of all learners. The model makes particular reference to three sources of knowledge that have been marginalised: indigenous, spiritual and community knowledge. The inclusion of subjugated and marginalised knowledges, must however, guard against the danger of an essentialised notion of indigenous knowledges, acknowledging the multiplicity of perspectives within these knowledges (Kincheloe, 2008). Since teaching is a political act, the successful integration of multiple centres of knowledge requires lifelong educators to exercise their critical consciousness in selecting teaching materials that reflect the knowledge and experiences of a culturally diverse student population. Another suggestion is to recruit minority teaching staff who represent a range of ethno-cultural differences and who will bring in alternative and oppositional forms of knowledge to their teaching. A primary objective is to create spaces for marginalised voices and promote alternative ways of knowing.

The second objective of the model is a recognition and respect for difference. This objective recognises the need to consider and value the complex identities of learners, and to ensure that teaching practices acknowledge and validate these identities. Difference within an integrative anti-racist framework must include an understanding of how forms of difference both intersect and interlock (Kelly, 1999). An intersecting analysis of difference moves towards an understanding of how specific kinds of difference (e.g. race and gender) intersect with one another to create multiple oppressions, and an interlocking analysis identifies the difficulty of separating these differences as well as a political commitment to addressing the multiple oppressions. Teaching about difference and power, as Mohanty (1990) suggests, is not an easy task and requires 'not only rethinking questions of learning and authority but also questions of center and margin' (p. 192). This can be done by designing learning activities that help minority learners make connections between their own selves and the cultural group that represents them. Lifelong educators also need to recognise and understand their own positions in relation to their learners and to work towards uncovering the beliefs, values and assumptions they themselves use to respond to cultural difference and diversity.

Effecting social and educational change through equity, access and social justice is the third objective of the model and requires that instructors acknowledge the existing inequities in educational structures and environments, understand their role in these structures and actively advocate for change. This requires a consideration of how policies and programs that address issues of equity can be formulated and implemented to respond to educational inequity. With this objective of the model, the role of instructors extends from the sphere of the classroom into the community and requires advocating for systemic change to impact decision-making practices, recruitment and reward systems, information systems and work structures. Systemic change calls on administrators, faculty members and learners to assess their positions, to be open to new ideas and to act in different ways. This level of change should have an impact on the mission and vision of an institution as well as the policies and practices used in both research and teaching. Thus, to bring about a truly transformed pedagogy requires fundamental and systemic change in the organisation itself.

The last dimension of the model focuses on teaching for community empowerment by building capacity and working towards increased individual and group self-esteem through the active involvement of all concerned groups in decision making related to the educational process. This requires collaboration among teachers, learners, administrators and the community to work for change at a broader level. It also requires mutual respect and respect for diverse perspectives and experiences among all stakeholders. By doing so, 'margins' will be brought into the 'centre'; education is no longer separated from the community; and change is not limited to the self but extends to society at large. This dimension particularly important for lifelong educators because learning to live together is one of the four pillars of lifelong education. We also understand that community development and empowerment are important sites for social transformation and emancipatory learning.

A critical integrative framework for inclusive education begins with the assertion that the creation of inclusive educational environments requires educators to be aware of how inequities in the classroom reflect inequities in the wider society, to consider the nature of these inequities and the power imbalances inherent in them and to employ approaches and strategies that challenge these inequities at all levels to respond to the needs of those who are 'in the margins'.

Toward inclusive education

The three models presented in the previous Part each address certain aspects of teaching and learning in culturally diverse classrooms and can be used as a starting point for creating inclusive lifelong learning environments at different levels of influence and in different contexts. The first model presented, the Individual Diversity Development Framework, can be used to understand how cognitive, affective, and behavioural attitudes towards diversity can be transformed to arrive at a deeper understanding of our complex identities and to encourage and promote multicultural attitudes in the lifelong learning environment. Instructors can use the model to reflect on their own growth in valuing diversity, as well as the growth of their learners. The model provides suggestions for activities and experiences that would promote and encourage movement along the various dimensions of the model to arrive at a better understanding of the many kinds of difference we encounter in our lives. However, this model only addresses change at the individual level and does not link to changes in policies and practices required at institutional and societal levels. As Gorski (2006) and Mohanty (1990) have noted, a growing acceptance of those who are different does not necessarily lead to a determination to participate in social action to create change; the focus on individual attitudes towards difference emphasises maintaining a discourse of harmony and civility disconnected from underlying structural issues. Furthermore, intercultural education is usually based on a depoliticised and static definition of culture. The emphasis on understanding the characteristics of culturally diverse groups can lead to reified and essentialist notions of culture, ignoring the fact that cultural characteristics are not fixed but fluid and dynamic, and are always mediated by differences within groups such as gender, class, language, religion, as well as varied histories and experiences (Fleras and Elliot, 2003). The Individual Diversity Development Model does not directly address issues of curriculum transformation, of pedagogical strategies, or of inequity at the institutional level.

In comparison, multicultural education provides a more comprehensive way of understanding inclusive education and implementing change at the classroom level. Banks' model of multicultural education can be used to derive appropriate strategies and activities for the culturally diverse classroom by examining how curriculum content and pedagogical practices can be transformed. The model includes five dimensions, and each of these can be used to derive specific strategies to create learning environments that respond to diverse needs. This includes either adjusting or transforming the curriculum, paying attention to the processes of knowledge construction and validation, and using culturally appropriate pedagogical methods that address the learning needs and different backgrounds of all learners, rather than focusing on the needs of the majority group. The dimension of an empowering learning culture is a reminder that changes at the classroom level can be more effective when supported by an environment that fosters a culture of respect and value for diversity. The multicultural education movement has played a significant role in addressing issues of diversity in lifelong education.

However, like intercultural education, multicultural education tends to focus on changes at the individual and classroom level. Despite the many different forms it takes, multicultural education has failed to nurture cultural diversity effectively in lifelong education due to its monoculturalism in terms of vision, content and style (James and Wood, 2005). Educational practices based on multicultural frameworks reflect what Gorski (2006, p. 167) calls 'a *compassionate conservative* [original italics] consciousness' rather than a focus on equity and justice. Much of multicultural education, he suggests, is about 'learning about other cultures' or 'celebrating the joys of diversity' rather than focusing on the elimination of different forms of oppression. For example, the dimension of curriculum integration in the multicultural education model usually takes an additive approach, which tends to be cosmetic and superficial. The focus on encouraging knowledge of different cultural groups, harmonious social relations with these groups, and curricular and pedagogical change is firmly located within a consensus paradigm that ignores existing inequities and asymmetries of power that influence social relationships. Under multicultural education, differences can be exoticised and trivialised. While minor differences may be gently affirmed in depoliticised and decontextualised forms such as food, dance and festivities, substantive differences that challenge hegemony and resist being co-opted are usually perceived by many as deficient, deviant, pathological, or otherwise divisive. In short, one fatal weakness of multicultural education is its depoliticisation and tendency to ignore issues of systemic and structural inequity that exist in the wider society and are reproduced in educational institutions (Dei et al., 2000; Marshall, 2002).

The criticism directed towards models of intercultural and multicultural education has led to a deeper examination of how educational systems can address the shortcomings of these models as well as modify and add to these approaches. One response has been the model of anti-racist education, which builds on the previous two models, but adds several new dimensions. The model is based on the assumption that changes at the institutional level cannot occur in isolation – they must be considered in light of the existing inequities in society that are reproduced in educational institutions; however, groups have the power and agency to resist and challenge these inequities by actively engaging in and advocating change.

In contrast to a consensus-based intercultural and multicultural education, anti-racist education moves beyond a narrow preoccupation with individual prejudice and discriminatory actions to challenge power differentials between socio-cultural groups in society. It explicitly names the issues of race and socio-cultural difference as issues of power and equity rather than as matters of cultural and ethnic variety. Whereas multicultural education focuses on the celebration and understanding of culture, anti-racist education questions how socio-cultural differences are used to entrench inequality. It interrogates White privilege and power and how they work together to construct and maintain social inequality. Furthermore, anti-racist education incorporates gender, class and sexuality into its analysis of race. As Kogila Moodley (1996) notes, the strengths of anti-racist education over multicultural education lie in its incorporation of historical analysis, its differentiated discussion of how different groups experience racism, and the interconnections it draws among different kinds of oppression such as gender and racial oppression.

Furthermore, this model highlights the need to move traditionally marginalised centres of knowledge away from the margins and towards the centre, and to focus on inclusive decision making which addresses issues of social justice, equity and power relations. It works 'against the grain' (Ng, 2003) in arguing that education is contested; educators cannot claim to remain neutral in the provision and utilisation of educational knowledge in lifelong education. An against-the-grain approach requires us to acknowledge explicitly that as educators we are all gendered, racialised and differently constructed subjects who participate in education in asymmetrical power relations; it also requires us to reveal how dominant forms of knowledge constrict human capacities. Through its analysis of the social construction of knowledge, it questions what is defined as valid knowledge and how such knowledge has been used to negate and devalue the experience of subordinated groups. In exposing the power relations integral to the knowledge construction process, anti-racist education calls for creating space for everyone, but particularly for marginal voices to be heard in lifelong education.

Conclusion

Responding to the needs of culturally diverse learners requires change at a number of different levels of lifelong education, starting from the self, and moving towards change at the classroom, institutional and community levels. The anti-racist education model presented in this chapter addresses the need for change at the individual and classroom levels, but suggests that social justice in educational settings can only be achieved if these changes are accompanied by changes at structural and institutional levels. As Mohanty (1990) stresses, 'curricular and pedagogical transformation has to be accompanied by a broad-based transformation of the culture of the academy, as well as by radical shifts in the relation of the academy to other state and civil institutions' (p. 191). The anti-racist education model is a critical integrative approach, which addresses issues of difference, power and social inequality, and provides a way to bring about change at the structural and institutional levels. This chapter concludes that to embrace cultural diversity in a context where teaching is a political act, the anti-racist education model is the most appropriate one for implementing change in a lifelong education setting. As a vehicle for social change, this innovative framework will help reclaim the radical roots of lifelong education for democracy and inclusive citizenship and achieve the goals of building an inclusive educational environment that is equitable and socially just.

Acknowledgements

An earlier version of this chapter appeared in the *Canadian Journal of Higher Education*, 37 (3). We thank the journal editor for letting us include a revised version here.

References

Banks, J. A. (2010a), 'Multicultural education: characteristics and goals', in Banks, J. and Banks, C. (eds), (2010) *Multicultural Education: Issues and perspectives*, Hoboken, NJ: Wiley, pp. 3–30.

Banks, J. A. (2010b), 'Approaches to multicultural curricular reform', in Banks, J. and Banks, C. (eds), (2010) *Multicultural Education: Issues and perspectives*, Hoboken, NJ: Wiley, pp. 233–256.

Banks, C. A. M. (2005), *Improving Multicultural Education: Lessons from the intergroup education movement*, New York: Teachers College Press.

Bennet, C. (2001), 'Genres of research in multicultural education', *Review of Educational Research*, 71: 2, pp. 171–217.

Bennet, C. (2003), *Comprehensive Multicultural Education: Theory and practice* (5th edn), Boston: Pearson Education.

Bowden, R. G. (2007), '*Scholarship Reconsidered*: Reconsidered', *Journal of the Scholarship of Teaching and Learning*, 7: 2, pp. 1–21.

Castañeda, C. R. (2004), *Teaching and Learning in Diverse Classrooms: Faculty reflections on their experiences and pedagogical practices of teaching diverse populations*, New York: RoutledgeFalmer.

Chang, M. J., Denson, N., Sáenz, V. and Misa, K. (2006), 'The educational benefits of sustaining cross-racial interaction among undergraduates', *Journal of Higher Education*, 77: 3, pp. 430–455.

Chávez, A. F., Guido-DiBrito, F. and Mallory, S. L. (2003), 'Learning to value the "other": a framework of individual diversity development', *Journal of College Student Development*, 44: 4, pp. 453–469.

Collins, M. (1998), 'Critical returns: From andragogy to lifelong education', in Scott, S. M., Spencer, B. and Thomas, A. M. (eds), (1998) *Learning for Life: Canadian readings in adult education*, Toronto: Thompson Educational Publishing.

Crowther, J. (2004), '"In and against" *lifelong learning*: flexibility and the corrosion of character', *International Journal of Lifelong Education*, 23: 2, pp. 125–136.

Cummins, J. (2003), 'Challenging the construction of difference as deficit: Where are identity, intellect, imagination, and power in the new regime of truth?' in Trifonas, P. P. (ed.), (2003) *Pedagogies of Difference: Rethinking education for social change*, New York: RoutledgeFalmer, pp. 41–60.

Dei, G. J. S. (1996), *Anti-Racism Education: Theory and practice*, Halifax: Fernwood Publishing.

Dei, G. J. S, James, I. M., Karumanchery, L. L., James-Wilson, S. and Zine, J. (2000), *Removing the Margins: The challenges and possibilities of inclusive schooling*, Toronto: Canadian Scholars' Press.

Dei, G. J. S., James-Wilson, S. V. and Zine, J. (2002), *Inclusive Schooling: A teacher's companion to removing the margins*, Toronto: Canadian Scholars' Press.

Fleras, A. and Elliot, J. L. (2003), *Unequal Relations: Race and ethnic dynamics in Canada* (4th edn), Toronto: Prentice Hall.

Freire, P. (1995), *Pedagogy of the Oppressed: New revised 20th anniversary edition*, New York: Continuum.

Gay, G. (2000), *Culturally Responsive Teaching: Theory, research and practice*, New York: Teachers College Press.

Ghosh, R. and Abdi, A. (2004), *Education and the Politics of Difference*, Toronto: Canadian Scholars' Press.

Gorski, P. C. (2006), 'Complicity with conservatism: The de-politicizing of multicultural and intercultural education' *Intercultural Education*, 17: 2, pp. 163–177.

Gurin, P. Y. (1999), [online] Expert report of *Patricia Gurin, Gratz et al. v. Bollinger et al.*, No. 97-75321, *Grutter et al. v. Bollinger et al.* Available from: University of Michigan Web site http://www.vpcomm.umich.edu/admissions/legal/expert/gurintoc.html [retrieved 8 February 2007].

hooks, b. (1994), *Teaching to Transgress: Education as the practice of freedom*, New York: Routledge.

Hu, S. and Kuh, G. D. (2003), 'Diversity experiences and college student learning and personal development', *Journal of College Student Development*, 44: 3, pp. 320–334.

James, C. E. and Wood, M. (2005), 'Multicultural education in Canada: Opportunities, limitations and contradictions', in James, C. E. (ed.), (2005) *Possibilities and Limitations: Multicultural policies and programs in Canada*, Halifax: Fernwood, pp. 93–107.

Jarvis, P. (2006), 'Beyond the learning society: globalization and the moral imperative for reflective social change', *International Journal of Lifelong Education*, 25: 3, pp. 201–211.

Jones, E. B. (2004), 'Culturally relevant strategies for the classroom', in Johns, A. M. and Sipp, M. K. (eds), (2004) *Diversity in College Classrooms: Practices for today's campuses*, Ann Arbor: University of Michigan Press, pp. 51–72.

Kelly, J. (1999), 'George Sefa Dei: Anti-racism: Education, theory and practice', *Aurora*, Issue 1999, http://aurora.icaap.org/index.php/aurora/article/view/22/33 [retrieved 2 June 2008].

Kincheloe, J. L. (2008), *Critical Pedagogy Primer* (2nd edn), New York: Peter Lang.

Kitano, M. K. (1997), 'A rationale and framework for course change', in Morey, A. I. and Kitano, M. K. (eds), (1997) *Multicultural Course Transformation in Higher Education: A broader truth*, Boston: Allyn and Bacon, pp. 1–17.

Knowles, M. (1980), *The Modern Practice of Adult Education*, Chicago: Association Press.

Kreber, C. (2006), 'Developing the scholarship of teaching through transformative learning', *Journal of Scholarship of Teaching and Learning*, 6: 1, pp. 88–109.

McLaren, P. (2003), *Life in Schools: An introduction to critical pedagogy in the foundations of education* (4th edn), New York: Allyn and Bacon.

Marchesani, L. S. and Adams, M. (1992), 'Dynamics of diversity in the teaching–learning process: A faculty development model for analysis and action', in Adams, M. (ed.), (1992) *Promoting diversity in college classrooms: Innovative responses for the curriculum, faculty, and institutions, New Directions in Teaching and Learning*, 52, San Francisco: Jossey-Bass, pp. 9–20.

Marshall, P. L. (2002), *Cultural Diversity in our Schools*, Belmont: Thomson Learning.

Merriam, S. B. and Cafarella, R. S. (1999), *Learning in Adulthood* (2nd edn), San Francisco: Jossey-Bass.

Mohanty, C. T. (1990), 'On race and voice: Challenges for liberal education in the 1990s', *Cultural Critique*, 14, pp. 179–208.

Moodley, K. A. (1995), 'Multicultural education in Canada: Historical development and current status', in Banks, J. (ed.), (1995) *Handbook of Research on Multicultural Education*, New York: Macmillan, pp. 9–20.

Morey, A. I. (2000), 'Changing Higher Education curricula for a global and multicultural world', *Higher Education in Europe*, 25: 1, pp. 25–39.

Newman, M. (1993), *The Third Contract: Theory and practice in trade union training*, Sydney: Stewart Victor Publishing.

Ng, R. (2003), 'Toward an integrative approach to equity in education', in Trifonas, P. P. (ed.), (2003) *Pedagogies of Difference: Rethinking education for social change*, New York: RoutledgeFalmer, pp. 206–219.

Palmer, P. J. (1998), *The Courage to Teach: Exploring the inner landscape of a teacher's life*, San Francisco: Jossey-Bass.

Pike, G. R. and Kuh, G. D. (2006), 'Relationships among structural diversity, informal peer interactions and perceptions of the campus environment', *Review of Higher Education*, 29: 4, pp. 425–450.

Rogers, A. (2006), 'Escaping the slums or changing the slums? Lifelong learning and social transformation', *International Journal of Lifelong Education*, 25: 2, pp. 125–137.

Samuel, E.and Burney, S. (2003), 'Racism, eh? Interactions of South Asian students with mainstream faculty in a predominantly White Canadian university', *Canadian Journal of Higher Education*, 33: 2, pp. 81–114.

Solomon, R. P. and Levine-Rasky, C. (2003), *Teaching for Equity and Diversity: Research to practice*, Toronto: Canadian Scholars' Press.

Statistics Canada (2007), *Immigration in Canada: A portrait of the foreign-born population, 2006*, Ottawa: Statistics Canada.

Tisdell, E. (1995), *Creating Inclusive Adult Learning Environments: Insights from multicultural education and feminist pedagogy*. Information Series No. 361. Columbus: ERIC Clearinghouse on Adult, Career, and Vocational Education, Center on Education and Training for Employment, Ohio State University.

Tuijnman, A. and Boström, A. (2002), 'Changing notions of lifelong education and lifelong learning', *International Review of Education*, 48: 1/2, pp. 93–110.

Wlodkowski, R. J., and Ginsberg, M. B. (1995), *Diversity and Motivation: Culturally responsive teaching*, San Francisco: Jossey-Bass.

Chapter 2

Informal community learning in traditional Africa

Mejai B. M. Avoseh

Introduction

This chapter presents items from indigenous African education with a focus on the components of community learning especially its informal and lifelong dimensions. With a special reference to institutions of 'higher education' as an aspect of community learning in traditional African education – including secret cults, divinities and some other aspects of traditional education – the chapter attempts to provide some 'outside' grounds for bolstering the drive towards innovations in contemporary dialogue and practice in lifelong learning.

The enormous diversity of Africa makes it difficult to define anything in a universal 'African' sense. However, traditional Africa is often understood in terms of sub-Saharan Africa because of the common bond of history and culture. Furthermore, traditional Africa also 'covers the cultures and traditions of Africa in its pure pre-colonial state' (Avoseh 2002: 8). Traditional Africa is used in this chapter within the framework of the definition above. The nature of education in traditional Africa especially makes it difficult to discern adult education from all other forms of education because education was a continuum that went along with life. It is in this sense of education being a synonym for life in traditional African communities that makes indigenous African education the pedigree of contemporary lifelong learning. If this is granted the above, then it is possible that lifelong learning in traditional Africa may have useful cues for innovations in twenty-first-century lifelong learning.

The history of adult education in Western societies has often been tied to social movements in quest of justice and equity (Youngman 2000; Finger and Asùn 2001). The same trend of using socio-political and economic issues to construct the history of adult education may not be applicable in traditional Africa. For one thing, there are unique differences between Western and traditional African value systems and patterns of thought. While the West generally interprets the world from a linear perspective, Africans have a holistic understanding of the world. Within the holistic way of life, there is a link between the unborn, the living and the dead. Within this setting, everything flows into everything else just as everyone exists because of everyone else in the family and community. The informal and the oral drive education, religion, morals, dancing, rituals and celebrations all of which dovetail in the community and run parallel with life. Consequently, everything presents an informal opportunity for learning because education is everything. This complex chemistry makes it almost impossible to separate education into primary, secondary, tertiary and so forth in traditional Africa, hence the concept lifelong is more apt to describe education. However, the institutions that service specific areas of indigenous education including age groups, trade and apprenticeship, can be used to figure out the different 'levels' of education in the lifelong process. The institutions that provide 'adult education' in addition to the focus of 'the education of adults' in traditional Africa provide the best pedestal for teasing out items from informal education in traditional Africa for contemporary innovations in lifelong learning.

Innovations in ideas may combine items from history to say old things in new ways that make sense in current or updated usage. It is in this sense that items from history are used to analyse and understand contemporary events. History as applied to informal learning in traditional Africa is used in this chapter in a qualified sense. History is applied here as an opportunity for understanding of institutions of adult education in traditional Africa. Bown (1981: 164) argued that this form of 'historical' study is one of the ways to compare 'adult education at different stages of a country's' or a people's growth.

Fajana (1960: 37) also uses the agencies and functions argument in his study of educational policy in Nigerian traditional society. He concluded, 'a study of traditional educational policy is therefore a study of the various agencies and their united efforts to achieve the communal goal'. Consequently, the history of informal education within the traditional African educational system is tantamount to understanding the place of cults, divinities, religion and morality, festivals and cultural dances in traditional African society. This chapter uses examples mainly from the Yoruba and Gu people of Southwestern Nigeria to offer a view into informal learning in traditional Africa. My use of the Yoruba and the Gu is based on proximity and common threads that run through both cultures. Furthermore, I was raised in both cultures even though I am Gu.

Inviting the outsider inside for innovations in lifelong learning

Lifelong learning and lifelong education are used interchangeably in this chapter because there is not such distinction between education and learning in traditional Africa. Even in modern usage, most literature still uses the concepts synonymously. Jarvis (1990: 203) admits: '*Lifelong education* and lifelong learning are used interchangeably because there is a tendency to treat *education* and *learning* as synonymous concepts'. What Jarvis calls the 'imprecise' use of the concept may have its foundation in Walters' and Watters' (2001: 471) assertion that 'an understanding of what lifelong learning means, varies across the globe'.

Lifelong learning, as indeed its parent discipline adult education, is still largely dependent on context and learners' needs. The importance of context and learners in defining and understanding lifelong learning often creates a problematic in arriving at universal definitions. Furthermore, there are some ambiguity in terms of the genesis of lifelong learning and its coverage. Duke (n.d.: 2) extends the ambiguity argument to assert that lifelong learning is a conceptual morass. He declares, 'From the outset the literature and its concepts (on lifelong learning) have proved problematic. They are often confused, and remain so today . . .' Gustavsson (1997: 238) addresses the ambiguity question in a stronger language thus: 'life-long education tends to be idealistic because it is seen to be applicable for any purpose, making it an empty concept filled with a content that is no longer able to face the problems in adult education'. Again Jarvis (2001: 4–11) in his review of the emergence of lifelong learning argues that the 'rise of lifelong learning' paints a complex picture of shifts in paradigm and socio-political and technological changes that led to the emergence of lifelong learning as we know it today. He further acknowledges the contributions of Yeaxlee's 1929 publications that came at a time when 'adult education was only just becoming established in the United Kingdom' (2001: 9). Cross-Durrant (2001: 31–48) corroborates Jarvis's submission that Yeaxlee is indeed one of the founding 'parents' of contemporary lifelong learning.

In addition to the works of Yeaxlee, other adult educators, including Dewey (1964), Lindeman (1961) and Nyerere (1978) all have emphasized the imperative of lifelong learning in different languages and contexts. In spite of the contributions of the adult educators cited above, almost every literature on lifelong learning credits the United Nations Education, Scientific and Cultural Organization (UNESCO) as the founder of twenty-first-century lifelong learning because it adopted the concept after World War II.

There is no doubt that there is copious literature on lifelong learning and that the debate on the concept has been quite robust. The quality and diversity of the debate on lifelong learning portends good things for the field of adult education. The robust debate and the efforts at innovations also guarantee that the products (in terms of the meaning and practice of lifelong learning) would have passed the tests of logic and rationality. The refinement through logic and rationality would help locate lifelong learning in the domain of being 'scientific' and 'systematic'. In this respect, lifelong learning would thus be useful not only for practice but also as a theoretical framework.

In spite of the advantages and benefits of the scientific approach to understanding and making innovations in lifelong learning, there is the possibility of the debate dovetailing with ideological and intellectual muscle flexing. The push towards ideology, if not checked, would leave the intended beneficiaries of lifelong learning – the learners and their communities – out of it all. Butler (2001: 65–66) warned of the dangers in the 'pervasive rhetoric of lifelong learning' and the attendant paradigm shifts in semantics 'from social citizenship to active contributor to global–national productive culture' because it may end up limiting lifelong learning to 'a metadiscourse for contemporary neoliberal public policy'. André Grace (2007: 186) cites the example of 'Canadian youths'' predicament in placing value on lifelong learning' (see also Chapter 5). André Grace (2007: 187) uses Canadian youths' discontentment with 'lifelong learning' as translating into the understanding of the 'learner–worker' as a 'commodity' and learning as a 'consumer product'. The author concludes, 'in its current reductionistic mode, Canadian youths experience a compulsory and conscripting lifelong-learning culture'. There is thus the possibility of lifelong learning becoming what Giroux (1988: 3) calls 'a pedagogy of chauvinism dressed up in the lingo of the great books'. Again Duke (n.d.: 3) points in this direction by admitting that 'lifelong learning as a grand idea is under threat . . . from *trivialization* . . . from *reductionism* . . . Thirdly there is the threat that it may fall out of favor or be dismembered since it has become a new "contested space".'

The picture of the background to innovations in lifelong learning painted above provides challenges as well as raw materials for permutations that will translate into lifelong learning not as coercion but as a way of life. As a way of life, everyone – especially learners – is a stakeholder in lifelong learning with the subtle but inescapable responsibility towards the community through active and productive involvement. Informal community learning in traditional Africa, in spite its being 'unscientific', presents lifelong learning neither as a matter of choice nor as an authoritarian imposition by experts. In the current efforts at innovations in lifelong learning, views from 'outside' the mainstream as in the example of the traditional African society may have some important import.

Institutions of adult education in traditional Africa

The complex and life-defining process of education in traditional Africa is designed in such a way that irrespective of one's age and disposition, there is always an opportunity to learn and to teach. Gustavsson's (1997: 239) definition of lifelong learning as meaning that 'learning and education are possible at any age, from cradle to the grave', aligns perfectly with the original meaning and usage of the concept in traditional African education. Although the learning and teachable moments are generally informal they are by no means haphazard. Most indigenous education is 'structured' along three main categories which Okello (1993: 28) put into three main compartments of 'Home-centered methods', 'Community-centered methods' and 'Institution-centered methods'. Each level of these methods sometimes helps to determine the 'grade' level of the participant(s). At all levels, the adult is either a teacher or a student but with most of the onus of educating the young falling on the adults. Irrespective of age, institution and methods, the overall aim of traditional education is the cultivation of what the Yoruba and the Gu of Nigeria call *Iwa* and *Wadagbe* 'good character' that contains the attributes of an active and ideal citizen who combines intellectual, moral, religious and professional values and skills to sustain family, community and self.

Some scholars of African indigenous education sometimes use 'moral education' as a synonym for *Iwa*. Adeyinka and Ndwapi (2002: 20–21) list the focus of moral education to include obligation to self, to family and the community. They further list 'honesty, truthfulness, hard work, tolerance, self-confidence, perseverance, humility' as moral norms. What they refer to as moral norms are the same attributes that define an individual who has *Iwa*. Ocitti (1994: 19–20) identified both formal and informal aspects of the lifelong learning through which the aims of indigenous education are accomplished especially at the level of adult education. The formal aspects were more consistent with adult education in that they focus on skills, vocational and related training, age groups and initiations. According to Avoseh (2002: 8), the most formal levels are in the 'apprenticeship training programs that blended the intellectual and practical elements of education so well by putting learning into action and action into learning'. At this level, secret cults serve as 'Institutions of Higher Education' and members of secret cults serve as the 'philosopher kings' – individuals with the highest *Iwa* and intellectual ability.

Although adults provide the essential leadership for learning at these levels, they too become learners. As Anyanwu (1981: 98) puts it, 'the adults continue to learn by teaching the young and introducing necessary changes into the life of the society'. With reference to the Yoruba, Anyanwu (1981) further explains how adult education both prepares an individual for the most esteemed status in the community and defines the 'real' adult. The educator of adults in traditional African education must 'guide other people on aspects of traditional education', and since such an individual does not possess all knowledge yet, he/she must immense self in continuing education and professional development. Anyanwu (1981: 104–105) provides further detail:

> [H]e/she (adult educator cum learner) must strive to belong to some of the cults, take part in civic assignments and through cultivated diligence, take part in discussions with groups of people on any aspect of traditional education and culture.

It is through such efforts in lifelong education that the adult educator can hope to advance his/her status to that of a 'revered elder' (and in most cases a revered ancestor), which is a synonym for 'ripe experience, accumulation of knowledge and a high level of intelligence' (Anyanwu 1981: 105), as well as good character. Based on the foregoing, it can be affirmed that the lifelong nature of adult education and indigenous education in general, allows a thin line between the educator and the learner. The indicators of adult education and one's level of advancement include the complexity of the content, advanced use of language, application of proverbs and stories, decoding myths, adjudicating, exhibiting patience, self-control, knowing how to keep secrets, knowing the depths of one's chosen career, the size of one's farm, knowing how to lead at prayers and pour libation, etc. These indicators are put into three broad groups: intellectual training and growth, vocational education and community education.

Intellectual training and growth includes coordinating experience through abstract reasoning, knowing the seasons and their relation to agriculture, knowing plants, animals and the geography of the community and its neighbours. Also included in the intellectual training are knowledge of proverbs, stories, poems and a good command of language. The second, vocational education includes a cluster of trades and professions including native medicine, music and arts, hunting, farming, forms of priesthood among others. The vocational education component is usually predicated on the apprenticeship scheme. All these forms of education converge in participation in the community and are therefore inseparable, irrespective of the fact that many avenues and institutions service the educational system. Avoseh (2007: 33) explains that learning dovetails with the community in traditional Africa.

> Learning in traditional Africa is generally inter-twined with other activities that give meaning to life and living in a community. It is therefore almost impossible to separate a community and the process of education because the community is education and education is the community.

Although community learning is generally informal, there are certain 'formalized' aspects that help meet the unique needs of individuals and deities. The formal aspect of community education especially at the adult level is entrusted to cults. Cults are in both the human and spiritual domains. The human cult is known as 'secret cults', while the cult of ancestors is the spiritual arm.

Cults and community learning

In most traditional communities, cults and secret societies were the highest institutions of learning just as membership of such societies was one of the highest 'degrees or qualifications' as long as an individual's character does not suffer blemish. In traditional societies of the Gu and the Yoruba, there are usually two categories of cults, mainly those of the living and those of the departed. The cults of the living are referred to as secret cults because they are the philosopher kings – individuals who have the highest moral and intellectual ability. The philosopher kings are akin to those who in *Plato's Republic* are virtuous and who should be entrusted with governing society – the highest moral task. The Yoruba call them *Ẹgbẹ Awo* or *Ẹgbẹ Imule* while the Gu refer to them as *Awono*. The second category of cults is that of the ancestors. The ancestors are the bridges between the living family and those of the spirit world. Hence, they are part of the family and part of all the community's efforts. Mbiti (1969: 85) explains that this is why they are known as 'the living dead [who] are partly "human" and partly "spirit"'.

Secret cults belong to those of the living and members usually form the intellectual cream of society. Avoseh (2001: 484) states that members of these cults are believed to exercise 'powers ranging from the intellectual, judicial, moral to metaphysical powers'. They put these powers to use in the educational process at the adult and higher levels through initiations and rituals. Olu Daramola ati Jeje (1975: 130) trace the history of *Ẹgbẹ Awo* (secret cults) in traditional Yoruba society to *àpàpọawọn agba ilu* (the council of elders). These authorities on Yoruba culture further establish the historical fact that the members of secret cults were same as the chiefs or titleholders in their different communities. They formed the king's advisory council and served simultaneously as 'checks and balances' should a king decide to be too absolute in his powers (***nwọn si maa ndá ọba l'ẹkun nigba-kugba ti o ba nfẹ gbe sáraá rẹ koja mọsalasi***). Members of secret cults wielded such powers because of their intellectual, moral and experiential advantage. Fafunwa (1974: 16) affirmed that the powers mentioned above are what make secret cults 'institutions of higher or further education', and put them in charge of the education of the 'select or the elect' of their communities. Fafunwa (1974: 16) added that at this level of the education of adults 'the secrets of power (real or imaginary), profound native philosophy, science and religion were mastered . . . [and] the curriculum was relevant to the needs of the society'.

The content of education was usually woven into initiation rites, rituals and other religious and advanced ceremonies of the community that belong more to what Ocitti (1994: 19–20) classified as 'formalized' aspects of indigenous education. Avoseh (2001: 484) insists that at such formal levels, 'learners may be kept incommunicado for weeks or months', because 'only the deep can call the deep'. Onabamiro (1983: 66) confirmed that as a matter of fact, the training of a priest by a master-priest takes more than a decade because in 'ancient times Ifa priests were the guardians, counselors, philosophers and physicians of their various communities'. He further states that 'if the training goes well without a hitch and if the trainee has a retentive memory the training lasts . . . ten to twelve years'. The master-priest will usually be a member of secret cults. In that case, members of secret cults have power over education in both the intellectual and the vocational realms and so are very powerful. It is pertinent to clarify the fact that irrespective of individual attributes of members of secret cults; their individual and collective powers are held in trust and on behalf of those who have held such powers before them, that is; the ancestors. Therefore, the cults of the living, in most cases, derive the authority of their powers from the ancestors who are the spiritual arms of the learning community.

Again, the holistic approach to life puts the ancestors at the center of everything because they are the spiritual arm of the extended family. Understanding the role of the ancestors in everything may provide the 'outsider' of traditional African value-system with what Fajana (1960: 34) refers to as 'an intelligent appreciation of traditional educational policy'. The ancestors' involvement in education is at all levels and the history of their involvement dates back to the first ancestors of any given community. Fajana (1960) puts it more succinctly in his explanation of the part that the ancestors play in the world of the traditional Nigerian. According to him (1960: 34):

> The spirits of the ancestral dead were incorporated into the social system as an intimate and integral part of the social group. Also *law and custom were believed to have been handed down from the spirit world from time immemorial, from ancestor to ancestor.* From birth onwards, there was a gradual

> education . . . into the various strata of the society, each stratum scrupulously distinguished from the others in rights and duties, until . . . the individual . . . became one of the elders and a repository of all the wisdom and lore of the tribe [emphasis mine].

Ancestors have been involved from time immemorial in the history of adult education in traditional Africa, and they have continued to sustain and overhaul the content of education especially at the higher level. Avoseh (2001: 484) argues that whereas secret cults derive their authority from the ancestors; 'the cult of ancestors is the source of its own authority and power'.

Although various communities express the involvement of ancestors in the educational system in different ways, most of the ways converge in rites and initiations. Among the Gu of southwestern Nigeria for instance, initiations into the *zangbeto* and *oro* cults are advanced level education processes that involve incarceration and/or nightly sessions in jungles for long periods. The ancestors through the *bokọnọ* (diviner) screened those who were selected at given points for this advanced education class. The ancestors advise if there is any danger ahead, and what sacrifices must be made in order to appease a particular god or great ancestor before the session begins.

I recall being involved in one of such educational process as a young adult. The format was usually semi-formal. Each session began with prayers and libation to the ancestors. There were codes of secrecy, of 'manliness' and the need for valor. The idea of nightly meetings in the jungle and of sneaking out of the village in the dead of the night, all added an air of awe to the process. The nightly sessions were rather inconvenient but the status and recognition pay for all the inconveniences in the world. The ancestors serve as the institutions and represent the history of such sessions as described above. Teffo and Roux (1998: 142) affirm that the ancestors' presence is a 'given' and this is one of their ways of fulfilling their obligation to sustain the community, its tradition and solidarity and 'to guarantee moral consistency'. The expectation of reinvestment of the dividends of education in the community through quality participation is also an obligation to community required of every graduate. Consequently, the cult of ancestors has a pervasive presence even in festivals, religious and cultural dances and celebrations because all these events provide learning opportunities in and for the community.

Festivals, cultural dances and community education

Traditionally Africans do not separate 'the inner world of spirits and the outer world of reality' but instead construct a 'unitary world of aesthetic continuum' (Anyanwu 1983: 105). There is a constant intercourse between the knower and the known and the context, between the process and the product, between the dancer, the music and the drum and so on. This aesthetic continuum is highlighted especially in the use of festivals, cultural dances and religious celebrations to foster community learning.

Idowu (1962), Mbiti (1969), and Frank Yerby (1971) all agree that most festivals in traditional Africa had their origins in religion. The interconnectedness between life, education, morality and living in the community is made more prominent by the role of religion in informal community learning. Most festivals were ways of adoring and expressing gratitude to the Supreme Being through His ministers – deities including *Sàngo, Oro, Ọsun*, and even through the ancestors. Such festivals, according to Michael Omolewa (1981: 20) 'provide the local population with "courses" in the history of the locality, accounts of origins, stories and legends of families and great men (women) produced in the society'. Also through such festivals, praise songs (*oriki*) are used to enliven the history of the community with references to the feats and failures of ancestors and the lessons that they affect. *Ewi* (poems) are used at such occasions to teach moral lessons. Even the dances on such festivals have educational impact. Again, Omolewa (1981) puts it well: '[T]he exquisite dancing steps and body contortions, and carefully worked out arrangements for order of appearances, embodies education.' The educational significance includes lessons in choreography, aesthetics and orderliness.

Idowu (1962: 192–194) further provides the history, moral and educational lessons of *egungun* and *oro* festivals in Yoruba culture. He outlines how both festivals are used to educate celebrants about the ancestors and the need to be of good conduct in readiness for life after death. The *Orìsà-nlá* festival is used, for instance, to teach and re-emphasize the need for good conduct and especially self-discipline in terms of alcohol consumption. Furthermore, any celebration of *Orìsà-nlá* is a lesson in character education for adults because in 'the theology of the Yoruba . . . *Orìsà-nlá* represents the norm of ethical and ritual purity'. *Orìsà-nlá* for instance, forbids palm-wine because 'wine is an intoxicant which is capable of spoiling man's (woman's) personality' (Idowu 1962: 151).

The *Ọsun* festival is another important Yoruba festival that doubles as informal community learning. It combines educational, religious and moral content for community learning. History has it that *Ọsun* was one of the wives of the god of thunder *Sàngo*, who was a powerful king of Oyo. He became a deity because he was an exceptional active citizen in his life. *Ọsun* is worshiped in most parts of Yorubaland as the goddess of fertility who is associated with the *Ọsun* River. The *Ọsun* festival in Oshogbo (Southwest Nigeria) is a process of teaching and learning morals, the virtue of hope especially for women who are barren in addition to emphasizing the importance of procreation. The rites and rituals of *Ọsun* Oshogbo festival are therefore more of community educational processes that further re-emphasize the complex mix of learning and living. The festival also confirms that the ancestors are involved in everything especially community education.

For the Gu and the Yoruba and indeed 'many societies of traditional Africa, formal education most strongly manifested itself in the initiation ceremony' (Datta 1984: 6). Datta explains that the selective nature of learning through initiation makes them very formal and rigid: '[T]he initiation ceremonies and the post-initiation training camps . . . were highly structured and formalized' (Datta 1984: 10). Ocitti (1994) further affirms the formalized nature of initiations and the fact that there are both 'prolonged formal' and 'short-formal' formats of learning through initiation. Ocitti also acknowledged the involvement of 'bush schools or secret societies' as key to selective learning especially with 'traditional societies of central and west Africa' (Ocitti 1994: 20). Community education through the media of initiations and dances combines both formal and informal. Initiations and certain cultural dances usually have religious-cum-educational content and significance in addition to the socio-cultural merriments that accompany the completion of different stages of initiation. Again, there are variations in the format and specifics of who does what at what point. What is constant across-board is the fact that the history of initiation carries with it advanced levels of indigenous community education woven around religious rites and age groups.

It is pertinent to clarify the fact that at the level of initiations, the learning opportunities are often selective and discriminatory and are therefore not open to the entire community as in other instances. Those to be initiated into certain cults and priestly roles are often 'chosen' directly by the deities and oracles through the chief priest or diviner (*hunno* or *bokono)*, hence the process is selective. The selective nature of learning through initiations makes most stages of initiation sacrosanct so much so that to violate them would lead to sanctions for individuals and the community from the deities and or the ancestors. In spite of being exclusive, the lessons learned in the confines of initiation are geared towards community values and sustenance. The initiated demonstrates the knowledge acquired through active participation in the community and through such involvement receives the recognition and respect due to a 'graduate' of a specific initiation.

The *Dan Votùn* of the Gu of Southwestern Nigeria is one of such initiations that combine religion and age in selecting its recruits. The new recruits for *Dan* deity are put in confinement for periods ranging from nine to twenty-four months. During their seclusion, the new *Votùnsì* in training undergo different forms of learning that include language peculiar to the deity, forms of greeting, dancing steps and new spirits of commitment to other devotees and the need to pursue the finest things in the interest of the self and the community after graduation. Consequently, they learn not just values, history, social and religious contents but also vocational education while in the 'seminary'. At graduation/initiation, they are entirely 'born again'. They take new names; have different types of incision on their faces and bodies. They are now *Votùnsì* ('wives of the deity') by virtue of which much is expected from them morally, intellectually and spiritually because of their advanced level of education. In return, they are accorded very high respect and recognition. At their 'graduation', the learning extends to the entire community through celebrations, eating and dancing. Those who aspire to be so initiated go for special prayers and make offerings so that when their time comes, the gods will not say no. The neo-*Votùnsì* also look forward to the next and higher level of their initiation-cum-education.

Mbiti (1969: 121–122) gave a list of initiation rites across Africa and summarized their significance. Mbiti's summary affirms initiation as a lifelong learning process that revolves around the essence of the community. It is community learning that includes ritually introducing the young adult into the art of communal living, into incorporation into adult life, and introduces them to the life of the living-dead as well as the life of those yet to be born. Mbiti (1969: 122) gives a succinct summary of initiation; according to him:

> Initiation rites have a great educational purpose . . . [which] often marks the beginning of acquiring knowledge which is otherwise not accessible to those who have not been initiated . . . a period of awakening to many things, a period of dawn for the young. They learn to endure hardships, they learn to live with one another, they learn to obey, they learn the secrets and mysteries of the man–woman relationship; and in some areas . . . they join secret societies each of which has its own secrets, activities and language.

Initiation rites from their commencement to the final stages of graduation and celebration, including the cultural dances that accompany such celebrations all combine to add to the complexity of education as a holistic continuum. The holistic continuum imposes the imperative of applied knowledge, the only evidence of 'graduation' – transcript, certificate, testimonial – that each individual showed for his/her education.

The limits and imports of the traditional African perspective

It could be argued that the traditional African informal community learning presented in this chapter is, not perfect. I am aware of criticisms such as too much emphasis on orality and age, the tendency towards authoritarianism, and overglorification of the past that make it all appear utopian. Most of these criticisms and observations are understandable especially coming from those who are 'outsiders' to the culture. Elsewhere (2007: 38) I have noted that it is not just 'outsiders' of the African traditional system that have criticized it. Wiredu (1980: 41) for instance criticizes the system on the grounds that it lacked intellectual rigor and encourages over reliance on 'rationally unsupported belief in entities of any sort'. Furthermore, Omolewa et al. (1998: 166) criticized the system on the basis that 'individuals . . . are less motivated to seek personal achievement or even to make use of new opportunities'. There is also Bodunrin's (1981: 166) classification of the traditional African system as being weak and of little significance in the face of money economy, urbanization and technology. Bodunrin's conclusion was based on the fact that the pre-eminence of the community in the traditional African system was based on modest populations and on a non-money economy.

There is much logic and sense in these criticisms of the traditional African system. However and in spite of their logicality, the fact remains that learning in traditional Africa is a lifelong process that subsists in the daily activities and values of the community. Its lifelong nature stretches to the ancestors through the cult of ancestors as the absolute measure of the endless nature of learning. Furthermore, informal learning has fostered the need to pursue self-interest within the broader community interest and active citizenship. Therefore, if we grant the logic of the critiques we must also admit the fact that these weak points are not sufficient to obliterate the goodness and utility of informal community learning for those societies. And more importantly, the critiques do not foreclose the import that lifelong learning in traditional Africa may have for today's innovations.

It is pertinent to point out the fact that this chapter has not tried to contrast lifelong learning in traditional Africa with the Western rendering of the concept. The danger in such contrasts is to create a dualistic view of the world and the concept along the fallacious pattern of one being 'good' and the other being 'bad'. However, I have tried to extract some difference as a basis for innovation. One notable difference is the genesis and use of lifelong learning in both contexts. Lifelong learning in traditional African communities pre-dated every individual because it was the way of the first ancestors. It has no author and it is not seasonal. The Gu and the Yoruba would call it *jọwa mọ* and *adaye ba* (something that exists before everyone) respectively. Furthermore, lifelong learning in the traditional sense is a compass for navigating the complex networks of educational, cultural, vocational, religious, social and other values of life and living in a community.

The story is different in its Western and academic understanding. In its Western rendering and application; the origin of lifelong learning is credited to organizations and/or individual scholars. In addition, lifelong learning is often invoked in response to critical socio-political and economic situations, as has been the case in recent years. For instance, UNESCO has been most associated with the popularization of lifelong learning in its contemporary focus on creating a class of twenty-first-century workers whose skills are updated via constant learning, that is, lifelong learning. Cross-Durrant (2001: 31) confirms the fact above by her assertion that 'the idea of lifelong education is generally regarded . . . as being attendant upon modern technological and societal changes, and as such, as being "new"'. Dae Joong Kang (2007: 207) strengthened this line of thought with the assertion: 'The focus of lifelong learning has shifted from humanitarian to economic objectives. It is taken for granted that lifelong learning could enhance employability in an uncertain, risky job market'. Merriam, Caffarella and Baumgartner (2007: 48–49) also observe that because 'lifelong learning is so pervasive throughout society; knowledge becomes a commodity that is produced, packaged, and sold to the consumer. Crass commercialization begins to define lifelong learning'. The reference to 'crass commercialization' reminds one of Lindeman's (1961: 64) arguments for adult education to be salvaged from the 'bread and butter' strangulation and evolve 'towards cultural ends'.

The idea of the learning society coupled with the imposing presence of 'specialists and experts' tends to affirm the fears and discontentment of Canadian youths with lifelong learning mentioned as an example earlier. These expressions of 'premonitions' for contemporary lifelong learning draw a clear line of difference between its African traditional rendering and application and its twenty-first-century understanding and drive. Whereas in traditional African societies lifelong learning was a way of life, a communion with the environment and the avenue to acquiring vocational skills; in Western and twenty-first-century usage, lifelong learning is more of a response to problems or perceived problems. The difference and the similarities between the two worlds and their uses of lifelong learning as community education should provide some lessons for efforts at innovation especially in terms of informal community learning.

Conclusion

This chapter has attempted to tease out the history of informal community learning in traditional Africa and its import for innovations in lifelong learning in spite of the heavy accent on orality. The more important issue I have tried to address is to determine the extent, if any, that an understanding of some aspects of informal community learning in traditional Africa may contribute to the debate on innovations in lifelong learning. In presenting community learning in traditional Africa, this chapter has used the 'history', institutions, forms and formats of education in indigenous Africa. At this point, the question remains: why the history of informal community adult education in traditional Africa? Given the complex nature of African traditional societies, this question cannot be answered in a definite and linear way. For one thing, the history of anything in traditional Africa almost implies the history of everything else because of the complex continuum I mentioned repeatedly above. Notwithstanding this holistic symmetry, I have been able to link the history of adult education with the genealogy of the community. The genealogical line extends to the first ancestors and thus the history of education, of religion, of culture, of trade and of adult education is the history of the people.

The institutions and formats that I have identified in this chapter are more like signposts that lead to more fundamentals that connect everyone to everyone else and establish education including adult education as a life's journey. The import lies in the symmetry that adds contrasting colour and beauty to life and living in the community, which is now called lifelong learning. Elsewhere (2007: 39) I have put the symmetry in greater detail: The symmetrical relationship between learning and communities in traditional Africa ensures that education is spiritual, moral, vocational, socio-political and lifelong. Education imposes commitment to group interest and teaches the imperative of good character as what makes an individual stand out. Individuality is emphasized and recognized as applied knowledge, as a reinvestment of knowledge via active citizenship. Thus, the purpose of education is to develop the Gu's *Medagbe* and Yoruba's *Omoluwabi* – the absolute measure of individuality.

Lifelong learning is about the individual in the community. The dividends of lifelong learning must first accrue to the individual before it can be re-invested into the community. The traditional African perspective of lifelong learning discussed in this chapter provides an example of symmetry of individual and community interests that make learning a definition of life and living in a community. The individual learner is the centre of lifelong learning and the community provided the 'classrooms' for learning as well as the avenue to put what has been learned into fruitful use through active citizenship.

References

Adeyinka, A. and Ndwapi, G. (2002). 'Education and morality in Africa', *Pastoral Care.*

Anyanwu, C. (1981). *Principles and Practice of Adult Education AND Community Development*, Ibadan: Abiprint Publishing Company Limited.

Anyanwu, K. C. (1983). *The African Experience in the American Marketplace*, Smithtown, NY: Exposition Press.

Avoseh, M. B. M. (2001). 'Learning to be active citizens: lessons of traditional Africa for lifelong learning', *International Journal of Lifelong Education*, 20:6, pp. 479–486.

Avoseh, M. B. M. (2002). 'Investigating the world of adult education in Africa', *AERC 2002 Proceedings*, proceedings of the 43rd Annual Adult Education Research Conference, North Carolina State University, Raleigh, pp. 7–12.

Avoseh, M. B. M. (2007). 'The symmetrical relationship between learning and communities in traditional Africa', proceedings of *Researching Adult Learning: Communities and Partnerships in Local and Global Context,* Belfast: SCUTREA.

Bodunrin, P. (1981). 'The question of African philosophy', *Philosophy*, 56, pp. 161–179.

Bown, L. (1981). 'History and adult education', in Bown, L. and Okedara, J. T. (eds), (1981) *An Introduction to the Study of Adult Education*, Ibadan: University Press Limited, pp. 159–167.

Butler, E. (2001). 'The power of discourse: Work-related learning in the "learning age"', in Cervero, R., Wilson, A. and associates (eds), *Power in Practice – Adult education and the struggle for knowledge and power in society*, San Francisco: Jossey-Bass, pp. 60–82.

Cross-Durrant, A. (2001). 'Basil Yeaxlee and the origins of lifelong education' in Jarvis, P. (ed.), (2001) *Twentieth Century Thinkers in Adult and Continuing Education*, 2nd edn, London: Kogan Page, pp. 31–48.

Daramola, O. ati Jeje, A. (1975). *Awon Àsà ati Òrisà Ilẹ Yoruba*, Ibadan: Onibon-Oje Press.

Datta, A. (1984). *Education and Society: The sociology of African education*, London: Macmillan.

Dewey, J. (1964). *Democracy and Education*, London: Macmillan.

Duke, C. (n.d.). 'Lifelong learning and tertiary education – the learning university revisited', University of Western Sydney.

Fafunwa, A. (1974). *History of Education in Nigeria*, London: Allen & Unwin.

Fajana, A. (1960). 'Educational policy in Nigerian traditional society', *Phylon*, 33:1, pp. 33–48.

Finger, M. and Asùn, J. (2001). *Adult Education at the Crossroads: Learning our ways out*, London: ZED Books.

Giroux, H. (1988). 'Literacy and the pedagogy of voice and political empowerment', *Educational Theory*, 38:1, pp. 61–75.

Grace, A. (2007). 'When lifelong learning goes awry: critical perspectives from Canada', *Researching Adult Learning: Communities and partnerships in local and global context*, Belfast: SCUTREA Conference Proceedings.

Gustavsson, B. (1997). 'Life-long learning reconsidered', in Walters, S. (ed.), (1997) *Globalization, Adult Education AND Training*, London: Zed Books.

Idowu B. (1962). *Olodumare: God in Yoruba belief*, London: Longman.

Jarvis, P. (1990). *An International Dictionary of Adult and Continuing Education*, London: Routledge.

Jarvis, P. (2001). 'Introduction: adult education – an ideal for modernity?' in Jarvis, P. (ed.), *Twentieth Century Thinkers in Adult & Continuing Education*, 2nd edn, London: Kogan Page, pp. 1–11.

Kang D. (2007). 'Rhizoactivity: toward a postmodern theory of lifelong learning' *Adult Education Quarterly*, 57:3, pp. 205–220.

Lindeman, E. (1961). *The Meaning of Adult Education*, Canada: Harvest House.

Mbiti, J. (1969). *African Religions and Philosophy*, London: Heinemann.

Merriam, S., Caffarella, R. and Baumgartner, L. M. (2007), *Learning in Adulthood*, 3rd edn, San Francisco: Jossey-Bass.

Nyerere, J. (1978). 'Development is for man, by man and of man: the declaration of Dar-es-Salaam' in Hall, B. and Kidd, J. (eds), (1978) *Adult Learning: A design for action*, Oxford: Pergamon Press, pp. 27–36.

Ocitti, J. (1994). 'An introduction to indigenous education in East Africa', supplement to *Adult Education and Development*, 42, pp. 1–126.

Okello, G. (1993). 'The conceptual and practical environmental orientations of African indigenous education', *Adult Education and Development*, 41, pp. 27–32.

Omolewa, Michael (1981). *Adult Education Practice in Nigeria*, Ibadan: Evans Brothers.

Omolewa, M., Adeola, O., Adekanmbi, G., Avoseh, M. and Braimoh, Dele (1998). *Literacy, Tradition and Progress*, Hamburg: UNESCO.

Onabamiro, S. (1983). 'Islamic, Christian, and indigenous religion in Nigerian education', in Obayan, P. and Arinze, E. (eds), *The Use of Cultural Heritage in Nigerian Education*, Lagos, National Commission for Museums and Monuments, pp. 59–68.

Teffo, L. and Roux, A. (1998). 'Metaphysical thinking in Africa', in Coetzee, P. and Roux, A. (eds), *Philosophy from Africa*, Johannesburg, International Thompson Publishing, pp. 134–148.

Walters, S. and Watters, K. (2001). 'Lifelong learning, higher education and active citizenship: from rhetoric to action', *International Journal of Lifelong Education*, 20:6, pp. 471–478.

Wiredu, K. (1980). *Philosophy and an African Culture*, Cambridge: Cambridge University Press.

Yeaxlee, Basil A. (1929) *Lifelong Education*, London: Cassell.

Yerby, F. (1971). *The Dahomean*, New York: Dell Publishing.

Youngman, F. (2000). *The Political Economy of Adult Education and Development*, London: ZED Books.

Chapter 3

Beyond the home

Informal learning and community participation for older women

Jan Etienne and Sue Jackson

Introduction

In this chapter we explore older women's informal learning and community participation. The chapter draws on the results of an Economic and Social Research Council (ESRC) funded research project entitled 'Learning Citizenship: Lifelong Learning, Community and the Women's Institutes'.[1] The key purpose of the study was to investigate the role and impact of informal learning on lifelong learning and citizenship, especially with regard to older women. Two specific aims of the research were to investigate (1) older women's engagement as active citizens and (2) the relationship between civic engagement and lifelong learning. A significant objective of the study was to increase knowledge of the extent and type of participation in lifelong learning and in active citizenship by older women.

The National Federation of Women's Institutes (NFWI) was chosen for the research primarily for two reasons. First it is the largest voluntary sector organisation for women in the UK; and second its mission seeks to enable women to provide an effective role in the community, to expand their horizons and to develop and pass on important skills, all central to any considerations of lifelong learning and active citizenship. The NFWI has a UK membership of around 215,000 women. The organisation has existed since 1915 and is made up of 70 regional Federations across England and Wales, each of which has a Chairman (*sic*)[2] and varying numbers of individual institutes. Today there are almost 8,000 Women's Institutes (WI) in the UK with different levels of membership. Members of the WI participate in lifelong learning through a variety of informal learning activities. Traditional images of the WI involve the construction of older women as homemakers, with the most dominant images being ones of jam and cake making, flower arranging and the development of other home craft skills. It is certainly the case that many of these activities abound. However, WI members also participate in talks on wide ranging topics often presented by fellow members with topics including anything from a recent holiday abroad to the role of a school governor. They also actively engage in constructing and supporting resolutions for national campaigns on a range of issues, including, for example, campaigns on global human rights issues such 'trafficking', nationwide health concerns such as healthy eating for schoolchildren, and local issues such as the closures of local community hospitals or post offices. It is these latter two activities (talks and resolutions) with which this chapter engages, considering how older women's informal learning developed through these and other activities take them beyond the home and into the community.

As Shibao Guo and Zenobia Jamal show in Chapter 1 of this book, pedagogies for adult learning are often separated from issues of community participation. Although the initial lifelong learning agenda for the incoming UK Labour Government in 1997 did explicitly link learning, community participation and social cohesion, as we show below, there was little if any focus on older people. There is to date little research on lifelong learning and community participation for older people and for women. Although the number of older women learners far outweighs the number men (NIACE, 2003), there is practically no research on older women as learners and active citizens. What work has been done has limited scope (see e.g. Cook et al., 2003). As successive UK Labour Governments complete their third term in office, lifelong learning and 'citizenship' look set to remain high on the political agenda, with continuing development of policies.

This chapter contributes to an understanding of lifelong learning and community for older women. It explores questions about older learners, social class, active citizenship and community and contributes to understanding the connections between informal participation in learning and community involvement for older women. After outlining the research project, the chapter begins with a discussion of active citizenship, community participation and lifelong learning. It goes on to explore ways in which the WI enables women to fully participate in communities of (informal) learning and community participation into old(er) age. Drawing on the data collected and analysed, we demonstrate how informal learning in the WI enables older women to be active beyond the home, with a strong political voice in their local communities and nationally. The chapter questions whether such experiences can be transferred to other sections of a growing ageing population in order to tackle loneliness, isolation and social exclusion.

The research

The research methods used in the study were largely qualitative with the use of focus groups and one-to-one interviews, although they also included more quantitative-based questionnaires. A total of 11 interviews were conducted with NFWI officers and Women's Institutes Advisers as well as 15 focus groups involving members from 24 local Women's Institutes across five selected Case Study Regions in England and Wales. In addition quantitative data was gathered and analysed from a total of 63 out of a possible 70 questionnaires received from Federation Chairmen and 155 from other WI members.

The five case study Federations were selected from a cross section of rural and urban areas in England and Wales:

- the largest Federation, with 248 institutes and 9,500 members, covering a large geographical area from the industrial south east of the England to rural villages;
- a Federation in a sparsely populated region, mainly consisting of rural farmlands and market towns, although it includes an affluent spa town and has a total of 101 institutes;
- one of the smallest Federations, with 33 institutes, covering a largely urban area, including institutes in socially and ethnically diverse communities;
- a Federation with 45 institutes in ethnically diverse towns and a range of villages in the North of England; and
- a Federation in Wales with 95 institutes and almost 4,000 members, covering a diverse geographical area, from a major city of Cardiff to the rural Welsh valleys.

Federations were chosen across England and Wales that were representative of a wide cross section of institutes, including those located in socially and ethnically diverse communities in Greater London and the West Midlands. However the social and ethnic diversity of the communities was not apparent in the research groups. The research encouraged self-classification of ethnic origin. The majority of participants who disclosed their ethnic origin described themselves either as white or through nationality or both (e.g. English, English White, Welsh, Irish or Scottish). Our selected case study Federations included areas in England and Wales with high percentages of multi-racial communities but this was not reflected in the participants. Although 'whiteness' has many categories and constructions (Frankenburg, 1993; Nakayama and Martin, 1998) it appeared to the researcher that all the participants were white. In his foreword to the interim statement introducing the work of the UK Commission on Integration and Cohesion, the Chair of the Commission, Darra Singh said:

> We are seeing new and complex pictures of diversity in our local communities, reflecting globalization and economic change. Communities with little experience of migration, particularly in rural areas, are experiencing significant change.
>
> (Department for Communities and Local Government, 2007)

However, there was no significant change apparent either in the membership of the WIs nor in the community work with which those members engaged.

Social class was a contested area. The majority of WI Chairmen classified themselves as 'middle class' (80 per cent), compared with 40 per cent of other WI members. A substantial proportion of members (40 per cent) chose not to disclose their social class status. Some participants felt strongly that the question on 'class' was irrelevant in today's society.

> Focus group 4:
> Interviewer: Do you feel class is an issue? Should it be an issue?

> Respondent 1: I don't think it should.
> Respondent 2: I must say I was rather surprised to see the question (on the questionnaire.

Others, too, did not want to engage with issues of 'class', or expressed concerns about class identity:

> I don't like the sort of class business. I am certainly not upper class, and middle class I don't know these days, these things get distorted. A lawyer, a dentist or something like that – that is my version of middle class, which I would not then be middle class. Then you say working class but for working class it's usually, as I understood it – the lower class and I don't consider I am lower class.

A significant number of the women came from a professional background, including teaching and the civil service. Seventeen per cent of the women hold a teaching certificate and 21 per cent possess a degree. A substantial number of participants are aged between 66 and 75 (41 per cent), with a significant amount aged over 75 (14 per cent). The majority of the women described themselves as married (68 per cent) or widowed (21 per cent). Although the study worked with Institutes located in urban areas (17 per cent) the vast majority (and representative of the NFWI as a whole) were located in rural areas (80 per cent).

Issues of ethnicity and class are discussed further, below. The quotations that are used in this chapter are taken from the interviews, focus groups and qualitative responses in the questionnaires, and are presented anonymously.

Informal learning and community participation

The NFWI engages in a range of learning activities for its members, including formal, non-formal and informal learning. For example, it runs some accredited courses through its own residential college, Denman College, in association with a local further education college. It also runs a range of non-accredited courses including training for various roles in the NFWI and, through Denman College, short taught programmes and courses (see Jackson, 2006 for more details). However, it is the informal learning that takes place within the local institutes that interests us in this chapter. Although informal learning is not always recognised as learning per se, taking place outside of dedicated learning environments (McGivney, 1999), there are around one and a half million learners in Britain between 50 and 75 participating in learning in a range of settings (Jackson, 2005), with a substantial number likely to be involved in informal learning in organisations like the NFWI. There is good evidence that older people can benefit substantially from continuing to learn both formally and informally as part of a fulfilling and active retirement. For example, 80 per cent of learners aged 50–75 reported a positive impact from learning in areas such as their enjoyment of life, self-confidence and their ability to cope with events such as divorce or bereavement, while 28 per cent reported an increased involvement in social, community and voluntary activities. For many, involvement in learning represents an important form of social activity (DWP Report, 2005).

In this chapter, we are interested in ways in which informal learning develops into the social involvement that we refer to as community participation rather than the possibly more politically influenced active citizenship. Although there are multiple and contested definitions of active citizenship, it is primarily about the inter-relations of rights and responsibilities within democratic societies, although definitions can be extended to include belonging and participation (Lister et al., 2007). Ruth Lister (1997) has described citizenship both as a political concept and a lived experience. However, for some groups and individuals, both politically and experientially, 'citizenship' is neither straightforward nor unproblematic (Jackson, 2004). It can exclude as well as include and depends on legal definitions as well as discursive practices as to who may be a member, with the resultant rights and obligations, and who may not. Active citizenship includes the transmission and strengthening of democratic values upheld by states (Arnot, 2009) and can involve regularly participating in the life of local communities through a range of activities. However, at the heart of the social representation of citizens is the concept of a male civic and public responsibility, with women 'not represented as legitimately successful and autonomous in public life' (Arnot, 2009: 15). Citizenship is not gender neutral and constructs women and men differently, and women have long been involved in maintaining the social relations of communities. There have been several critiques of a 'citizenship' located in the male public arena which pays scant attention to women's so-called 'private' work in the home, including for example the relationship between active citizenship and women's roles in undertaking home-based childcare and other care work (see e.g. Lister et al., 2007; Jackson, 2004).

Rather than focus on the rights, responsibilities and politics of 'citizenship', we are instead interested in community participation, which we take to be the direct or indirect involvement of members of a community in decision making processes and activities that affect the development and wellbeing of their community. This is not to suggest that any of us live and participate in clearly identified singular communities: we all exist in multiples communities simultaneously, which might involves places and spaces as well as identities, politics and constructions of power. Teresa Cairns (2003: 112) describes community participation as 'an uneasy shifting process involving ambiguous relationships and motives that reflect inequalities of resources and power', and 'spaces created by the powerful may be discursively bounded to permit only limited citizen influence, colonising interaction and stifling dissent' (Cornwall, 2002: 52). This is apparent, for example, in ways in which boundaries are negotiated or imposed through the discursive spaces of social class, or ethnicity, or religion or gender. As shown above, spaces created by the powerful include many of the public spaces occupied by men or through the discourses of masculinities implied in concepts of 'citizen'. However, it is the case that some members of the WI also act in exclusionary and colonising ways:

> Focus group 2:
> Respondent: I think there is a class distinction. I really do.
> Interviewer: There is?
> Respondent: 'I think so. If I was poor and needy . . . I think the WI would benefit you but you wouldn't benefit the WI because they couldn't cope with this.
> Interviewer: Explain a little more.
> Respondent: . . . They couldn't cope with the way we do things, the structure . . . In that regards there is a class distinction . . . because . . . the lower down the scale you are the less intellectual you are . . . They wouldn't feel comfortable talking to us.

Here there is a smooth transition from the empathy of the first person ('if *I* was poor and needy'), to sympathy ('the WI would benefit *you*'), to a movement towards a clear distinction between them ('*they* wouldn't feel comfortable') and us ('talking to *us*') [italics added], and with an association clearly being made between class, intellect, and in/abilities to cope. Working-class women, for example, are not seen as 'people like us':

> Focus group 1:
> Researcher: If I said that the WI is traditionally made up of middle-class women, what might be your view?
> Respondent 1: I think it's right!
> Respondent 2: It's not that others are excluded, it's just that they don't join us.
> Respondent 3: 'I think people have different values. We are people with similar values and expectations . . .

There was very little discussion of ethnicity or 'race' and, where there was, it came from WIs in urban areas. Members at two urban WIs considered issues of 'race' in their interviews. There was some recognition of 'difference' and of shared learning experiences, although in part this was located within similar discourses to that of social class: here of Asian women not being 'like us':

> I think we are probably more open minded [than WIs in rural area] . . . For example, we have an Asian lady that comes and she educated us to their way of life . . . We did think of setting up a WI in an Asian community, but because of the way they work men control the money side of it and they would want the right to come . . . We are thinking that perhaps now, because there is another generation that it's more, that it has picked up more about our ways, that perhaps we can now go and have a WI.

> I did . . . make an appointment to see the then Lord Mayor of [city], who was a Jamaican and a woman, and I implored her to help me set up some ethnic WIs but I wasn't successful . . . We did try very hard to set up some WIs within the Asian community . . . and we couldn't because the men wanted to control the purse strings and to dominate. And of course the WI can't do that.

For some minority ethnic communities and individuals, even after many years, or a lifetime, of living in the UK, they still face exclusionary practices in accessing meaningful lifelong learning opportunities (Dadzie, 1993). Field (2006: 17) reminds us that 'research so far has told us little about the experiences of different ethnic groupings' in lifelong learning, and the literature relating to ethnicity, learning and older women learners remains sparse. Over the next fifty years the current proportion of Black and minority ethnic (BME) elders is set to grow significantly (PRIAE, 2003). Older BME elders remain absent from existing learning provision for numerous reasons, including that provision available to them is often irrelevant, culturally inappropriate and inaccessible (NIACE, 2003).

Gerontological research (see e.g. Moriarty et al., 2001) has increasingly recognised the diversity of older people's lives, highlighting the differing experiences of women and men, including women and men from different minority ethnic groups. Moriarty and Butt's ESRC funded empirical research (2004) demonstrates growing numbers (350,000) of people from minority ethnic communities in the UK aged 65 and over – more than twice the number in 1991. Maynard's research into women from different ethnic and economic backgrounds reveals a growing number of women clearly wishing to play an important role in developing the world around them (Maynard et al., 2003). As suggested above, women traditionally have high levels of active participation in their local communities and there is a strong history of women's participation in community groups that have grown out of and developed from women's networks (Reiger, 2000; Jackson, 2004). A prime example of this would be the Southall Black Sisters, a group which started as a local community network supporting Black women who suffered at the hands of violent men in one London borough (Southall), which moved to prominence in a number of high profile national campaigns. This is true, too, of the Women's Institutes. As one member stated, 'the WI grew from just housewives to something more important for the community'. There are clear benefits to the community through participation of the members of the WI, and another member told us that 'the whole community benefits from the work of WI members'.

One aspect of networks that develop through community participation and/or through active citizenship, which has received high political profile, is social capital. Social capital is about the development of networks, norms and trusts, and is said to contribute to social cohesion and inclusion. The capacity for reciprocal trust and co-operation, at the centre of the development of social capital, is thought to be a major factor in promoting high levels of civic engagement and participation. According to Putnam (2000: 322), when social networks flourish social capital develops and individuals, neighbourhoods and 'entire nations' prosper. The regular meetings and networking of the local institutes of the National Federation of Women's Institutes help develop social capital for WI members, and there is a very high degree of reciprocity and trust, although the social capital developed through women's networks does not often carry high public value (Jackson, 2004).

Putnam (2000) describes social capital as a feature of social organisations that facilitates coordination and cooperation for mutual benefit and such social relations are traditionally important aspects of women's lives. The women who participated in this research identified reasons for belonging to the WI that include involvement, getting to know neighbours, having more involvement in village life and meeting people. Important, too, was the quest 'to be part of my community' and to have an 'involvement in community work' (Jackson, 2006). Older women can be, and are, involved in developing social capital and well able (if they choose) to fully participate in and work alongside their communities. However, social capital can exclude as well as include, and 'communications may not be shared with outsider groups, and new ideas and skills may be ignored because they come from outside the network' (Field, 2000: 129).

As we indicated above, the tight networks of the WI do appear to exclude as well as include, and the research was inconclusive as to the degree to which the development of social capital was leading WI members into greater community participation with diverse groups, and how much they were developing the social capital to remain with 'people like us'. It may be that until women from a broader cross section of society are actively involved with the WI, the more exclusionary aspects of social capital will continue within the institutes.

There is a popular notion that adult informal learning in community contexts can contribute to a greater sense of social justice and critical democracy (Coare and Johnson, 2003) although there are 'difficult questions about . . . the role and impact of adult learning . . . in fostering social inclusion at both national and local level (Johnson, 2003: 5). Kilpatrick, Field and Falk (2003: 426) noted:

> There are two types of positive outcomes possible from interactions that use social capital. One is some action or co-operation for the benefit of the community or its members; the other is the building or strengthening of knowledge and identity resources, such as constructing an agreed, or shared vision for the future.

We shall go on to explore this further in the next section. In particular we are interested in two related aspects of informal learning in the WI: learning through invited speakers through the regular talks at local WI meetings; and learning through political campaigning through the development of resolutions for national campaigns led by the Federation.

Beyond the home: developing learning and participation

Lifelong learning can take many forms but may be best described as the learning that takes place throughout our lives and which is not necessarily formally accredited, tested or measured. With the older women learners of the WI this primarily takes the form of informal learning which can promote social responsibility and includes the capacity to motivate others; the ability to appreciate networking; the skills to be able to pursue, pass on and share knowledge; and the ability to take direct action to challenge others.

In considering ways to develop a pedagogy for learning that supports and promotes citizenship (and, presumably, what we are describing here as community participation) Coare and Johnston (2003: 207) set out ten propositions for practice:

- promoting social learning;
- building social capital;
- fostering collective identities;
- finding common purpose;
- listening to voices;
- negotiating the curriculum;
- connecting formal and informal learning;
- embracing participation;
- working with social movements;
- influencing policy.

We have shown (above) some of the ways in which members of the WI develop their social capital, although we have been sceptical about views that automatically link social capital and community cohesion and inclusion. We have shown elsewhere ways in which the WI fosters collective identities and promotes social learning and how its members are able to connect formal and informal learning and negotiate curricula (see Etienne and Jackson, 2010 forthcoming; Jackson, 2006). In this section we draw on others of these propositions to explore ways in which informal learning in the WI enables its members to move beyond the home and towards their communities. We consider the extent to which such learning supports and promotes community participation, and are particularly interested here in the ways in which women engage with listening to invited speakers which can lead to their developing resolutions for campaigns which impact on their local and wider communities. As the NFWI website explains:

> Every year WI members have the chance to put forward issues or 'resolutions' that they would like the national body to campaign on. These resolutions go through a year long debating and consultation process by the membership. Once the resolutions have been short-listed by the membership a select number are chosen for discussion at the AGM in June. If passed, these then

> become mandates and form the basis of campaigning activities in the years ahead. (http://www.thewi.org.uk/standard.aspx?id=10606)

In order to put forward suggestions for resolutions, WI members explore a range of issues through listening to speakers invited to talk at their local institutes, and we begin by exploring the learning that takes place through listening to the invited speakers who give talks at local WI meetings. These talks appear to be central to members' informal learning. In exploring informal learning opportunities inside the WI, members participating in the research were asked what activities they found most helpful to their learning. Ninety per cent of the respondents placed 'Listening to an invited speaker' at the top of their list. These talks are extremely popular:

> There are key speakers in perhaps issues like healthy eating or children and exercise and sometimes it is just an excellent and amusing speaker which will inspire. And I think inspiration is important as well.

The ways in which members of the WI interact with speakers and each other is of course influenced by their life experiences and their attitudes to learning. This in turn affects what they learn through the process of developing their knowledge about the range of issues discussed. As Reece and Walker (2003: 98) have shown, 'such knowledge can be said to be a type of 'wisdom', since it is a recognition that experience is not just a side effect of living, but a major factor in people's successful approach to learning'. In exploring theories of 'expert' and 'novice' learners, Reece and Walker (2003) show how older learners can take on the roles of both 'experts' and 'novices' through the ways in which they learn from and teach each other, drawing on and developing learning from experience. This is particularly pertinent for older learners:

> No one can have failed to notice that as we experience more of life, no matter what age we are, we begin to approach things differently, and we begin to be able to bring our experience to bear on any solution. But further as we *do* get older, by the simple virtue of having lived longer, chances are that we *will* have experienced more situations. (Reece and Walker, 2003: 98)

The women draw on their experiences in their active participation in selecting, and sometimes becoming, speakers. For example, speakers may be drawn from the members themselves, eliciting talks as diverse as 'how I began bee keeping', 'my recent holiday' or 'becoming a parish councillor'. Despite its image, the WI is no longer predominantly concerned with jam making,[3] but is an increasingly challenging environment in which its members can engage in campaigning on issues that impact on the local and global communities, including for example adult education, health and the environment. For these wider issues of local, regional and/or national concern, a more extensive range of speakers are approached, often drawing on the expertise, knowledge or social capital of the members:

> As soon as we know what the subjects are we have to say 'Who do we know?' or 'Who should we go to?' this organisation or that organisation or whichever and then we try and get speakers.

This reliance on 'who we know' can be limiting, with an over-dependence on 'like-minded people' (Jackson, 2006), although there is usually an emphasis on getting two speakers to develop arguments for and against particular propositions. As one officer told us, this has proved to be very popular with members:

> They love coming to the meeting where the speakers are speaking for and giving an alternative view on the issues. We get 100s attending and they really do enjoy it.

This gives the women opportunities to develop their critical thinking and explore their values and attitudes as a result of engaging in discussion and critique:

> And the other thing about learning is that we always choose really good speakers, powerful speakers, who are able to speak. It's usually balanced so that you have got to have speakers who speak for and against the resolution, so everybody is learning and learning how to weigh up information and of course some of them may want to change their minds and vote in a different way from the information they have been given.

Speakers more often than not come from outside the organisation to speak on issues that affect not just the lives of the WI member but the lives of others around them. Within the informal learning settings of the local WIs, the women are briefed by a variety of 'expert speakers', who share their experiences and knowledge and enter into challenging dialogue where WI members question speakers and members, and present their own viewpoints. Learning takes place when the women network and engage in controversial debate with others. For the women such issues may be highly challenging, such as the sex trafficking of women and children, child prostitution or domestic violence. Following the talks there are opportunities for questions and feedback and a resolution may emerge based on the determination by a member to take action to address the issue. Such activities value the experiences and contributions of older women learners and potentially stand the women in good stead to support the learning of others, widen community participation and influence change for the benefit of local communities, especially when linked to the development of confidence to speak and to act:

> Belonging to a WI gives you the confidence to voice your opinions and help your community. You are respected because you are a member of the WI. You are learning in your own way. You are definitely learning from the speakers who come in.

> I feel that with the resolutions, you learn something while you are researching them. It opens your eyes continuously.

The development of resolutions begin an important journey for older women in enabling them to move their horizons beyond the home:

> It was whilst we were discussing the resolutions and I discovered that more people died from Aids each day . . . than the total number of people who died in the 9/11 tragedy. I think if I had not been involved in working on that resolution I would never have known. I feel I need to do something about those children really suffering in Africa.

This new learning can lead to active community participation and political engaging. As one member told us:

> They came and spoke to us about the issue and they asked us to sign petitions and a couple . . . went down to the County Hall when the planning permission was given, to march against it.

This type of pedagogic practice relies on presenting issues with which members will engage, listening and deciding if they wish to take learning further through the formulation of a resolution which stands to benefit themselves, fellow members as well as members of the wider community. The initial step to a resolution begins with a talk from a speaker chosen by a fellow WI member. Learning outcomes are achieved when the women retire to formulate resolutions; conduct independent research; network; present proposals and eventually work with other WI members to develop local campaigns that matter to them.

> If you are actually presenting a resolution you have got to have done an awful lot of research to make sure that it's a sensible resolution that they can be taken forward. For the woman who actually has to present it, it's a huge learning curve.

It is here that the women are involved in research to develop a resolution and to present their ideas to the rest of their Institute involving much preliminary planning and preparation:

> When I had to present resolutions I had attended the meeting which is held where the speakers come along to give us information etc. And then I have to prepare the resolution to present to all our members. Bear in mind that we have 100 members. It is pretty daunting because I haven't ever done public speaking before and I have now presented 3 resolutions!

The women interviewed appeared to be learning informally within their local institutes, both from the invited speakers and from their involvement in the creation of the resolution. 'It does open your eyes on what is happening really', one said. Another woman stated: 'It pushes you in all different directions.' One woman described her experience of presenting a resolution with which she was involved:

> The resolution was about children and carers and that was the first resolution that I have presented. It was actually gathering that information because although when one is studying one does all these things on an academic basis, it was doing something that mattered today to the children that we were dealing with or I was dealing with as well because it was whilst I was still teaching. It was so relevant to two sides of my life.

For many women, if a local concern emerges this can be a first step towards helping to understand the lives of others and helping to make a difference outside the WI:

> In terms of resolutions they hear that and hopefully they could be inspired to go back to their federations and help with the campaigning whether it is raising the awareness among the membership locally or the wider community or whether it's raising the issue with their local assembly member or local Councillor depending on the issue.

One woman described a resolution impacting on her local community:

> We are also involved in Resolution 2, on juggernauts to be kept out of the town. They are going through small towns and villages. That one was not chosen but when a resolution is rejected you can put it forward each year.

Older women learning through informal learning activities such as the development of resolutions – whether adopted or not – are demonstrating a certain level of commitment to tackling challenging issues in their communities. Their success may be determined by their level of understanding of the needs of the communities around them. The engagement in exploring resolutions that focus on wider issues that impact on society as a whole is a useful first step to promoting social cohesion in an ageing and culturally diverse society. In participating in local campaigns the women are able to pass on their learning to others and, through the interactions that follow, resolutions are developed with the potential for benefiting the wider community, and have the possibility of involving any member. As one member explained:

> Any member who has the burning desire to bring something to the attention of the federation or the whole of the movement submits a resolution which goes to national. They get short listed down to about 10 or 8 and those are then given out to the WIs at this time of the year. And then without not too

> much explanation, just a sort of minimal amount of explanation about those resolutions all the WIs then vote to which 3 they consider most important to be brought for further discussion. Now, this happens all over the whole country.

Major resolutions that begin in local institutes are taken up by the national federation, normally with an aim to influence policy. As one officer told us:

> One of the campaigns that we are working on . . . at the moment . . . is the closure of rural schools. . . . But the reasoning for closing them doesn't make sense because they perhaps instead of looking at the wide benefits to the community they say: 'They have to go and that's it'. If you lose the school you lose the heart of the community. This campaign has really grabbed the members' attention. I have never known them to respond as they have to anything . . . We issued a petition calling on the minister for education to really look at the criteria. Because nobody will admit to it . . . nobody will admit who has written this policy, whose responsibility it is. So there is this huge battle. [We] issued a petition among [the] membership and so far we have had 4,500 signatures and more than that, and they are coming in daily. We have had 50% of the WIs responding which is an absolutely fantastic response.

The projects that form part of local and national campaigns can seem particularly relevant to women's lives and encourage them to participate in their communities, both locally and nationally, with an aim of influencing policy makers. The officer continued:

> I think the projects play quite a big part . . . because the projects are very much focused in the community, they do then impact on the wider community. So certainly through the project we see that happening [women's involvement]. . . . So many members say to me, 'Oh, because of the WI I have had the confidence to go to A, B or C'. . . . Members have gone to Brussels [European Commission] and they have lobbied the MEPs [Members of the European Parliament] and they have spoken with authority and knowledge about the issues and the concerns. I suppose the campaigns play quite a big role as well and put women into that forum. . . .

The ability for (older) women to develop their voices in political arena is clearly important:

> We can say what we want to say and actually we will make a point. I think Tony Blair was quite surprised. Because they don't expect women to have a view, the men are running the place and the women have been following behind. And all of a sudden, that's not the case.

As this section has demonstrated, the development of resolutions through listening to and engaging with speakers on a variety of topics has enabled members of the WI to find common purpose to work with or for social movements and to aim to influence policy on a range of issues of local, national and global concern. However, although they listen attentively and carefully to the voices of invited speakers, whether these are internal or external to the institute, the voices are in the main limited to those within their own communities of practice rather than extending to wider and more diverse communities. Nevertheless, the practices of the WI enable older women to be recognised beyond the home, and help promote and develop social learning and community participation, although there is little evidence that such practices are developed out of more radical pedagogic traditions.

Conclusions

In this chapter we have shown how the NFWI enables its members to actively participate in communities of (informal) learning and community participation in their old(er) age. Both the leadership of the National Federation and the members of its local women's institutes are well aware of the benefits of lifelong learning, especially for older people, and the connections between lifelong and informal learning and community participation:

> I think because people are living longer, lifelong learning is important; to keep people as active citizens, to keep people engaged in society, to keep people engaged with other people, learning brings people together.
>
> I think lifelong learning generates a community feel good factor, people get much more involved with their neighbours, people who are stimulated by learning are happier people, are more likely to volunteer, they are more likely to get involved, less likely to get depressed.

The enthusiasm for learning can be clearly seen inside the WI, where members encourage and support each other. Older women in the WI have demonstrated their effective practice through well thought out strategies that demonstrate their common purpose. Learning is promoting community participation of a sort, which is vital to avoiding the social exclusion in which older women can find themselves. However, the 'feel good factor' described above is unlikely to be inclusive of all community members, and the chapter has questioned whether such experiences can be transferred to other sections of a growing ageing population in order to tackle loneliness, isolation and social exclusion. For example, the 2001 UK Census (Arber et al., 2003) revealed that among the non-White population, Black Caribbeans were the largest proportion of people aged 65 and over (11 per cent) reflecting the first large-scale migration of non-White groups to Britain back in the 1950s. So far, the specific involvement of ethnic minority older women learners has rarely been commented upon and does not feature in the lifelong learning literature (Field, 2006).

The chapter has outlined ways in which learning through listening to speakers and the subsequent development of resolutions has helped WI members to participate in their local communities and engage in policy issues of local, national and global concern. Nevertheless, there is little to show that the NFWI has an overtly radical approach to education or learning. Freire (1972: 56) describes and critiques a 'banking' tradition in education, where 'knowledge is a gift bestowed by those who consider themselves knowledgeable upon those whom they consider to know nothing'. The members of the WI both receive the gift of knowledge from those they think of as experts and specialists, and give the gift of knowledge to those perceived as less knowledgeable than themselves. Foucault (1972) has demonstrated how knowledge is inextricably linked to power, and the knowledge held by the members of the WI is based in the privileges of 'race' and class (although not of gender or of age).

In considering the role and impact of adult learning in fostering social inclusion, Johnson (2003) turns to the process of 'detraditionalization' (Beck et al., 1994, in Johnson, 2003: 5), where traditions become subject to interrogation, enabling dominant assumptions to be destablised. However, far from destablising traditions, the NFWI holds firmly to its own traditions for community participation. The NFWI campaigns, which are conducted from the relatively safe spaces of the local institutes and mainly in rural communities, are at a geographic, political and ideological distance from many of the social issues occurring in more diverse urban settings. Nevertheless, the spaces created for learning from speakers, for developing resolutions and for participating in political campaigns do enable the members of the WI to move beyond constructions of older women located in the home into developing both learning and community participation, albeit from positions of privilege of class and 'race'.

The lack of will of governments to offer safe, accessible and funded learning opportunities for older people can present barriers not only to learning but also to active community participation in later life. In an ageing society, governments should look closely at the lifelong learning options available to older people in the community, and could look to the WI to develop informal learning and community participation for others. At a time when the potential for loneliness and isolation looms ahead for many older women, the type of informal learning delivered by the NFWI could become a model from which to develop good practice for lifelong learning and community participation, securing meaningful roles for many older (women) learners.

Notes

1 ESRC RES-000-22-1441.

2 Whilst the organisation is run for women by women, and operates in a women-only environment, it is customary in the WI to refer to the role as 'Chairman'. Our attempts to discuss this at interview were largely met with bewilderment.

3 If it ever was – for example, the NFWI campaigned on issues around equal pay as far back as 1945 – see http://www.thewi.org.uk/standard.aspx?id=10606.

References

Arber, S., Davidson, K. and Ginn, J. (2003) *Gender and Ageing: Changing roles and relationships*, edited by S. Arber, K. Davidson and J. Ginn, Buckingham: Open University.

Arnot, M. (2009) *Educating the Gendered Citizen: Sociological engagements with national and global agenda*, London: Routledge.

Beck, U., Giddens, A. and Lash, A. (1994) *Reflexive Modernization: Politics, tradition and aesthetics in the modern social order*, Bristol: Policy Press.

Cairns. T. (2003) 'Citizenship and regeneration: participation or incorporation?', in Coare, P. and Johnson, R. (eds) *Adult Learning, Citizenship and Community Voices: Exploring community-based practice*, Leicester: NIACE, 108–123.

Coare, P. and Johnston, R. (eds) (2003) *Adult Learning, Citizenship and Community Voices: Exploring community-based practice*, Leicester: NIACE.

Cook, J., Maltby, T. and Warren, L. (2003) *Older Women's Lives and Voices*, ESRC Growing Older Programme, Research findings 21, University of Sheffield.

Cornwall, A. (2002) 'Beneficiary, consumer, citizen: Perspectives on participation for poverty reduction', Study, No. 2, Swedish International Development Agency (SIDA), Stockholm.

Dadzie, S. (1993) *Older and Wider: A study of educational provision for black and ethnic minority elders*, Leicester: NIACE.

Department for Communities and Local Government (2007) *Improving Opportunity, Strengthening Society, Two Years on – A progress report on the Government's strategy for race equality and community cohesion*, London: Department for Communities and Local Government.

Department of Work and Pensions (2005) *Opportunity Age: Meeting the challenges of ageing in the 21st century*, London: DWP.

Etienne, J. and Jackson, S. (2010 forthcoming) 'Lifelong learning in later years: choices and constraints for older women', in Jackson, S. Malcolm, I. and Thomas, K. (eds) *Gendered choices: Learning, work, identities in lifelong learning*, Dordrecht: Springer Academic Press.

Field, J. (2000) *Lifelong Learning and the New Educational Order*, Stoke-on-Trent: Trentham Books.

Field, J. (2006) *Has Lifelong Learning Had its Day? Adults Learning*, 17 (8): 16–17.

Foucault, M. (1972) *The Archaeology of Knowledge*, London: Tavistock.

Frankenburg, R. (1993) *White Women, Race Matters: The social construction of whiteness*, London: Routledge.

Friere, P. (1972) *Pedagogy of the Oppressed*, New York: Herder and Herder.

Johnson, R. (2003) 'Adult learning and citizenship: clearing the ground', in Coare, P. and Johnson R. (eds) *Adult Learning, Citizenship and Community voices: Exploring community based practice*, Leicester: NIACE, 3–21.

Jackson, S. (2004) 'Widening participation for women in lifelong learning and citizenship', *Journal of Widening Participation and Lifelong Learning:* 4 (1): 5–13.

Jackson, S. (2005) 'When learning comes if age? Continuing education into later life', *Journal of Adult and Continuing Education*, 11 (2): 188–199.

Jackson, S. (2006) 'Jam, Jerusalem and Calendar Girls: Lifelong learning and the WI', *Studies in the Education of Adults*, 38 (1): 74–90.

Kilpatrick, S. Field, J. and Falk, I. (2003) 'Social capital: an analytical tool for exploring lifelong learning and community development', *British Educational Research Journal*, 29 (3): 417–433.

Lister, R. (1997) 'Citizenship: towards a feminist synthesis', *Feminist Review*: 57: 28–48.

Lister, R. et al. (2007) *Gendering Citizenship in Western Europe: New challenges for citizenship research in a cross-national context*, Bristol: Policy Press.

McGivney, V. (1999) *Informal Learning in the Community: A trigger for change and Development*, Leicester, NIACE.

Maynard, M., Afshar, H. and Franks, M. (2003) *Empowerment and Disempowerment: Comparative study of Afro-Caribbean, Asian and White British women in the Third Age*, Generations Review.

Moriarty, J. and Butt, J. (2004) 'Inequalities in quality of life among older people from different ethnic groups', *Ageing and Society*, 24 (5): 729–753.

Moriarty, J., Sin, C. H., Brockmann, M., Butt, J. and Fisher, M. (2001) 'Quality of life and social support among people from different ethnic groups', *Generations Review*, 11 (4).

Nakayama, T. and Martin, J. (eds) (1998) *Whiteness: The communication of social identity*, London: Sage.

NIACE (National Institute of Adult Continuing Education) (2003) *Cultural Diversity – Responding to the learning needs of older people from black and minority ethnic communities*, NIACE briefing paper.

PRIAE (Policy Research Institute on Ageing and Ethnicity) (2003) *Minority Elderly Care in Europe: Country profiles*, Leeds: PRIAE.

Putnam, R. (2000) *Bowling Alone: The collapse and revival of American community*, New York: Simon and Schuster.

Reece, I. and Walker, S. (2003) *A Practical Guide to Teaching, Training and Learning*, Sunderland: Business Education Publishers.

Reiger, Kerreen (2000) 'Reconceiving citizenship: the challenge of mothers as political activists', in *Feminist Theory*, 1 (3): 309–327.

Chapter 4

Men's informal learning and wellbeing beyond the workplace

Barry Golding

Introduction

My concern in this chapter is about what informal learning men seek and undertake when not in the paid workforce and the potential benefits of that learning to their wellbeing. It is one outcome of my 15-year Australian research journey from mainly vocational and formal learning in the 1990s, to my current interest in non-vocational and informal learning. In that journey my interest has changed from equity and recognition for formal participants in education and training to the arguable inequity, exclusion of learners and lack of recognition of valuable learning experienced in non-formal contexts. I have slowly but surely come to regard educational formality, based around what Livingstone (2001: 3) calls a formal knowledge tradition of 'scientific cognitive knowledge which emphasizes recordable theories and articulated descriptions as cumulative bases for increased understanding', as one part of the problem of widespread disengagement from formal education, particularly in compulsory years. I have at the same time come to regard so called 'informal learning', acquired through what Livingstone (2001: 3) calls 'a practical knowledge tradition which stresses direct experience in various situated spheres', as one of several informal solutions.

I acknowledge the groundbreaking work of Veronica McGivney in demonstrating the potential and value of informal learning (McGivney, 1999a) and identifying some of the reasons why some groups of men are disengaged from formal learning and tend to be perceived as 'missing' from adult education and training in the UK (McGivney, 1999b, 2004). I have since come to understand that there are broader international insights that can be drawn from McGivney's research, particularly for people not in paid work: retired, unemployed or withdrawn from the workforce. I regard the problem as being particularly acute for men not in paid work, since not having access to learning or identity through work *and* being disengaged from both formal learning and informal learning in the community is a difficult and potentially dangerous trifecta. I have also come to realize, as Lave and Wenger (1991) have shown, that most people learn most effectively *through* particular informal contexts rather than *about* formal content. Learning is most problematic for people not in paid work, including older people in retirement, unless they have access to a context that is conducive to social learning with others. I contend, like Findsen (2005: 21), that there has been a predominant preoccupation in older adult learning 'with describing what is rather than what *could* or *ought to be*'. I therefore share Findsen's (2005: 61) contention that older people potentially have more freedom and less compulsion to learn:

> [O]lder adults do not have to adopt predominant work and life patterns. In sociological terms they have considerable *agency* and their identities are not necessarily predetermined by prevailing social norms or stereotyping.

I introduce learning through community-based men's sheds part way through this chapter (Golding et al., 2007) as one example of what role agency can play in informal learning, particularly for men not in work. In doing so I am aware of the likelihood, through research, of elevating informal and tacit learning to a status or importance not necessarily understood, shared or recognized by men who participate. As Livingstone (2001: 5) puts it, my attempts to sensitize both 'learners and researchers to previously taken-for-granted learning processes' makes me prone to unjustified presumptions whenever I go beyond respondent's self reports. There is also a risk that my own research interventions into informal learning will impose definitions of 'learning' and 'learners' on men who participate informally in a grassroots activity and who benefit for many other reasons than those derived from learning per se. By formally identifying benefits of informal, 'grassroots' learning such as occurs in community men's sheds, there is a consequent likelihood that government interventions to support that learning (such as outcomes-based funding, safety regulations and supervisor training) will in turn lead to greater formality and reduced access.

My interest and concern

A useful starting point in this discussion about informal learning is my agreement with Colley, Hodkinson and Malcolm's (2002: 1) conclusion, in their UK-based mapping of the conceptual terrain of non-formal learning:

> [T]here are few, if any, learning situations where either informal or formal elements are completely absent. Boundaries or relationships between informal, non-formal and formal learning can only be understood within particular contexts.

The particular contrary 'hook' that got me started on this chapter was a claim by Smith (1998: 9) in an article about informal learning, that policymakers, academics and practitioners have been too eager to go beyond accepting 'that much learning takes place beyond the formal confines of the classroom'. Smith argued that to substitute learning for education 'at a cost of thinking about education (and the values it carries)', was constituting 'a grave disservice . . . to all involved'. I will be exploring and contesting Smith's claim for a moral elevation of education, and related claims: i.e. that unlike learning, which happens 'all the time', on the other hand 'education involves intention and commitment. Education is a moral enterprise that needs to be judged as to whether it elevates and furthers well-being' (Smith, 1998: 9).

As an education practitioner, teacher and researcher based in an Australian 'higher' education context I admit to being acutely aware of and subject to the prevailing preeminence of formal, academic knowledge and the relatively high value attached in this university context to formal education compared to training, learning and doing. As a previous teacher in schools I have always felt uncomfortable 'professing' to school students who are being compulsorily educated, many without intention and commitment and who, if they progress to 'higher' levels of education in increasingly formal contexts, become subject to (and in many cases victims of) more formal assessment specifically designed for sifting and sorting university and job applicants.

As an adult education researcher I am also aware of evidence from a wide range of studies (Livingstone, 2001: 6) that 'well over two thirds of most adults' intentional learning efforts occurred completely outside institutionalized adult education programs or courses, hence the image of the adult learning iceberg' (2001: 6), and that 'virtually all adults are regularly involved in deliberate, self-directed learning projects beyond school and training programs'.

My central point in this chapter goes well beyond what I argue is the relatively minor role played by schools and universities in a sea of informal, lifelong and life-wide learning. I contend that education as espoused and practiced in schools and universities in most countries is not necessarily a moral enterprise that on balance can be judged as universally elevating and furthering wellbeing, particularly in comparison to learning generally and informal learning in particular. To take up Livingstone's (2001) iceberg analogy, higher education is so visible not because it is bigger, but because it is conventionally viewed as higher and above water.

My simplified argument goes something like this. Schools are essentially designed for compulsorily socializing and educating young people. University is the education destination for a relative minority of school students seeking professional careers. All school and university students learn, but less than the majority are educated in a 'moral' sense, as teased out and defined by Long (1992) in his analysis of *Higher Education as a Moral Enterprise*. In a postmodern and poststructuralist world there is less universal agreement in schools or universities than there ever was about 'orthodoxy' (right beliefs as to the ultimate nature of things), 'orthognosis' (right ways of knowing) or 'orthopraxis' (right ways of practicing in a community of learning).

My research interest and particular concern about men not in the workplace is fundamentally about some men's wellbeing and the role that learning can and might play to enhance their social inclusion and wellbeing. By some men, I particularly refer to what Hearn, et al. (2003: p. 27) identify in their comprehensive European study of the *Social Problem of Men* as:

> The social exclusion of certain men [which] links with unemployment of certain categories of men (such as less educated, rural, ethnic minority, young, older), men's isolation within and separation from families, and associated social and health problems.

You will notice that my specific interest is in the relationship between inclusion, learning and wellbeing. My perception is that learning is increasingly perceived by governments as formal, individual, accumulative and able to be delivered free of context. My experience and belief is that learning is seldom undertaken alone and for learning's sake. I perceive most learning to be informal, recurrent, social and embedded. Further, my contention is that the primary purpose and essential benefit of most learning is and should be social inclusion and improved wellbeing.

Having been a teacher in schools, technical and further education and university in Australia I am well aware of the effort that goes into the formal, 'front end' of education and training, directed particularly at getting young people into work and to re-educate and retrain adults over their paid working lives. Governments are understandably concerned with providing formal learning for getting people, particularly young people, into paid work and keeping industries, enterprises and their nations productive. Research into school-based education in other nations confirms that despite this concern, what occurs at school tends to replicate and reinforce existing parental, family, community and regional inequalities. My interest is therefore about what difference adult learning makes, or more accurately might or should make, to individual, family and community wellbeing beyond that benefit directly associated with paid work.

There are a number of reasons for encouraging learning and wellbeing for adults who are not in the paid workforce. First, there is a strong statistical correlation between levels of education and training, employment and wellbeing. People not in work can therefore use further learning as a means of increasing their employability and re-entering the workforce. Second, adults in work, compared to adults not in work, have reasonable access to further learning, through the encouragement or assistance of an employer, through their own initiative and funds while working, or informally through work itself. Third, for people not in the workforce and not seeking to re-enter it, learning creates opportunities for enhancing individual, family and community inclusion and wellbeing.

So why bother about men's learning, particularly for men not in work, given that men are already more likely that women to be in the paid workforce and be paid more than women for doing the same work? My interest in men arose after over a decade of researching equity in vocational and adult and community education (ACE) in Australia. My interviews were typically with female adult learners. I openly wondered in my research interviews where all the men were. The women I spoke with who had male partners typically made excuses for their men, all of which were sensible. They were working and busy on the farm or in their other small business; they had tended to become disengaged by the formality of school-based learning; they had not accessed or embraced the new information and computer technologies; they thought they could get work in the previously booming Australian economy without the need for formal training, just like their fathers had; or negative experiences at educational formality at school had turned them off learning for life. I therefore set out to find out where the men were learning, what men's attitudes to learning were, and what learning contexts do and would encourage and include them.

In part men were missing in research by default because they were not regarded as an 'equity target group' by Australian governments. Indeed to suggest in the 1990s in either policy or academic circles that some men might be disadvantaged was revolutionary and heretical. Australian educational participation data in the decade since show a progressive increase in female educational participation and outcomes in every education and training sector in Australia to the point that women now comprise a majority of participants and completers in every post-compulsory sector. The counter argument goes that despite these numerical improvements in women's participation in education and training and particularly adult, further and community education, the fields and occupations that women and men go into are different, and those that women go to tend to have less status and lower average incomes. Women on average are still not achieving the same status in work and on average are earning less than men.

As a male I need to clarify my interest and motivation in this area of research. My concern and interest with men's learning specifically is based on my experience that not all men achieve status and wealth through education and training. I contend that some men have had very difficult lives, shaped and determined in part through negative experiences of formal learning. I further contend that there are new and innovative ways to make a difference for such men by making learning contexts and pedagogies attractive and inclusive of men, taking particular account of class and ethnicity. Concentrating on *some* men and arguing a case for equity and greater inclusion in education is nevertheless difficult in terms of gender politics. O'Rourke (2007: 3) summarized some of the dilemmas in this 'complex and still contested issue of men and their masculinities in post-compulsory education'. Like me, O'Rourke is at pains to stress the importance of being concerned about men and boys with 'nuanced specificity', and identifies the 'missing men' as 'those with low basic skills, little or no qualifications and skills who have, or are experiencing chronic unemployment often accompanied by offending or anti-social behaviour' (2007: 3–4).

I note O'Rourke's two broad areas of unease as a feminist about projects particularly targeting men. Her first concern is that some interventions to widen men's participation and 'overcome the feminization of educational provision' (2007: 4) are not based on a critical understanding of adult education or lifelong learning as a form of gendered practice. Her second unease is that men have adopted community development through education methodologies drawn from feminist models of women's education, and that the new interventions tend to confirm rather than confront traditional gender roles. I agree with each of these contentions along with her important contention, demonstrated in community men's sheds, that it is 'how men are worked with rather than who works with them, that makes the difference' (Golding and Foley, 2008). What I do not share as a male is O'Rourke's unease. I turn later in my comparison of community neighbourhood houses and men's sheds as to why is desirable and acceptable for some women and some men to sometimes have access to separate and different gendered spaces in which to maximize their learning, particularly about themselves as women and as men. I refute O'Rourke's less than nuanced profile of 'men as learners' as universally 'impatient, instrumental and individualistic and as such [being] less capable than women of becoming co-collaborators or co-constructers of learning'. I am in agreement with Tett (1996: 63) that single-sex work needs to focus on which 'men/women; in which context; and for what purpose', an organizing principle I apply to community men's sheds in the section that follows.

Men's sheds in community contexts

The case of community men's sheds, though only one of many possible examples from other national contexts, is illustrative of how recent, educational innovation in Australia need not start from the top down. Men's sheds in Australia are a loose network of grassroots organizations, recently organically created, shaped and disseminated across Australia to allow for some men, most of whom are not in paid work, to learn together informally and for improvements in wellbeing to be achieved. In brief, men's sheds in community contexts (Golding et al., 2007) are a relatively new, diverse, loosely coupled and poorly known set of community-based, grassroots organizations – until the first community sheds were opened in New Zealand in 2008, found only in Australia. These informal, workshop-based spaces and programmes in community settings have grown recently and rapidly in mainly southern Australia. The 250-plus Australian sheds in early 2009 (see www.mensshed.org for updates) are widespread, diverse and only very recently networked. Unlike personal, 'backyard' sheds, they are available to groups of men and are typically organized by and auspiced through existing community organizations. Some sheds are organized around rural retirees and ex tradesmen, some around men with a disability, others around war veterans, with most organized around health, learning and aged care organizations. Though individual and diverse, they usually provide a safe, group workshop space, tools and equipment and an adjacent social area in a public, shed-type setting mainly for men not in paid work including older, retired men.

Men's backyard sheds, while iconic culturally for some Australian men, are not attractive to or suited to all men. Golding et al. (2007) identify a detailed profile of men they *do* attract. Participants tend to be older, not in paid work, and seeking or in need of sharing the caring company of other men for some of their week while being manually productive. Participants become, to use O'Rourke's (2007) words, not learners or students but 'co-collaborators or co-constructors of learning' in a place they feel at home with other men, producing socially useful objects and products in the process. The wellbeing and health benefits are multifaceted and significant to participants, as well as for partners, carers and families. The range of projects they are enthusiastically involved with and the impact of those projects on the men who participate is remarkable. If one were to design an ideal context and purpose for some men with negative previous experiences to mentor each other and learn informally in a community setting, as identified as desirable by McGivney (1999a, 1999b, 2004) in the UK, as anticipated by our research (Golding, Harvey and Echter, 2005) into rural men's learning in Australia, and as theorized by Lave and Wenger (1991) as 'communities of practice', it might look very like a community men's shed. The international potential for men's sheds-based learning, necessarily adapted to differing national and cultural contexts, is further explored in Golding, Foley and Brown (2007).

Sheds are effective when they network across and are fully supported by the communities and neighbourhoods they serve, and when they met the particular need of groups of men, as men themselves determine. While Australian community men's sheds may not have the same iconic attraction for some men in other national and cultural contexts, the broader idea and attraction of retired and unemployed men having a culturally appropriate workshop-type space other than home to feel at home, to learn informally and to and contribute to community, group and individual wellbeing in a safe and supervised place with other men for around one day a week, appears from our reconnaissance to be widely understood internationally.

Fundamentally, community men's sheds, unlike personal, backyard sheds, create a means, place and purpose for some men to engage with their own lived experience as men and to regularly share and learn from other men's lived experiences. This purpose is identified as desirable in single-sex work by Tett (1996: 63). It is not insignificant that the shed-type setting is effectively a workshop, where, as a consequence of a lifetime of enculturation at work and home in shed and workshop-type settings with other men, many older men feel at home with other men. This fundamental requirement that the shed space be particularly familiar and attractive mainly and specifically to some men can certainly be criticized from a feminist perspective as confirming rather than confronting gender roles for men. My response is that, on balance, it is more important in some instances to meet some people's fundamental needs and rights for the company of people of the same gender, to encourage informal learning, good health and wellbeing, and also to contribute positively to families and the wider community, than to confront all men's and women's traditional gender roles in all places and spaces, regardless of age, ethnicity and class. I argue that this is effectively what adult and community education providers and neighbourhood houses have done so successfully for decades, mainly, positively, deliberately and therapeutically for women.

Choosing the appropriate theoretical lens and data for informal learning

Research into informal learning, including but extending beyond what happens in community men's sheds, does much more than benignly observe an activity. It is a political intervention with the capacity to subvert, redefine and change what learning does, can and should happen. As Eraut (1999: 40) puts it in a review of research into workplace learning, 'the limitations to making tacit knowledge intentional are formidable, and much of the discussion about it in the literature is ill-informed if not naïve'. To press the point, if men's sheds were instead to be studied and reported through alternative theoretical lenses such as from health, aged care, human capital, social capital or wellbeing perspectives, each study would produce findings and practical outcomes that are a relic of the research lens employed.

The commonest theoretical lens employed in pragmatic, contemporary education studies is that of human capital: the idea that participation in more formal learning leads on average to increased likelihood of employment, income and economic benefit. Consistent with human capital theory, there are government sponsored economic incentives (including research incentives) in most modern economies, fundamentally to get young people selected into their first jobs as qualified as they can be, and to provide opportunities to get all other people of working age off income support into work through recurrent education and training. Whilst human capital theory is limited in its focus to economics, one of several other benefits of education including broader wellbeing and health benefits, it is widely employed because it is relatively simple to apply to education. Data are readily available on both average income levels and completed formal educational qualifications that allow for mathematical predictions about what average economic benefits extra formal training might produce for individuals by age, gender, socioeconomic status and ethnicity. Whilst in Europe 'Social class continues to be the key discriminator in understanding participation in learning' (Smith, 1998: 2), work status is shown via such data to also be a key determinant. 'Those who are not working (23 per cent) and retired people (20 per cent) have almost half the levels of participation of people in work or seeking work (Smith, 1998: 2).

Quantitative survey data are also available from many countries that demonstrate 'a correlation between poor health, including the poor health of some men, and various forms of social disadvantage associated with factors such as class and ethnicity' (Europa, 2004: 2). These data demonstrate the important intervening role played by social exclusion/inclusion on some men's wellbeing and health at home and at work. The greatest variance in mortality rates of men of prime working age (25–64 years) is for men working in blue-collar, manual jobs (Ballinger, 2007) as well as for those men who are unemployed or underemployed (Abraham and Krowchuk, 1986). Such men also experience significantly higher rates of disease, cancer and accidents compared to other men, higher rates and earlier mortality and suicide, increased use of health services, reduced social support networks, increased depression, reduced family cohesion, increased conflict and greater socioeconomic impoverishment. Each of our Australian research projects have shown that men in these groups are less likely than other men to have positive recollections of school and be less engaged over a lifetime as adults in positions of responsibility in community organizations. They are also shown from interview data to have had significantly more difficult lives, including work and family relationships.

Determinants of some men's disadvantage

There has been a tendency to seek to blame men as a hegemonic group, and men's negative hegemonic masculine behaviour in particular, for many of the circumstances that some men experience in life, in work and beyond work. It is possible to argue on solid evidence that men in the workforce are already advantaged on average compared to women; that women have generally been better at constantly reinventing themselves through lifelong learning for the changing world of work; that women have historically suffered the indignity of less stable, part time and casual work, and that it is men's self-perceived life role as a breadwinner (and of their partners' roles as housewives) that leads some men without or beyond work into such dark, difficult and sometimes violent places, behaviours and mental spaces.

There are other, arguably more productive ways of identifying some of the social determinants of men's disadvantage that do not label all men as having deficits or all men as *the* problem, and therefore some positive, alternative, education and public policy-related interventions. The World Health Organization (WHO, 2003) listed nine such social determinants that are known to impact on health and wellbeing, italicized in the sentences that follow. Around one half of these social determinants can arguably be improved through improved access to all forms of lifelong learning. Informal learning can decrease *social exclusion*, improve access to *work*, decrease the risk and duration of *unemployment*, improve the foundations for men's and boys' *early lives*, including the early lives of men's children and grandchildren. Learning is also a powerful tool for reducing *stress*, including anxiety, insecurity, low self-esteem and lack of control over life, as well as a means of understanding more about the link between *food* and health and *substance abuse* and wellbeing.

My broader contention is that quite apart from being inequitable and inhumane *not* to recognize and act on known and obvious disparities in some men's health, longevity and wellbeing compared to women's wellebeing, it is likely to be economically rational for governments to spend more funds encouraging some men and boys to become more engaged in all forms of learning in order to make them healthier and more independent later in life. The typical political caveat is that this targeted funding for men's programmes should not be 'at the expense of funding for services to women and/or children' (Europa, 2004: 5). An alternative argument is that some men would be less of a problem to themselves, families and communities if they were encouraged to learn to exercise more agency over their lives, and that governments should act on known and persistent regional and intergenerational inequalities in order to broaden the reach of adult learning in ways that can save health and welfare funds that might otherwise be wasted.

Informal learning and wellbeing

I turn to Livingstone's (2001) Canadian learning research for some definitions and general findings about informal learning in order to try and pin down the broader nature and importance of informal learning. Livingstone's (2001: 4) generic definition of informal learning is 'any activity involving the pursuit of understanding, knowledge or skill which occurs without the presence of externally imposed curriculum criteria'. My Australian research in its totality reinforces Livingstone's Canadian, survey-based contention that estimates of such informal learning 'very likely substantially underestimate the total amount of informal learning that people do because of the taken-for-granted character of this tacit learning' (2001: 5). My optimistic research hypothesis is that informal learning has the capacity to be inclusive, equitable and valuable for adults of any age, particularly for those adults previously excluded from formal learning by negative experiences at school. My hypothesis is supported by Livingstone's (2001: 16) finding, based on Canadian data, that there is no evident relationship 'between level of schooling completed and the incidence of informal learning. . . . Everyone can participate on their own terms if they are interested. Most people apparently are interested.' Livingstone also concluded that 'ageing does not appear to represent a major obstacle to continuing informal learning' (2001: 17). Our Australian community men's sheds research confirms each of these findings.

The field of informal learning is beset by a range of definitional problems that hinge around distinctions between education, training and learning, degree of learner identification and intentionality, the site and context in which the learning takes place and the role of the teacher-mentor in shaping the learning (pedagogy, curriculum, assessment). Perhaps the hardest one to deal with as a researcher within the least formal contexts is intentionality: whether or not participants consciously identify as learners, whether the activity is fundamentally about learning and whether the outcomes are learning-related.

Researching informal learning, including identifying tacit knowledge, poses significant theoretical difficulties that include issues to do with researcher presuppositions. In the case of researching informal learning through community-based men's sheds, while there is copious evidence using direct observation, in depth interviewing and surveying that significant learning *does* take place for older men, with remarkable and significant benefits to their wellbeing, the research subjects are best described as co-participants and certainly not as students, clients or learners. The irony is that if community men's sheds were to describe or name themselves as learning centres (or literacy, employment preparation, health and wellbeing centres) they would likely cease to be as attractive to and as effective for men who participate.

While informal learning in community settings, by virtue of its encouragement of increased social inclusion, appears likely to have a positive impact on men's health and wellbeing, there is no simple way of measuring or demonstrating its extent or impact largely because learning is not the only process happening. Because of the few perceived (or objectively identifiable) human capital benefits of informal and lifelong learning generally, there are very few government incentives for older people to learn 'later in life' (Jarvis, 2001) including after retirement from work, particularly for older men to learn to retire and to seek a new identity in retirement. The option of turning to any form of formal learning in later life has typically been more difficult for men from lower socio-economic backgrounds for a range of other reasons. In part it is because such men tend to have less positive recollections of formal education, mainly of school, than women. In part it is because men generally, particularly those who have had both hard and dangerous working lives and limited wider socialization, tend to die several years earlier than women, making late older adulthood (as well as the institutions, people and services that cater for their learning and other needs) remarkably feminized (Findsen, 2005: 62). Men with limited knowledge or experiences of new information and computer technology through work or home are particularly alienated from most standard ICT-based learning platforms. They also tend to feel alienated from adult and community education providers where women tend to predominate as returners to education as mature aged adults (McGivney, 1996). If they do participate, the quality of men's engagement on average tends to be lower than that of women.

There is evidence of significant men's informal learning from other community organizational types. My other research into informal learning has included studies of volunteers (85 per cent of whom were male) in rural fire brigades in small towns across Australia (Hayes, Golding and Harvey, 2004). Our research showed that as town size decreases, the importance of learning informally increases and the opportunities for formal learning decrease. Volunteer fire brigades in rural Australia, along with sporting clubs and land care organizations, become critically important sites for men to interact socially and learn informally. Organizations with firmly embedded informal learning functions or regular hands-on training (in the case of volunteer fire stations and sporting clubs) are particularly important informal learning sites for men from lower socio-economic backgrounds who have negative recollections of school. I am interested, in future research elaborated later in the chapter, to investigate whether community volunteer work-related informal learning, found to be important in Australia, is also important in other cultural and national contexts. Such learning is dismissed as being relatively unimportant by Livingstone (2001) in Canada, on the basis that it comprised a relatively low numbers of hours of participation (on a 1998 social survey that included a few questions on informal learning). My hunch, as Livingstone (2001: 9) suggests, is that such surveys 'very likely produce serious underestimates of the actual current extent of intentional informal learning . . . It is likely that [they] have merely rediscovered the iceberg of intentional informal learning rather than plumbing its depth.'

Livingstone (2001: 13) surmised that the relatively low, average reported levels of community-related informal learning in Canada were 'consistent with the fact that this is the most discretionary type of work in advanced industrial societies and many people simply choose to opt out'. Nevertheless around 10 per cent of respondents devoted more than ten hours a week to such learning. What interests me in future research inclusive of other nations and cultures is what role such learning plays when cut by age, gender, socioeconomic status and work status. My contention is that people not in work have more to lose by 'opting out' of other forms of learning, and are particularly prone to experience increased risk of social isolation and consequent risk to health and wellbeing. I was fascinated when in Nova Scotia, Canada to find that the many of the CAP (Community Access Program – public internet facilities) were collocated in rural fire stations alongside other community-learning infrastructure where social connections could be maximized. It was what our volunteer fire brigade research in Australia had predicted would be desirable.

Duke, Osborne and Wilson (2005: 65) reviewed research into social capital and learning and concluded that many adult and young people 'derive educational advantages from their social connections'. They cited Tuijnman and Boudard's (2001: 40) analysis of International Adult Literacy Survey data from seventeen countries that 'showed a positive association between levels of participation in adult education on the one hand, and membership of voluntary associations . . . on the other.' This complementarity, as Duke, Osborne and Wilson (2005: 9) note, makes good theoretical and practical sense since:

> Knowing is essentially a relationship among subjects: Knowing is social . . . Learning to cooperate, communicate and engage for a more open, tolerant and active civil society is important for the development of social capital and wellbeing.

My research interest is more about identifying the negative consequences to wellbeing for community involvement and informal learning *denied* to older adults not 'enrolled' in 'programs', than identifying the wellbeing associated with those that *are* enrolled. The overwhelming tendency in all education systems characterized by formality (measured by researchers as enrolment and program completion) is that educational cultures, families and communities have tended to self-reproduce and entrench existing inequality. As Pearce (1991) summarized, the tendency even in most 'third age' learning contexts, despite their great value to those older persons who participate, has been for people with better than average educational credentials to receive this kind of learning opportunity first. I am therefore particularly interested in the longer term and inter-generational exclusionary effects of educational formality, and conversely in the power of informal learning in community contexts to include and to heal. If all this seems at first glance to be located toward the outer edge of international educational research, I concur. In other ways, I now regard research beyond but through the academy of learning in the least formal contexts as a powerful and sobering exploration of a wide and powerful base of a poorly recognized informal learning 'iceberg'. My underlying thesis is that academics like myself have a lot to learn from, and responsibility to write in an accessible way about the least formal types of learning, which the 'higher' education sector typically and formally defines itself as being above.

The group I am particularly interested in, men not in paid work, already comprise more than one-third of all adult men in Australia. Livingstone's data cited above identified at least four out of ten Canadians not in work. While the group of men not in work is diverse it is mainly comprised of men of retirement age, but also includes men with a disability who are otherwise withdrawn from the workforce or else are unemployed. The total proportion of men not in paid work is predicted to increase to around one half in forthcoming decades as longevity increases and as the average age of Australians continues to increase. The average gap between retirement from paid work and death for Australians has widened to around thirty years. In effect most boys will spend as much of their adult lifetime out of work as in work, with a greatly increased opportunity and need for new discretionary and essential learning in retirement.

The international 'men's informal learning and wellbeing' research project

This researching and thinking has led me to wonder about – and collaboratively plan and implement – an international research project about the learning and wellbeing of men not in paid work in other national and cultural contexts. Our international project is a major field-based study of men's learning and wellbeing beyond the workplace that seeks to answer some of the unknowns identified above. The Anglophone stakeholders and researchers planning Phase 1 of the research are from Australia, New Zealand, the UK (England and Wales, Scotland, Northern Ireland) and the Irish Republic. Phase 2 is proposed in other less Anglophone cultural contexts. The overall project aims to investigate and compare men's attitudes towards and experiences of learning, and in particular non-formal and informal learning, in different cultural, national and regional contexts. The intention is to identify and study contexts where men of various ages, cultural, economic and social backgrounds are already learning informally and non-formally through voluntary community engagement in groups. The purpose is to identify and analyze the nature and benefits of engagement in learning beyond the workplace to the wellbeing of the men, their families and communities. The overall aim is to find out what is attractive, common and different about group settings that work for men, including but not restricted to men not in paid work, to identify better ways to engage and benefit men in learning through active community involvement beyond the workplace.

Research into men's learning through informal community contexts is considered timely and of interest to nations experiencing concerns about men's attitudes to and involvement in formal, lifelong, community and adult learning and concerns about wellbeing for the growing proportion of men not involved in the paid workforce (unemployed, working voluntarily, retired or with a disability). It is being undertaken in the context of pessimism in the literature (Lattimore, 2007) about the value of formal training for re-integrating displaced males into the workforce and perceptions that some perceived 'skill shortages' may be associated with some men's early withdrawal from the workforce, ageing in regional and rural communities and retirement.

Our research particularly seeks to explore the attitudes towards learning of men beyond the workplace and how these attitudes are affected by location, class, culture and men's different masculinities. It seeks to identify which informal, group learning environments, contexts and organizations engage men not involved in paid work, for what reasons and with what outcomes. It has the potential to tease out the relationship between informal group affiliation and learning in community contexts, and the wellbeing of men, their families and communities. By looking across different formal and informal learning organizations and types where men are already participating, it has the potential to identify informal learning roles each type of organization plays as well as men's preferred pedagogies, with the potential to positively re-engage other men in learning through community engagement.

I will revert to the plural 'we' in these final sections of the chapter to include Mike Brown and Annette Foley, my Australian research partners in the Australian strand of this international research. We present this broad research plan including its Australian strand in an unusually and deliberately open way in order to help others to critique our intentions as well as to assist in our endeavours. It is more usual for academics to keep their intentions to themselves to prevent others 'stealing' their methods. We consider that if our method is open to debate and change it will inform and involve other researchers in the field and inevitably lead to more useful research of impact and benefit to more men in similar circumstances internationally.

Our international research is designed to answer questions about men's informal adult and vocational learning that census and enrolment data cannot. By building in at least some 'common core' in terms of method (sampling rationale, interview and survey questions) we anticipate the potential to make some useful and unique international comparisons. The research builds on findings about benefits of informal, community-based learning from research into men in socially disadvantaged and geographically isolated areas in Australia (Golding, Harvey and Echter, 2004). The Australian strand of our study whose rationale is outlined in the final section of this chapter is deliberately designed to complement separate but parallel research into men's learning being conducted by and with other national research teams. This research will expand on the small amount of recent international research in this field including that by Hearn et al. (2003)

in Europe, Kenway, Kraack and Hickey-Moody (2006) on *Masculinity Beyond the Metropolis* in Australia, by Ruxton (2002) on men, masculinities and poverty and McGivney's (1999a, 1999b, 2004) groundbreaking research in the UK on some men's avoidance of formal learning and the benefits of informal learning in communities:

> By deliberately focusing on men's informal learning, our research also has the potential to directly inform studies of men's vocational, adult and community education and training for men in disadvantaged regions seeking work-related training. It will also add to the knowledge of links between the benefits of learning and men's sense of wellbeing (Stanwick, Ong and Karmel, 2006), including their health, employment and fatherhood. Our research is innovative in that it will 'hear' what men have to say about their experiences of active engagement in 'safe' spaces and voluntary organisations with other men. By deliberately collecting data in different regions with higher than average levels of social disadvantage, our research will identify factors (such as access to education training, access to computers, remoteness, age discrimination in employment, sickness and disability, caring and family roles) that can and do make men vocationally redundant and reluctant to learn that can be addressed by ACE, VET and family-friendly government policies. (HREOC, 2007)

The proposed international research strand in Australia

As elaborated above, our *Men's Sheds in Australia* research (Golding et al., 2007) used field research to provide a window into the informal learning needs and grass-roots, community-based responses of some older men, most over 45 years. It identified a new and surprising community of participants committed to working together and improving their own and community wellbeing. We have since argued that the very recent Australian 'shed movement' for men and the 1970s neighbourhood house movement for women have some interesting similarities and differences. As we have recently identified (Golding et al., 2008), there are some tantalizing parallels between the grassroots development of neighbourhood houses in Australia in the mid-1970s and men's sheds since the mid-1990s. While the sectors developed separately in different contexts at least twenty years apart, what they share is a commitment to the different needs of women (in the case of neighbourhood houses) and men (in the case of men's sheds).

We concluded that while neighbourhood houses and men's sheds in Australia identify the preferred territory for establishing their communities of practice, neither has been able, at least overtly in public spaces funded in part by governments committed to gender equity, to promote one particular form of masculinity or femininity (Golding et al., 2008). We have claimed that sheds (mainly for men) and houses (mainly for women) in community contexts in Australia are simultaneously both conservative and revolutionary:

> On one hand they both reinforce the status quo of gender stereotypical roles – of houses as places for women and sheds as places for men. On the other hand they are revolutionary in that they both draw lines in the gender sand and recognize there are times and places where some women and some men benefit from gendered communities of practice.
>
> (Golding et al., 2008: 245)

We suggest that both neighbourhood houses and sheds, in their acceptance of women's and men's activities for their own sakes provide an altogether new position from which women and men may examine and possibly question the alternatives that are available to them in terms of their current gendered roles and future aspirations.

The Australian strand of the international field research seeks to extend our research to wider areas of men's community involvement. It specifically seeks to explore intersections between Lattimore's (2007) desk-based research into the particular needs of men not in work in Australia and Vinson's (2007) careful and nuanced desk-based research into the distribution of social disadvantage in Australia. It specifically seeks to focus on and identify the learning needs of some men (unemployed, withdrawn from the workforce or retired) in some Australian regions (metropolitan, rural or regional) known to be experiencing socioeconomic disadvantage.

The selected organizations are inclusive of men across the community including: adult and community education; sporting; religious or culturally diverse/ indigenous; voluntary community; fire or emergency service; age and disability related; and men's social organizations (such as a community men's sheds in Australia). We regard the research method and instruments, similar to those used in our men's sheds research, as effective and highly ethical. We deliberately seek to work *with* communities and community organizations and feed the information back in ways that respect and value respondents and their organizations.

Lattimore (2007) identified a number of good reasons for including Australian men who are economically inactive in future research apart from the fact that they comprise a large and growing proportion of all men. The significant loss of economic activity associated with men's non-participation in the labour market can have a devastating social impact on some men, their families and communities and require costly social welfare intervention and support. Lattimore (2007) identified a reduced tolerance in contemporary economies for employing men with disabilities and lower skills as well as the feminization of many new forms of work as some of the factors affecting men's non-participation in paid work. Lattimore also showed that economically inactive men tend to group together spatially. Our research shows that un-partnered men, men without other community connections and men who did not enjoy or benefit from school are particularly vulnerable to labour market withdrawal. Our research also shows that such men benefit socially and in terms of their attitudes to learning from regular and informal community involvement with other men. The particular issue for the Australian ACE and vocational education and training (VET) sectors in Australia is that the very men who appear most to need formal literacies and vocational retraining are the least likely to have the attitudes and skills necessary to participate in and benefit from it.

The research rationale, design and sample locations for our research in Australia are informed by intersections between our Australian field research into aspects of informal men's learning and very recent findings by both Lattimore (2007) and Vinson (2007). There is a striking similarity between the distribution of men of prime age not in work (in Lattimore) and the distribution of social disadvantage (in Vinson). Research into ageing (Ageing Australia, 2001; Productivity Commission, 2005) suggest that while men age 40–49 years are the largest ten-year age cohort in Australia they are increasingly likely to leave paid employment early. These economically inactive men of working age are much more likely than other men to have no formal post-school qualifications and live or move to areas of concentrated and intersecting social and labour market disadvantage similar to those targeted by our research.

Finally, the research is consistent with international developments through OECD (2001: 66) that identify *all* learning environments as important for adults. Kearns (2006) reviewed international experience with equity in adult learning and concluded that equity objectives will be best achieved by integrating social and economic objectives with a focus on the adult learner rather than on vocational objectives alone. Access Economics (2005: 22) provided evidence that Australia lags best practice on participation at all mature age cohorts above 25 years. Given other evidence of men's lack of participation in both VET (Lattimore, 2007) and ACE in age cohorts over 45 years, there are particularly good social and economic arguments for raising participation by men in adult learning generally in the context of an ageing population, particularly for those Australian men unable to work, for whatever good reasons.

Conclusion: anticipated outcomes of the research

Schuller, Hammond and Preston (2004: 192) concluded that '[h]uge costs are incurred where learning is absent including poor physical and psychological health, malfunctioning families and communities lacking in social cohesion'. They also concluded that '[l]earning outcomes should be assessed within a framework which goes beyond the acquisition of qualifications and includes the learner's capacity to sustain themselves across a range of domains' (2004: 192). The learning opportunities we hypothesize are available through men's community involvement are seen as important pathways to many domains that include but go well beyond paid work and which are consistent with government policy in that they are both economically rational and equitable.

One important outcome of our research is an identification of learning strategies that are positive and therapeutic for many men. It starts from the premise that men not in work *pose problems for themselves, their families and the community* but that men in this situation are not *the* problem. The research therefore has the potential to identify ways of breaking intergenerational cycles of unemployment for men through community involvement. One final but important outcome of the research is an identification of a range of opportunities for marginalized men who are 'living on the edge' to develop positive masculinities and to enhance informal learning through mentoring with other men in community contexts.

References

Abraham, I. and Krowchuk, H. (1986), 'Unemployment and health: Health promotion for the jobless male', *Nursing Clinics of North America*, 21: 1, pp. 37–47.

Access Economics (2005), 'The economic benefit of increased participation in education and training', report to Dusseldorp Skills Forum, Glebe: Access Economics.

Ageing Australia (2001), *The National Strategy for an Ageing Australia*, Canberra: AGPS.

Ballinger, M. (2007), *More Than a Place to Do Woodwork: A case study of a community-based men's shed*, Master of Health Sciences Thesis, Bundoora: La Trobe University.

Colley, H., Hodkinson, P. and Malcolm, J. (2002), *Non-formal Learning: Mapping the conceptual terrain: A consultation report*, www.infed.org/archives/e-texts/colley_informal_learning.htm, accessed 4 January 2008.

Duke, C., Osborne, M. and Wilson, B. (2005), *Rebalancing the Social and Economic: Learning partnership and place*, Leicester: NIACE.

Eraut, M. (1999), 'Non-formal learning in the workplace: The hidden dimension of lifelong learning: A framework for analysis and the problems it poses for the researcher', plenary paper at First International Conference on Researching Work and Learning, Leeds University, 10–12 September.

Europa (2004), *Men and Social Problems: A new approach?* European Commission, www.ec.europa.eu/research/social-sciences/knowledge/projects/article_3551_en.htm, accessed 8 February 2008.

Findsen, B. (2005) *Learning Later*, Malabar, FL: Krieger.

Golding, B., Brown, M., Foley, A., Harvey, J. and Gleeson, L. (2007), *Men's Sheds in Australia: Learning through community contexts*, Adelaide: NCVER.

Golding, B. and Foley, A. (2008), 'How men are worked with: Gender roles in men's informal learning', paper to SCUTREA Conference, Edinburgh: University of Edinburgh, 2–4 July.

Golding, B., Foley, A. and Brown, M. (2007), 'The international potential for men's shed-based learning', *Ad Lib – Journal for Continuing Liberal Adult Education*, pp. 9–13.

Golding, B., Harvey, J. and Echter, A. (2005), *Men's Learning through ACE and Community Involvement in Small Rural Towns: Findings from a Victorian survey*, final report to Adult, Community and Further Education Board, Victoria, February, Melbourne: ACFEB.

Golding, B., Kimberley, H., Foley, A. and Brown, M. (2008), 'Houses and sheds: An exploration of the genesis and growth of neighbourhood houses and men's sheds in community settings', *Australian Journal of Adult Learning*, 48: 2, pp. 237–262.

Hayes, C., Golding, B. and Harvey, J. (2004), *Learning Through Fire and Emergency Services Organization in Small and Remote Towns in Australia*, Adelaide: NCVER.

Hearn, J., Muller, U., Oleksy, E., Pringle, K., Chernova, J., Ferguson, H., Holter, O., Kolga, V., Novikova, I., Ventimiglia, C., Lattu, E., Tallberg, T. and Olsvik, E. (2003), *The Social Problem of Men: Final report 2000–2003*, The European Research Network on

Men in Europe: The social problem and societal problemisation of men and masculinities, HPSE-CT-1999-008.

HREOC (2007), *It's About Time: Women, men, work and family*, Canberra: Human Rights and Equal Opportunity Commission.

Jarvis, P. (2001), *Learning in Later Life: An introduction for educators and carers*, London: Kogan Page.

Kearns, P. (2006), *Equity in Adult Learning: Integrating social justice and economic success*, paper to Adult Learning Australia, Canberra: ALA.

Kenway, J., Kraack, A. and Hickey-Moody, A. (2006), *Masculinity Beyond the Metropolis*, Basingstoke: Palgrave.

Lattimore, R. (2007), *Men Not at Work: An analysis of men outside the labour force*, staff working paper, Canberra: Australian Government Productivity Commission.

Lave, J. and Wenger, E. (1991), *Situated Learning: Legitimate peripheral participation*, Cambridge: Cambridge University Press.

Livingstone, D. (2001), *Adults Informal Learning: Definitions, findings, gaps and future research*, WALL working paper No. 21, Toronto: Centre for the Study of Education and Work.

Long, E. (1992), *Higher Education as a Moral Enterprise*, Washington, DC: Georgetown University Press.

McGivney, V. (1996), *Staying On or Leaving the Course*, Leicester: NIACE.

McGivney, V. (1999a), *Excluded Men: Men who are missing from education and training*, Leicester: NIACE.

McGivney, V. (1999b), *Informal Learning in the Community: A trigger for change and development*, Leicester: NIACE.

McGivney, V. (2004), *Men Earn, Women Learn: Bridging the gender divide in education and training*, Leicester: NIACE.

OECD (2001), 'Closing the gap: Securing benefits for all from education and training', in *Education Policy Analysis 2001*, Paris: OECD, pp. 73–98.

O'Rourke, R. (2007) 'Men, margins and the mainstream: Feminist reflections on changed times', *Ad Lib – Journal for Continuing Liberal Adult Education*, pp. 3–6.

Pearce, S. (1991), 'Toward understanding the participation of older adults in continuing education', *Educational Gerontology*, 17, pp. 451–464.

Productivity Commission (2005), *Economic Implications of Ageing in Australia*, Canberra: AGPS.

Ruxton, S. (2002), *Men, Masculinities and Poverty in the UK*, Oxford: Oxfam.

Schuller, T., Hammond, C. and Preston, J. (2004), 'Reappraising benefits', in Schuller, T., Preston, J., Hammond, C. and Brassett-Grundy, A. (eds), *The Benefits of Learning*, London: RoutledgeFalmer, pp. 179–193.

Smith, M. (1998), *Participation in Learning Projects and Programmes*, www.infed.org/biblio/b-partln.htm, accessed 3 January 2008.

Stanwick J., Ong, K. and Karmel, T. (2006), *Vocational Education and Training, Health and well being: Is there a relationship?*, Adelaide: NCVER.

Tett, L. (1996), 'Theorising practice in single-sex work', *Studies in the Education of Adults*, 28: 1, pp. 48–63.

Tuijnman, A. and Bouchard, E. (2001), *Adult Education Participation in North America: International perspectives*, report no. 89-574-XPE, Ottawa: Statistics Canada and Human Resources Development.

Vinson, T. (2007), *Dropping Off the Edge: The distribution of social disadvantage in Australia*, report for Jesuit Social Services and Catholic Social Services Australia, Sydney: Social Policy Research Centre.

WHO (2003), *Health Promotion Glossary*, Geneva: World Health Organization.

Part I: Conclusions

Sue Jackson

The four chapters in this Part have been concerned with ways in which inclusive learning environments can be built and sustained through learning communities. They have all, in their different ways, critically engaged in discussions of current policies and practices of lifelong learning, including hierarchies of privilege and the prioritising of knowledges that emanate from Western thinking in the 'developed' world. The chapter authors have demonstrated that pedagogies of and for lifelong learning are too often separated from learning within communities, and have explored innovative practices that can lead to sustaining communities, and to ensuring more inclusive and participatory practices for individuals and groups, including those currently marginalised in lifelong learning agendas.

The next Part continues some of the themes raised in Part I, including discussions of power, privilege and innovative practices, to explore participation and non-participation in lifelong learning.

Part II

Participation and non-participation

Introduction

Sue Jackson

Part II centralises debates about learning participation and (apparent) non-participation in lifelong learning, of concern to governments and non-governmental organisations across the globe. In Europe, for example, 16 core indicators of learning were developed (European Commission, 2007) with participation measured by the Eurostat Classification of Learning Activities.

> The benchmark appeared low enough, calling for 12.5% of the population of the EU member states aged between 25 and 64 to participate in lifelong learning by 2010. However, early survey results indicated that an average of just 9.7% of 25–64-year-olds participated in some form of lifelong learning activity (although there were notable differences between member states).
>
> (Badescu and Saisana, 2008)

Nevertheless, despite over 90 per cent of the population of the EU population apparently not participating in lifelong learning, non-participation is most often described through notions of deficit and 'lack' (Crowther et al., 2001). This Part challenges such definitions.

Whilst Part I focuses primarily on informal learning, in considering participation and non-participation Part II turns in the main to more formal structures and institutions. All of the chapters in this Part are interested in some of the barriers, challenges and choices for participation, including choices that are made in conditions not of our own choosing (Jackson et al., 2010). Whilst the chapters describe participation and non-participation mainly with examples from North America and the UK, the authors draw broader international comparisons, including the impact of demographic changes on and for diverse groups of learners (see also Chapter 1).

The chapters in this Part outline debates about participation and non-participation for marginalised groups and individuals, including women of colour and otherwise marginalised women, older learners, and those who have been otherwise previously distanced from learning. They aim to break down some of the neo-liberal complacencies about 'choice' and participation that assume that gender for example (Chapter 5), or 'race' (Chapter 6) no longer matters, or that lifelong learning is about the development of particular skills sets for particular learners (Chapters 7 and 8). In Part II we see an extension of some of the debates and discussions of Part I. For example, like Etienne and Jackson (Chapter 3), Patricia A. Gouthro (Chapter 5) is concerned with citizenship; and Keith Percy and Fiona Frank (Chapter 7) with issues of community and with older learners. Like Avoseh (Chapter 2), Yvonne Hillier (Chapter 8) is concerned about the loss or non-recognition of histories, and Frank and Percy (Chapter 7) with a need to blur distinctions between learners and teachers.

Chapter 5 opens the Part by considering the difficulties that women face when they attempt to advance their education by returning to university or when they decide to participate in formal politics. Patricia A. Gouthro argues that it is helpful to make such comparisons as in both situations it is evident that the non-linearity of women's life trajectories impacts upon their learning experiences and ability to participate, whether it is in higher education or the formal political sphere. A category of 'women' is of course not homogeneous: to begin to consider how gender impacts on women's learning pathways it is also important to consider the diverse range of backgrounds and experiences that women have. Women who are immigrants, who are older, who come from minority status cultural or racial backgrounds, who are not heterosexual in orientation, who have experienced abuse or been through traumatic family experiences, are all examples of women who face additional challenges in learning and active participation (see Cotterill et al., 2007), whether in formal education or the informal community sphere where politicians are often mentored. The difficulties and adversity that some women face may serve as a motivator for them to engage in learning, to take a proactive stance to right inequities and social justice, and to prove that they are capable and able to initiate change (Jackson et al., 2011, forthcoming). For many women, however, the consistent social, structural, cultural, and political barriers that are entrenched in both the formal education and political spheres, serve to limit participation and learning opportunities.

In the following chapter (Chapter 6) Lisa Baumgartner and Juanita Johnson-Bailey continue a discussion of participation and non-participation of marginalised groups by exploring how race and racism affect participation and learning in higher education. Despite an increased presence of African Americans and other minority ethnic groups on US and other college campuses in the last three decades, barriers remain. For Black students, the barriers include the discouragement of White school administrators towards Black applicants to programmes; a history of racism at predominantly White institutions; and a sense of isolation in the classroom. A culture of racism manifests itself in intimidation, hostility, isolation, and indifference. In contrast, White students cite family responsibilities and an inflexible institutional environment as barriers to participation. The authors examine White privilege by drawing on their personal stories as a White woman and a Black woman to show how race affected their respective graduate school experiences, including the under-researched role of emotion in the learning process (see Burke and Jackson, 2007).

Continuing debates raised in the first two chapters, in Chapter 7 Keith Percy and Fiona Frank engage with strategies for participation by a further minoritised group of learners, in this case older learners, developing issues also raised in Chapters 3 and 4. Like Golding (Chapter 4) they raise issues about wellbeing, lifelong learning and older learners, although they take a critical look at what this means with regard to policy and practice. They draw on a case study of a Senior Learners' Programme within a British higher education institution, whilst making broader international comparisons. Like Hillier (Chapter 8), as well as some of the authors in Part I, this chapter considers learning spaces in different contexts and settings. The aim of the Senior Learners' Programme was to give older learners space to learn about themselves and their past and to re-design their future. One way in which this space occurred was through a research circle (see also Freire, 1972) within the programme where students were able to engage in and develop their own research interests. However, the authors note that the programme exists within the realpolitik of a twenty-first-century British university. The authors conclude that with regard to the learning of older adults it may be time to move beyond the restrictions of the dichotomous terminology of teaching and learning, of directed and self-directed learning, of formal and informal learning, and of theoretical and experiential learning. They argue the need for a more extended and sophisticated paradigm that does not have unnecessary barriers and that extends new understandings, identities and futures.

The final chapter of this Part, Chapter 11, turns from higher education to adult education. Yvonne Hillier begins by outlining ways in which adult learning has been influenced at policy level over three decades, before drawing on one key area of adult learning – adult literacy and numeracy – to show how innovations in informal learning have developed and subsequently influenced mainstream adult learning. One area of innovation described by Hillier is that of learning technologies, although she notes that despite its proliferation, 'technology does not have to be very grand to be useful'. Hillier concludes that one key strand of adult learning – adult literacy, language and numeracy – has been a fertile area in which practice has been creatively developed and where tutors have been innovative. However, echoing some of the concerns of the previous chapter, she argues that as this strand becomes drawn into the compliance and accountability culture that pervades much of education (Chapman et al., 2006), there is a danger that innovation will become stifled. Like the other authors in this Part, Hillier states that activists need to find ways to continue to meet and engage with new interests and challenges in order to develop innovations in lifelong learning.

References

Badescu, M. and Saisana, M. (2008) *Participation in Lifelong Learning in Europe: What can be measured and compared?*, Luxembourg: European Commission.

Burke, J. and Jackson, S. (2007) *Reconceptualising Lifelong Learning: Feminist interventions*, London: Routledge.

Chapman, J., Cartwright, P. and McGilp, J. (eds) (2006) *Lifelong Learning, Participation and Equity*, Dordrecht: Springer Academic Press.
Cotterill, P., Letherby, G. and Jackson S. (eds) (2007) *Challenges and Negotiations for Women in Higher Education*, Dordrecht: Springer Academic Press.
Crowther, J., Hamilton, M. and Tett. L (2001) *Powerful Literacies*, Leicester: NIACE.
European Commission (2007) *A Coherent Framework of Indicators and Benchmarks for Monitoring Progress towards the Lisbon Objectives in Education and Training*, communication from the Commission to the Council, COM 61 final, Brussels, April.
Freire, P. (1972) *Pedagogy of the Oppressed*, New York: Herder and Herder.
Jackson, S., Malcolm, J. and Thomas, K. (eds) (2011, forthcoming) *Gendered Choices: Learning, work, identities in lifelong learning*, Dordrecht: Springer Academic Press

Chapter 5

Women, learning and equity

Recognizing non-linear life trajectories for women learners in political life and in higher education

Patricia A. Gouthro

Introduction

Deciding to return to higher education or deciding to run for political office are two very different life experiences, but they both require adult learning. For women, there are often issues around equity that affect participation in learning, whether it is in formal contexts, such as in higher education, or informal contexts, such as in the political sphere. Despite the commonly held perception that gender equality has been achieved in most Western societies, women still face numerous barriers around participation often linked with the fact that women tend to have non-linear life pathways. To explore this, this chapter draws upon three recently completed research studies conducted within Canada. The first of these examines women's learning trajectories around continuing in higher education as mature students, while the other two look at issues around active citizenship and participation in governance. These research studies reveal that women face similar sorts of barriers to participation when they seek to advance themselves, regardless of whether it is by going back to university or by running for political office. The 'politics of participation' seem to be linked to gendered differences in life experiences and expectations that often create non-linear life and learning trajectories. Women face numerous social structural barriers that cannot simply be attributed to personal circumstances or individual capabilities, but rather, are indicative of entrenched patriarchal values that constrain women's opportunities to participate in both formal and informal learning contexts that may lead women to having greater power in society.

The chapter begins with a discussion of current educational contexts and the influence of neoliberalism on lifelong learning policies and practices. A critical feminist analysis that draws upon Habermasian theory and uses a feminist lens is used to explain how social structural issues impact upon what may otherwise be perceived as individual 'choices' or decisions around learning. This framework for analysis also provides a context for understanding the barriers that impact on participation for women in higher education and in politics.

To understand how barriers that impact upon participation in higher education and in political life are connected, four particular areas of concern for women around learning and equity are taken up in this chapter. These include (1) how the issue of gender is complicated by diverse backgrounds and experiences that shape women's lives, (2) concerns around financial resources, (3) issues around a lack of self-confidence and (4) women's non-linear life and learning trajectories. Examples are provided from the three research studies to highlight the points that are argued. The chapter concludes with some suggestions and recommendations for acknowledging gender diversity issues in both formal and informal learning contexts in order to create more equitable opportunities for women to be successful in both higher education and in the political sphere.

Women in higher education and the political sphere

Over the last few years I have been awarded three external research grants, one funded through the Social Science and Humanities Research Council of Canada (SSHRC) on Understanding Women's Learning Trajectories: Implications for Adult and Higher Education in Canada, focusing on the experiences of mature women learner's pathways in Canada. The other two were funded by the Canadian Council on Learning (CCL). The first CCL study focused on Women as Active Citizens in Nova Scotia, and the other CCL grant was a national study called Grassroots and Governance: Examining Connections Between Community-based Organizations, Lifelong learning and Active Citizenship. The SSHRC grant and Active Citizens study used a combination of life history interviews and interviews with 'key informants', while the Grassroots and Governance study combined case studies with interviews with key informants. By 'key informants' I refer to individuals in 'key' positions to provide insights into the topics being discussed. In the SSHRC study this included people in the administrative and policy sector around higher education, while in the CCL studies, the key informants were politicians and leaders in the policy and not-for-profit sectors. In the three studies the identities of all individuals were kept confidential with the exception of the women interviewed as 'active citizens' in the Active Citizens study. Two of these women served as politicians in Canada – one is a member of the Senate (Jane Cordy), while Yvonne Atwell served as an MLA (Member of the provincial Legislative Assembly). The identities of all other participants are not revealed in the examples and quotes included in this chapter. This includes a number of mature students who participated in the SSHRC study, and some politicians who were involved in the CCL research studies as 'key informants'.

In conducting these three studies, it became apparent that many barriers that impact on women's ability to run for political office are similar to the challenges that women face in continuing in higher education. By drawing a comparison between these two examples, we can see that the obstacles that women face are not just individual problems, but rather systemic social concerns, that impact on women's abilities to participate equitably in all facets of life, particularly when they wish to engage in learning that will provide them with opportunities to have more of an impact on social, political and economic sectors.

Neoliberalism and lifelong learning

Increasingly our educational contexts are shaped by the discourses of neoliberalism that emphasize individualism, competition, and the values of the marketplace. In recent years, many educators have noticed the emphasis on linking educational policy with an economic agenda (Warren and Webb, 2007; Grace, 2007). Neoliberalism shapes educational policies and learners' expectations and is characterized by 'discourses of choice, education, work and lifelong learning [that] are connected to the market' (Bansel, 2007, p. 283). As broader definitions of lifelong learning have gone by the wayside,

> the notion of lifelong learning has moved to embrace the market orientation that places the learner not so much within a strong civil society as within an economic environment in which he or she must take responsibility for a whole range of economic imperatives and choices.
>
> (Axford and Seddon, 2006, p. 167)

This discourse of individual choice and responsibility eschews notions of social accountability and responsibility for equitable participation in learning and democratic engagement. The emphasis on personal 'choice' creates an illusion that all citizens and learners can choose to participate in higher education or in the political sphere. In reality, however, there are still significant social structural barriers that impact upon women's abilities to participate fully in a 'learning society'.

Critical feminist analysis

Using a critical feminist analysis that examines critical Habermasian theory with a feminist lens, the detrimental impact of neoliberal influences that foster a climate of individualism, competition, and an emphasis on values of the marketplace, can be used to consider the barriers and challenges that must be addressed to create more equitable opportunities for learning and engagement. Critical theorists drawing upon Habermas, such as Newman (1999) and Brookfield (2005) point to the impact of the 'system' – political, economic and social structures on the 'lifeworld' – the everyday world of experience we are immersed in through our local communities and in the home. Habermas theorizes that as our societies have become more sophisticated and complicated, the communicative linkages between the system and the lifeworld have eroded. In his introduction to Habermas's *Theory of Communicative Action*, McCarthy explains that Habermas believes that increasingly 'the lifeworld is subordinated to system imperatives, moral-practical elements are driven out of the public and private spheres, and everyday life is increasingly "monetarized" and "bureaucratized"' (1981, p. xxxii). This can be seen in the way that the marketplace is shaping educational discourses, whereby students become customers and clients. Education becomes an accounting game through assorted 'assessment' exercises whereby true criticality is undermined, thus creating a source of concern and contention for critical educators.

Feminist theorists such as Hayes and Flannery (2000) and Burke and Jackson (2007) point to the way that gender (as it is complicated by other intersecting variables of race, social class, ability, age, and sexual orientation) also shapes learning opportunities. Critical feminist Nancy Fraser (2003) argues that to attain equality we must address both redistribution and recognition. By this I take it that she means that we need to look at the issue of equality in terms of more equitable distribution of resources and power (i.e. having a higher number of women serve as politicians), and at the same acknowledge differences around identity and positionality (i.e. that women's experiences, needs, and priorities are not going to always be the same, nor should they be the same as men's experiences, needs and priorities). Fraser argues, 'Only an approach that reddresses the cultural devaluation of the 'feminine' precisely *within* the economy (and elsewhere) can deliver serious redistribution and genuine recognition' (2003, p. 66).

In bringing a feminist lens to critical theory, I look at the notion of communicative learning as a means of exploring alternative frameworks of making sense of the values that shape our worldviews. Habermas (1998) has developed a communicative theory of understanding, applied by some educational theorists, such as Mezirow (1991) as a communicative theory of *learning*. Habermas believes that language serves as the centre of our understanding of society, how social systems are developed and reproduced, and how, through dialogue and engagement in civil society, for example, it can be changed and altered. In discussing the centrality of language in creating and sustaining possibilities for understanding, Habermas explains, 'The structure of language maintains and renews itself solely through the linguistic community's practices of reaching understanding' (1998, p. 184). So language continues to exist, and to develop, because it is consistently used between active participants to negotiate and renegotiate their understandings of the world and their roles within in. Therein lies the power of communication action or communicative learning – there is always the potential for change, for growth, and for movement in a different direction. The most effective tool for social change, according to critical Habermasian thought, is this essential component of being human – we can use language to communicate with one another to work towards reaching consensus and thus work towards changing the way that we understand ourselves and the world that we inhabit. As Michael Newman explains, in discussing how Habermas has worked to broaden our conception of what is meant by the term 'reason':

> There is no such thing as pure reason. Rather, reason is tied up in language, and so 'enmeshed' in communicative action and the lifeworld upon which communicative action is premised.
>
> (1999, p. 207)

In other words, within the lifeworld, the world of everyday interaction and shared experience, we can learn from one another. Through communication we can discuss differences in perception and experience, and from this we can make decisions around changes in our actions and behaviors, if we so choose.

In critically examining a neoliberal context, therefore, Bansel argues that '"Choice", then, is not understood as a single rational act, but as a discourse and practice located within a network of multiple other discourses that together constitute a repertoire or network' (2007, p. 284). Currently, the responsibility for participation in higher education and the political sphere is represented as personal decisions made by individuals who must assess the options and accept the consequences of their 'choices'. However, a critical feminist perspective reveals that these 'personal' choices around participation are embedded within a larger framework whereby individuals are hampered by barriers and impediments beyond their own making. To move beyond the level of 'personal' choice and responsibility requires an understanding of these broader social, political, cultural and economic factors that shape individual decision-making. Burke and Jackson argue that 'pedagogies for lifelong learning should make explicit ways in which human knowledge develops in the course of relationships with others and their social contexts' (2007, p. 158–159). Through critical dialogue, it is possible for educators to explore these concerns and suggest alternative frameworks for making sense of the circumstances that impact upon women's experiences in both education and the political sphere.

Diversity and women's learning experiences

'Women', of course, is not a uniform category – to begin to consider how gender impacts on women's learning trajectories it is also important to consider the diverse range of backgrounds and experiences that women come from. As Merrill (2009) notes, 'adult learners are not homogenous and as a result learning careers and identities are shaped by issues of class, gender, ethnicity, disability and age' (p. 11). Women who are immigrants, who are older, who come from minority status cultural or racial backgrounds, who are not heterosexual in orientation, or who have ability issues often face additional concerns in learning and active participation, whether in formal education or the informal community sphere.

Acknowledging diversity means that educators must consider that many learners face additional challenges not just because of personal circumstances, but also because of social structural factors. The difficulties and adversity that some women face may serve as a motivator for them to engage in learning, to take a proactive stance to right inequities and social justice, and to prove that they are capable of initiating change. For many women, however, the consistent social, structural, cultural and political barriers that are entrenched in both the formal education and political spheres also serve to limit participation and learning opportunities.

In my SSHRC study examining the experiences of mature women students returning to higher education in Canada, it was clear that minority women often face additional challenges in continuing their formal educational studies. Issues of discrimination, feelings of marginalization and concerns around acceptance were all raised, although some students did seem to feel that the increasing number of visible minorities in the current Canadian context has helped to ease some of the sense of exclusion they faced earlier in their educational careers. For example, one student talked about when she first came to Canada as a student from the Caribbean in the 1970s, 'there were a few West Indian people, so some of the people that we hung out with were West Indians, as opposed to being in an all White environment . . . but Montreal at that was . . . an extremely racist place'. Similarly, another Black student discusses how Canada is becoming far more diverse, noting that when she did her undergraduate degree: 'In my undergrad years it was horrible. I think that's one reason I didn't do well . . . out of three hundred students in the class there were maybe three Black students so you felt very different'. As Guy (2009) points out, however, racism in educational settings is rarely overt anymore. Instead, he believes that there is often a subtle centering of White experience that tends undermine the significance of contributions and concerns of minority students.

Often it is difficult for learners to easily articulate the challenges that arise around diversity issues, whether these are around race or other concerns. After some thought, one Asian student in my SSHRC study explained:

> If you say it's race, actually, it's not about the colour of your skin, but about culture . . . For instance, at my centre there are age differences too. We have Caucasian students and when we have a party they tend to socialize together. Sometimes I don't even understand what they are talking about, so it's kind of harder for me to join their conversation . . . Those younger groups have different things to talk about. I feel left out. I'm older than them. They go to bars and talk to the boys. I don't feel it's about the skin colour, but about culture.

Certainly power plays out in many ways within academic settings. One minority student pointed out that in getting to the levels of graduate studies, 'the dynamics of class come into it. Economic status is a factor in who procures education at that level'. A White student acknowledged the privilege she had from her skin colour and middle class background, but also noted the challenges of being the only women in her cohort with extensive caregiving responsibilities, while she also struggled with ongoing health issues from a chronic and debilitating illness; 'Through my disability I see you can be on the margins in a number of ways.' A student from the Middle East pointed out the complex dynamics around race in one class she was taking: 'Power is important. Who has power, try to dominate. So in that class the Black [students] have . . . the power, so they dominate.' Instead of seeing racism as a binary opposition between Whites and other visible minorities, she argues that claims for voice and privilege often play out in multiple ways. The different kinds of diversity and power issues that exist within higher education often make it difficult to create inclusive learning environments.

My research on citizenship also raised concerns about additional challenges around running for political office that women from diverse and minority status backgrounds face. In their study on 'nascent political ambition', a quantitative US study that used a large scale survey to assess the factors that contribute to a citizen's decision as to whether or not they would consider running for political office, Fox and Lawless (2005) note that individuals from 'historically excluded groups' are much less likely to consider running in an election. Certainly women, particularly minority women, are poorly represented in most Western governments. As one of the 'key informants' in my Grassroots and Governance study said:

> There's only 20% of women in the House of Commons, and that is a travesty. I mean Afghanistan has better percentage. Rwanda has a better percentage. I mean nations we regards as less developed than we are for a variety of reasons are doing a lot better.

In my study on Women as Active Citizens, one of the participants, Yvonne Atwell, described some uncomfortable experiences a Black female politician:

> And what I didn't like when I showed up on behalf of the [New Democratic Party] NDP meetings or something like that, people thought that I was in the wrong room or that I was looking for the washroom [toilets] down the hall . . . that was my portfolio and people don't expect to see you, right? They don't expect to see a Black woman to be there. It becomes difficult . . . those were the hardest pieces of the work was trying to force myself to shake hands with people that I didn't particularly want to do that with.

While Yvonne felt that she was able to make important contributions that were beneficial to the members of her riding, and to the Nova Scotian Black community as a whole, she found that being one of a very few visible minority women in political leadership was often challenging.

A couple of participants in my Grassroots and Governance study raised the point that for many New Canadians it usually takes a few years, or in many cases a generation, before immigrants are able to reach a point of being ready to engage in the formal political process by running for government. As one 'key informant', now in political office and who grew up in an immigrant household, said:

> From my observation the active connection to the community is usually through their association or these groups. It's like a sequence of steps . . . they come in, it's the first couple of years of survival. Then it's finding out who you can be part of, what other members of your like community are organized and how they're organized and then through that they become active.

Finding connections to community seems to be an important first step for engaging citizens in the political process, so the support of different ethnic communities through social clubs and support groups seems to be a way to ensure more diverse participation in the political process. In my first CCL grant on 'active citizens', several of the participants noted that it was through involvement in local, community-based organizations (within the realm of what Habermas would call civil society) that they learned how to collectively raise their concerns to government, and in some instances, decide to eventually run for political office. Similarly, in his research on a Chinese immigrant community-based organization in Canada, Guo (2006) found that the supports offered by grassroots community organizations play an important role in fostering active citizenship capacities amongst New Canadians.

In both education and in politics, women who cope with issues around diversity often recognize the importance of power, since it is so often denied to them. Through both formal education and the political sphere, they see that it can be used to make a difference. Participation in higher levels of education may allow women with diverse backgrounds the opportunity to take up their own experiences to inform their research. For example, one SSHRC participant explained: 'My studies were about the early educational experiences of Black women, from their formative years, and how it affects their outcomes in higher education. It is almost like an autobiography. That's why I was so passionate about it.'

Similarly, a First Nations student talked about continuing with graduate studies:

> My motivation is that our history needs to get out there. It has never been told, not even to us. The history of colonization is very hush hush. And when I get these letters behind my name I . . . want to write books at different levels and distribute them in our community so people can actually read and see what our history is.

These learners believed that through their studies they could share their stories and they would be taken seriously because of the legitimacy attached to formal academic research.

A similar sense of motivation and purpose was expressed by one of the 'key informants' in the Grassroots and Governance study who grew up in an economically poor family. The deprivations she and her family experienced when she was a child motivated her to seek political office so that she can work to foster social justice issues. She argues passionately:

> There are no disposable people. There are no throwaways. Everyone matters. Their [economically marginalized people's] concerns and needs have to be at the centre of political decision making.

At the same time, however there are still numerous barriers that women of minority status face, in being able to effect the kinds of changes that they would like to see happening. Amongst these are financial concerns that may limit women's ability to pursue their educational or political goals.

Financial concerns

Women consistently earn lower incomes and have less access to financial resources than men do. McGivney (2001) notes that the decision to return to higher education is perceived as more risky for people from lower income backgrounds, as they have to invest more with less to fall back on if their education does not lead to better financial security.

Many of the women in the SSHRC study worried about the amount of student debt that they were accumulating, and whether or not they would be able to find employment that would pay them enough that they could repay it without finding themselves in financial difficulties during retirement. While some women had male partners who were financially supportive, many were 'on their own' – even if they had financed their husband's education earlier during their relationship. As one woman who had put her husband through law school before eventually getting a divorce and deciding to continue with her studies explained:

> I didn't get any support from my husband, aside from being able to live in the house and being able to eat the food from the fridge while I was there [during the alternate weeks that she provided caregiving for the children] . . . and it dropped to a rather risky level by the end of the doctoral process.

In addition, very few of the women in my SSHRC study had their studies paid for by their employers. One of the key informants thought back over situations where students had their education paid for: 'I think in every case I knew they were men . . . being sent there by the military [or] employers.'

Minority women also raised some interesting points about cultural differences with regards to financial issues. For example, one student who was of Caribbean background explained:

> I find that students of colour, especially Black students, don't want to ask, we don't want to get the hand out . . . my culture kind of puts that restriction on you. If you don't have food you don't let anybody know and you just put your chin up and bear it. It's a pride thing for West Indians. You don't share that information. You don't let anybody know that you are damning out. So for you to let White community know that you need help, that you're struggling, just compounds what they already think about you. That's one of the reasons you don't ask. But . . . I said, 'I am a Canadian. I have been here for all of these years. My parents are not about to be supporting me or helping me in any way. I am going to get what I can get'.

A number of students raised concerns around how lack of financial support creates serious barriers for women who want to continue their education. For example, one participant, when discussing the decision of women to return to school later in life explained:

> It is not the same for someone who is going back to school in their forties and their fifties . . . it is no small thing. It is not, 'Oh, I think I will go to school'. This is a life decision that means that a number of key foundational concepts of self have had to shift to go back this late. Some really hard work has gone on to get back to school . . . there ought to be some recognition of the value.

This points to the fact that lifelong learning, as discussed in the recently released Schuller and Watson (2009) report, *Learning Through Life*, too often focuses on narrow skill sets and economic returns rather than broader societal benefits. For example, if the physical and mental well being of a person is improved, if they are better able to parent and be caregivers, and if mature learners become more active as citizens because of their return to schooling, there needs to be some acknowledgement of these wider concerns. The 'costs' of going to school for people later in life are often higher, because they have to sacrifice more than younger people – but the benefits can also be very positive – so many participants felt that there needs to be a recognition of this.

Similarly, in the political sphere, having connections and financial resources are an important factor in determining whether or not a woman can decide to run for political office. Fox and Lawless note that 'individuals with time, money and civic skills are significantly more likely to engage in various forms of political activism' (2005, p. 645). One of the key informants in the Active Citizens study who was a politician noted that it was important to have connections with people who would be able to raise money for you to run a campaign – and it is often men who have these stronger networks with people who are able to make solid financial contributions. Another concern that Yvonne Atwell (an Active Citizen participant) raised was that once a person's political term is up, they need to have a job to go to. She noted that once her political party was out of power, most of the women were left seeking employment, while the men were taken care of by their friends and connections. Atwell points out that the reality is that being a politician is 'a temporary, part-time job' and that 'women don't often get those benefits that some of the men get who are in politics'. Therefore, the 'risks' for women to enter into politics, like continuing on in post-secondary education, are higher if they have lower incomes and less access to financial networks and supports.

Self-esteem and self-concept

Concerns around a lack of self-esteem consistently arise in research on women and learning (Belenky et al., 1986; Hayes and Flannery, 2000). This does not appear to be caused by an individual anomaly or 'weakness', but rather is a reflection of widely held social values that serve to diminish women's confidence in their abilities to be successful and to have something important to contribute. Yet once again, in a neoliberal climate of competition and individualism, this is framed as a problem of personal feelings of inadequacy, rather than as a structural problem of gender inequality.

Brookfield (2005) notes that many students returning to higher education, particularly at the graduate level, experience feelings of 'impostership' – the sense that everyone else belongs, but they have somehow managed to slip in and do not really deserve to be there. Many of the women in my SSHRC study discussed their struggles with self-esteem and self-concept in regards to schooling. As one participant said simply, 'I never saw myself as smart.'

Life histories help to uncover some of the stories that contribute to women's difficulties around developing and sustaining high self-esteem. For example, one participant talked about a musical audition early in her academic career:

> Someone made a remark and it just crushed me . . . because I was so crushable. I had no internal resources . . . when I was accepted to [University] . . . it was hard because [of] my self image, my own constructed life story . . . when I got accepted into Graduate Studies, it took me a year to feel comfortable . . . that I belonged.

Messages from educators and other significant people in student's lives often serve to perpetuate feelings of inadequacy and low self-worth. One SSHRC participant said that the first time she brought up the idea of returning to graduate school, her husband laughed at her. Another student talked about her divorce from her first husband: 'In fact, what broke us up was that I really didn't feel that I measured up'. After several relationships, and the decision to ultimately chart her own life course, which involved returning to higher education, this participant said:

> It is only since I have made the decision to go my way on my own that I realize that men have been amused by me in many ways. I feel that there has not been the respect that I thought there was. The amusement comes in [the form of], 'She's a woman who has this knowledge and it is really great talking with her . . . but . . .' at some point and time there is dismissal that I have noticed now for the first time in my life.

In taking a step back from her relationship with men, she is able to wryly acknowledge the subtle ways in which patriarchy often manifests itself in relationships, working to undermine women's abilities to feel confident and self-assured. A difficulty in addressing patriarchy is that it is often difficult to recognize and name. Being amused or dismissive are not violent or aggressive acts, but these kinds of behaviours reinforce an aura of masculine superiority that can erode a woman's sense of confidence and self-efficacy. Many women struggle with doubts about whether they are intelligent and have the ability to be successful because for years they have received subtle or not-so-subtle messages that reinforce a sense of inadequacy and incompetency – even if at some level, they know they are capable.

Other participants discussed the feedback that they received from educators and the impact that it had on them. While some educators provided positive support and encouragement, others undermined their confidence. For example, one participant who had spent years in therapy as a survivor of childhood sexual abuse talked about 'doing one practicum and I ended up withdrawing from this practicum when an advisor, a male advisor said to me "I bet men walk all over you"'. She explained that this was after

> a big bee flew into the classroom and sort of chaos erupted. And I was getting things back under control and very nervous having this man watching me. And so he was criticizing how I handled that, that I needed to be more assertive . . . I remember my sponsor teacher just being horrified by what he had said. And she had spent weeks with me and knew that I was doing okay. And I think that is was probably different because he was there.

At the time, this was rather devastating feedback, that reinforced her feelings of inadequacy. In retrospect, she considers the impact of this incident and explains:

> At that point I don't think I was conscious of it, I think that women sort of still make things okay and we took responsibility if something went wrong. Somehow it was our fault. I don't think it was just my experience of being a good girl and not making waves. I remember thinking, and especially I think during my early twenties, my university years, I had always hoped or wished that I could be a boy because they were permitted, they had more license to do things . . . I had gone through a lot of the Girl Guide program, and the mottos there just reinforced the abuse that I had experienced. You know a Girl Guide smiles and sings even under difficulty, thinks of other people before herself, and puts up with all of these things.

In my SSHRC interviews, it became apparent that relationships with family members were also very important in shaping self concept. For example, an Aboriginal student said:

> I had no confidence. I had no self esteem. I was sure that everything I did was wrong and that is because of what I heard at home, what Mom yelled at us all the time, 'You'll never be anything. You'll never do anything right'. Which looking back I can surmise is what was yelled at her at the residential schools or from her mother . . . she was just repeating it.

A number of the women in my SSHRC study shared stories of coping with trauma and dealing with adversity, such as growing up in alcoholic families or struggling with their own issues around substance abuse. All of these factors are linked with a learner's self perception and sense of self worth.

On the positive side, however, almost all of the women in the SSHRC study, regardless of facing challenges during their study or in seeking employment afterwards, commented on how obtaining further education increased their sense of confidence and self worth. One participant described her experience of being a mature student, which was very different from her earlier schooling experiences: 'When I came to university I was enjoying it. I was doing well and being asked to join this Honours program . . . and I thought, ooh, look at me go!'

Similarly, in my research on citizenship, concerns about self-esteem and beliefs in personal efficacy frequently arose. One of the Grassroots and Governance 'key informants', when asked to identify barriers that might inhibit active citizen participation, explained:

> I think it's a belief that an individual is too small to make a difference, that whole notion 'you can't fight City Hall', and a feeling of helplessness . . . a good example, I think, would be women living in poverty, in situations where they haven't the economic control over their lives. They feel trapped and [have] a sense that there aren't any avenues, there aren't any doors open to them.

In order for women to become involved in political life, they have to believe that it is possible for them to make a difference. Generally speaking, both male and female politicians that I spoke to in my CCL research noted that women often lack the confidence of their male counterparts in believing that they had the capabilities to be political leaders.

Fox and Lawless found that 'Women are more than twice as likely as men to consider themselves 'not qualified' to run for office' (2005, p. 654). In my Active Citizenship study, when asked about women entering into political office, Senator Jane Cordy said, 'Women, I think they say "Well, am I trained to do that? Do I have a background to do that" . . . they start second guessing'. In contrast, men often work on the assumption that they are quite capable of serving as a politician, regardless of their skills or educational background. One of the key informants in the Active Citizenship study echoed Senator Cordy's beliefs, noting that he never had a man question whether or not he would be well qualified to serve in any role in government, while women frequently did so. Of course, one could argue that it is not a fault that most women actually think you should have some skills or expertise to offer before taking on a political portfolio!

Fox and Lawless (2005) found that the combination of being mentored politically, and being involved in political activism, were the two most significant variables in determining whether a person would seriously consider running as a political candidate. Similarly, in my CCL research, women who did decide to go into politics often had a family background where politics were actively debated. They usually had extensive experience in working in community, and encouragement from friends, other community members and sometimes other politicians that led them to the decision to run for political office. This suggests the importance of sustaining grassroots organizations, where many people are informally mentored around participating in political life. In addition, it reinforces the importance of learning in the homeplace to create active and engaged citizens.

Women's non-linear learning trajectories

The main reason women, from a variety of backgrounds, continue to have non-linear life experiences, is that women continue to be the caregivers and have stronger ties to responsibilities connected with the homeplace than men do (Gouthro, 2009). Despite the neoliberal rhetoric of choice and decision-making that presupposes that individuals are responsible for putting their own interests first in order to be successful, many women continue to make choices about participation in learning, the workplace, and the political sphere, that are based primarily on accommodating the best interests of others. The values that shape these decisions are often radically different than the values of the marketplace.

Many of the SSHRC participants discussed the challenges of combining family responsibilities with returning to education. As one participant said 'it seems like it's held against you if family matters to you, which is so odd, because we're all part of families and want our families to be healthy'. She noted that programs that demanded full time residency and lacked flexibility created challenges particularly for women who tend to have 'complicated lives' with multiple responsibilities. As Marks, Turner and Osborne (2003) found in their study exploring reasons why individuals choose not to participate in higher education, many women feel guilty if they take time away from caregiving activities to pursue their own interests by returning to university. The participants in my SSHRC study frequently deferred their return to school and or selected alternative (and often otherwise less desirable) programmes because they worked better to accommodate their responsibilities around childcare. For example, a single mother explained her decision to take a programme with compressed weekend courses because 'it could be hard to find babysitters who would want to stay up that late on a weeknight'. Rather than making decisions with their own self-interest as the primary motivator, women consistently make educational choices that accommodate the needs of others.

Similarly, the one of the main reasons that women often do not enter political careers is because of their responsibilities within the homeplace. Yvonne Atwell reflects, 'Some people say "Oh, women should get into politics" . . . but women's agendas are very different at certain stages of their life.' She notes, 'It would be hard if you had little kids . . . or an unsupportive mate.' One of the key informants also commented on the 'family unfriendly' hours of political office, noting it would be next-to-impossible for a single parent to juggle the time demands of being a politician without other support networks. These comments point to the social structural design of our political system, that creates barriers and challenges for more inclusive participation because it directly conflicts with the values and expectations assigned to women in the broader society.

Women, more than men, are expected to prioritize caregiving activities and responsibilities. This consistently means that women 'choose' to put the perceived needs of other family members first, regardless of whether it is in their own 'best interests' in furthering their education or their career. This was seen time and time again in my SSHRC grant, when women dropped out of programmes, juggled caregiving with part-time education options, or deferred their return to school because of concerns that their formal education was conflicting with their family responsibilities. Having children or moving to accommodate a partner's career often meant breaks in both career and educational paths.

Other factors not linked with caregiving, but connected to concerns within the homeplace, also impacted on women's educational 'choices'. Some women had to deal with financial fallout after a divorce and needed to become financially capable of supporting their children. Other women emigrated to Canada to escape violence in their own country, leading them back to school to regain credentials. A couple of women had to flee from abusive husbands at different stages in their lives. All of these factors led to disruptions, changes in educational trajectories, and non-linear career paths.

In speaking with politicians, it was clear that childcare responsibilities often interfere with women's possible interest in running for electoral office. In my first CCL grant, one of the key informants noted that when she decided to run for office, her mother came and looked after the kids and the household while she campaigned. Her mother said she wanted to do this because she believed that was the only way her daughter could have a fair chance of being elected. The participant acknowledged that even though her husband was supportive, her mother was right – without her support, she would have been at a disadvantage compared to male politicians because their wives took on so much of the unpaid labour and caregiving activities within the home. Since many women do not have someone else who can provide that kind of support, mothers will often defer from entering the formal political sphere until their children are grown – a 'choice' that may have a detrimental effect on their ability to have a successful political career.

Several politicians commented as well that it was rare for women to plan a career as a politician, whereas young ambitious men often begin as political aides, get a degree, and then move into the political sphere. Women are more likely to have other careers or be at home with children first, and then because of their involvement in grassroots activism or community volunteer work, may eventually be encouraged or come to a decision that they would like to consider running for office. Therefore women are less likely to plan to engage in learning, even at an informal level, to prepare for a life in politics.

Implications for adult and higher education

The non-linearity of women's learning pathways should not be viewed as a problem unique to individual women, but rather as a systemic response to the multiple demands and expectations placed on women. If we are seriously concerned with the notion of 'widening participation in Higher Education', Hunt argues that it is would be beneficial to draw upon an adult education perspective that traditionally has had an emancipatory focus, and in which educators believe that 'working explicitly with the life experiences of course participants is usually as important as imparting subject knowledge' (2007, p. 767).

While most of the policies and systems we currently have in place in higher education and the political sphere do not acknowledge a gendered difference in life and learning experiences, there have been some positive innovations in both the higher education and the political system that have been beneficial in terms of creating greater participation amongst women. In higher education, while many of these programmes are not specifically targeted to women, women often benefit the most from having childcare options on campus, loan forgiveness programmes from government based on income after graduation (since women usually earn lower incomes), and they are more likely to take advantage of counseling and support services on campus. Transition year programmes, designed to ease the experience of entering into higher education by providing additional supports to marginalized groups in Canadian society such as First Nations students and African-Canadian learners, are beneficial to female as well as male learners.

Whilst there are some problems in suggesting that flexible, distance, and compressed educational delivery methods 'solve' all the problems that women face in juggling their many responsibilities, it is true that these options are the main reason many mature women are able to continue with their formal education. For women who want to continue their studies in a part-time capacity, these options enable them to create a better balance between the demands of academe and the other commitments that women have in their lives. The only problem is that too often women 'choose' educational options that are not ideal, but are a compromise so as not to 'rock the boat' too much at home. If the consequences of these 'choices' are that women are less likely to get into graduate school, less likely to be get the type of employment desired, or are less satisfied with their educational experience, then one is left wondering if these types of innovations in some ways are as beneficial as they might appear to be on the surface. In some instances, the options of flexibility mask the underlying issues in equality, whereby women often have fewer options than men do around prioritizing their own needs or interests in determining their educational pathways.

With regards to the political sphere, there are some innovative programmes in Canada that encourage women to consider electoral politics for a career. For example, my university, Mount Saint Vincent, runs a short-term non-partisan campaign school for women who are considering running for office. Most political parties in Canada provide women with a small extra budget to cover additional costs that women might face during campaigning, such as requiring childcare or a more extensive wardrobe than their male counterparts. However, the sums for this are quite small (equivalent to one or two hundred pounds sterling). While a good idea, to make a real difference, they need to be more substantial. The other policy that can make a significant difference, is when political parties (such as our NDP) insist on having an equitable number of women candidates and women politicans serving on various committees. This, in a sense, forces other politicians and leaders to seriously consider how they can mentor and support women entering into and participating equitably in the political sphere. As one political leader noted, it may take more work and encouragement to seek out and support female candidates, but this is perceived to be a more worthwhile investment of time and resources if there is a commitment to gender equity.

There are still numerous barriers, however, in both formal and informal learning contexts, that women are expected to negotiate in order to be successful. By taking a critical feminist lens for analysis, the systemic nature of some of these challenges that shape women's participation in both returning to formal education and participating in the political sphere can be seen. These are the same sorts of challenges that impact on women's ability to be successful in the paid workplace, or to move into positions of authority and power in any social structure (i.e. churches). The sense of complacency that 'gender no longer matters', and that it no longer needs to be taken up as an issue of social justice needs to be challenged. The neoliberal discourse of 'choice' must be called into question, to recognize the social structural factors that shape women's participation in learning in both formal and informal contexts. There needs to be shifts in policies, educational practices, and in the political sphere that would provide greater access and equity for women while recognizing and validating the contributions that women have to make regardless of whether they often follow non-linear pathways through life.

References

Axford, B. and Seddon, T. (2006). 'Lifelong learning in a market economy', *Australian Journal of Education*. 50: 2, pp. 167–284.

Bansel, P. (2007). 'Subjects of choice and lifelong learning', *International Journal of Qualitative Studies in Education*. 20: 3, pp. 283–300.

Belenky, M. F., Clinchy, B. M., Goldberger, N. R. and Tarule, J. M. (1986). *Women's Ways of Knowing: The development of self, voice and mind*. New York: Basic Books.

Borden, L. and Serido, J. (2009). 'From program participant to engaged citizen: a developmental journey', *Journal of Community Psychology*. 37: 4, pp. 423–438.

Brookfield, S. D. (2005). *The Power of Critical Theory: Liberating adult learning and teaching*. San Francisco: Jossey-Bass.

Burke, P. J. and Jackson, S. (2007). *Reconceptualizing Lifelong Learning: Feminist interventions*. Abingdon: Routledge.

Fraser, N. (2003). 'Social justice in the age of identity politics: Redistribution, recognition, and participation', in Fraser, N. and Honneth, A. (2003) *Redistribution or Recognition? A philosophical exchange*. London: Verso.

Fox, R. and Lawless, J. L. (2005). 'To run or not to run for office: Explaining nascent political ambition', *American Journal of Political Science*. 49: 3, pp. 642–659.

Gouthro, P. A. (2009). 'Neoliberalism, lifelong learning and the homeplace: Problematizing the boundaries of "public" and "private" to explore women's learning experiences', *Studies in Continuing Education*. 31: 2, pp. 157–172.

Grace, A. P. (2007). 'Envisioning a critical social pedagogy of learning and work in a contemporary culture of cyclical lifelong learning', *Studies in Continuing Education*. 29: 1, pp. 85–103.

Guo, S. (2006). 'Adult education for social change: The role of a grassroots organisation in Canada', *Convergence*. 39: 4, pp. 107–122.

Guy, T. (2009). 'Just democracy: Ethical concerns in teaching', *New Directions for Adult Continuing Education*. 123, pp. 43–52.

Habermas, J. (1998). *On the Pragmatics of Communication*. Cooke, M. (Ed.) Cambridge, MA: MIT Press.

Hayes, E. and Flannery, D. (2000). *Women as Learners: The significance of gender in lifelong learning*. San Francisco: Jossey-Bass.

Hunt, C. (2007). 'Diversity and pedagogic practice: Reflections on the role of an adult educator in higher education', *Teaching in Higher Education*. 12: 5/6, pp. 765–779.

McCarthy, T. (1981)'Translator's introduction', in Habermas, J. (1981). *The Theory of Communicative Action: Volume one: Reason and the rationalization of society*. Boston: Beacon Press.

McGivney, V. (2001). *Fixing or Changing the Pattern? Reflections on widening adult participation in learning*. Leicester, UK: NIACE.

Marks, A, Turner, E. and Osborne, M. (2003). '"Not for the likes of me": The overlapping effect of social class and gender factors in the decision made by adults to participate in higher education', *Journal of Further and Higher Education*. 27: 4, pp. 347–364.

Merrill, B. (2009). 'Introduction: Moving beyond access to learning careers and identity', in Merrill, B. (ed.) (2009) *Learning to Change? The Role of Identity and Learning Careers in Adult Education*. Frankfurt am Maim: Peter Lang.

Mezirow, J. (1991). *Transformative Dimensions of Adult Learning*. San Francisco: Jossey-Bass.

Newman, M. (1999). *Maeler's Regard: Images of adult learning*. Sydney: Stewart Victor Publishing.

Schuller, T. and Watson, D. (2009). *Learning Through Life: Inquiry into the future for lifelong learning*. Leicester: NIACE.

Warren, S. and Webb, S. (2007). 'Challenging lifelong learning policy discourse: Where is structure in agency in narrative-based research', *Studies in the Education of Adults*. 39: 1, pp. 5–21.

Chapter 6

A field of flowers and broken glass

Contrasting stories of 'race', participation and higher education

Lisa M. Baumgartner and Juanita Johnson-Bailey

Introduction

Racism and white privilege work in tandem and conspire to preserve the white status quo whilst oppressing people of colour. Institutional racism includes 'the collective effect of acts, policies, unwitting prejudice and the invocation of stereotypes that sustain an atmosphere which is hostile to the full participation and success of racial minorities' (Foster, 2005: 494). Oppression differs from prejudice because prejudice is an individual act, whilst oppression 'involves institutional control, ideological domination, and the imposition of the dominant group's culture on the target group' (Sensoy and DiAngelo, 2009: 345). White privilege, the unseen and often unacknowledged partner to oppression, is 'an invisible package of unearned assets that [whites] can count on cashing in each day, but about which [they are] meant to remain oblivious' (McIntosh, 1992: 76–77).

In this chapter, we explore how racism and white privilege influence higher education participation. In addition, we investigate how emotion interacts with these forces to create barriers to participation and learning. Though our personal stories, we demonstrate how racism and white privilege affected our respective graduate school experiences. Last, we offer recommendations and strategies for improving the learning experiences of the racially privileged and marginalised in higher education. During our collective 45 years as graduate students and teachers in the academy, we have focused on how race affects the processes in the academy; student admissions, tenure, and graduation; and student/professor/institutional relations. In this chapter, we offer innovative strategies that have been used in formal educational settings to encourage equity in accessibility and participation in lifelong learning.

An example of how 'race' affects education is seen in nursing school admissions in the U.K., where data indicate that 70 per cent of the applicants are white and 30 per cent are from minority ethnicities (Admission Statistics Show BME People Under-Represented, 2006). However, 17 per cent of those completing the program are minority ethnicities and 83 per cent are white. Likewise, blacks are underrepresented 'in undergraduate programs at traditional British universities' (Taylor, 1998: 131) and tend to be disproportionately admitted to lower-tier universities in Britain (Ratcliffe, 2006), and Israel (Shavit et al., 2007), compared to their white counterparts. Minority ethnicities are also underrepresented in Dutch higher education (Brug, 2006). So although the chapter focuses on 'race' and participation in higher education in the United States, we recognise that these factors affect higher education participation and retention in other countries.

The demographics on college campuses in the United States are increasingly diverse. In 1976, minority ethnicities comprised 17 per cent of undergraduate enrolment and 11 per cent of graduate enrolment. By 2004, those figures had risen to 32 per cent and 25 per cent respectively. African American undergraduate enrolment increased 103 per cent between 1976 and 2004, and 181 per cent for graduate enrolment. Black females composed 54 per cent of black undergraduate enrolment in 1974 and by 2004, this increased to 64 per cent. In 1976, 59 per cent of blacks enrolled in graduate school were female and by 2004, this increased to 71 per cent (KewalRamani et al., 2007).

Despite increased access to higher education, rates of completion at the undergraduate levels differ. Overall, 58 per cent of those enrolled in 1995 as freshman completed their degree by 2001; 14 per cent were still working on a bachelor's degree; and 21 per cent had discontinued pursing the degree (Snyder, Dillow and Hoffman, 2009). Bachelor degree completion varies by 'race': 59 per cent of whites complete their bachelor degrees within six years whilst the percentage for Latino/as is 47 per cent, 41 per cent for African Americans, and 39 per cent for Native Americans (Snyder, Dillow and Hoffman, 2009).

Doctoral degree completion rates are also generally lower for minority ethnicities than for whites. The Council of Graduate Schools (CGS) funded a study that used data from 29 participating US universities, primarily predominantly white institutions (PWI), representing 316 PhD programs across the nation. Although graduate school enrolment has increased for people of colour in all fields between 1997 and 2007 (Bell, 2008), data on ten-year completion rates suggests that 'white students have the highest cumulative ten-year completion rate at 55 per cent, compared to 51 per cent for Hispanic Americans, 50 per cent for Asian Americans and 47 per cent for African Americans' (Heiser, 2008: 1). Completion rates vary by field. Ten year PhD completion rates for African Americans as compared to whites are as follows: engineering, 47 per cent to 60 per cent; life sciences 60 per cent to 60 per cent (i.e. equal); Maths and Physical Sciences 37 per cent to 52 per cent Social Sciences, 47 per cent to 57 per cent; Humanities: 52 per cent to 51 per cent (Heiser, 2008: 1–2). In all fields, whites have the highest 10-year PhD completion rate or are within one percentage point of the ethnic group with the highest completion rate (Heiser, 2008).

Participation in and completion of higher education is affected by racism and white privilege, which manifests through institutional testing policies that benefit whites during the admissions process (Sacks, 2000) and curriculums that focus on and celebrate knowledge created by whites, excluding or minimising knowledge of people of colour (Margolis and Romero, 1998). In the classroom, student/faculty and peer interaction can influence students' sense of self-efficacy and feelings of belonging (Solorzano, Ceja and Yosso, 2000; Schwartz et al., 2003). A feeling of isolation affects students' emotions, which in turn can disrupt their ability to learn (Dirkx, 2008). In order to demonstrate how 'race' affects participation in higher education, we offer our admissions and retention stories as doctoral students of different races enrolled in the University of Georgia's adult education programme to illustrate how the tandem forces of racism and white privilege operate in higher education.

The admissions process

Undergraduate and graduate programmes generally require applicants to submit test scores, transcripts, recommendations and writing samples. Prospective undergraduates must submit their SAT (originally an acronym for the Scholastic Aptitude Test) or ACT (originally labelled for the American College Testing programme) (Zwick, 2002) scores whilst prospective graduate students are required to take such tests as the Graduate Record Exam (GRE), Millers Analogies Test (MAT), Law School Admissions Test (LSAT), Graduate Management Admissions Test (GMAT), or the Medical College Admissions Test (MCAT), depending on their area of graduate study.

Whilst research shows that standardised tests are biased against marginalised groups, they continue to be heavily weighted in admissions decisions for many programmes. Standardised tests disadvantage those who come from lower class households or who use non-standard English (Micceri, 2007). For example, since the vocabulary section of the GRE exam is normed on white middle-class subjects, international students (Mupinga and Mupinga, 2005) and economically disadvantaged students (Spencer and Castano, 2007) do more poorly. Freedle (2003: 1) notes that there are 'non-random ethnic test bias patterns found in the SAT'. The test items are classified as easy, medium and hard. The easy SAT items favour whites, which accounts for much of the difference in test scores. In addition, those who suffer from test anxiety perform poorly on timed tests, and the learning disabled are disadvantaged on standardised tests (Micceri, 2007).

Scholars assert that the reliance on standardised tests serve more of a gatekeeping function given that academic success is not highly correlated with standardised test scores (Sacks, 2000). As a result, some schools have revised their admissions policies. For example, in the 1990s, the University of Texas weighted class rank much more heavily than test scores in admissions decisions. Hence, students ranked in the top 10 per cent of a struggling high school had the same opportunity for admission as a person in the top 10 per cent of an elite high school (Sacks, 2000). Of the 2,675 four-year institutions serving undergraduates (US Department of Education, 2008), over 815 do not use SAT or ACT scores to admit 'substantial numbers of bachelor degree applicants' (Test Score Optional List, 2009: paragraph 1). Likewise, the University of Berkley Law School reduced the importance of the LSAT in admissions decisions in the 1990s and Texas

A & M's medical school waived the MCAT requirement for those committed to work in rural areas or for those who took internships in rural areas whilst maintaining an above-average grade point average (Sacks, 2000).

The graduate school admissions process for most graduate programmes also includes letters of recommendation and often interviews at the doctoral level. As professors who have served on admissions committees, we have witnessed examples of how a letter of recommendation can affect a prospective student's opportunity for admissions. A phrase such as 'This is the most intelligent Hispanic student that I had the pleasure to teach' contains hidden messages that negatively influence admissions committees. The speaker is comparing the student with an ethnic group and perhaps inferring inferiority. Why did the referee not write, 'This is one of the most intelligent students that I have had the pleasure to teach', as a way of offering a somewhat more meaningful and unqualified statement? A third part of the graduate school process that can affect access is the personal and often informal contact that can precede the application period. This exchange can serve a welcoming or unwelcoming function. This event, which is usually not monitored or recorded, could be the potential student's first contact with the programme. It can encourage or discourage the student from continuing the application process. For instance, a black woman graduate who was initially enrolled in one institution explains why she switched to another school:

> At the reception, the professors acted as though they were afraid to talk to me. . . . I said, 'No way.' Then the opening statement from the chair of the department sent vibes that convinced me that I was in the wrong place. He said that the program had a level of expectation that I might not be able to reach . . . I felt like if I had been successful in three graduate institutions across this country [U.S.], I wasn't going through those games. I went to another school the next day. The other campus was quite different . . . I had a friend [a black woman] who stayed in the other program. As we compared notes about the style of the two programs, her experiences were miserable. Mine were better.
>
> (Johnson-Bailey, 2001: 63)

Personal stories

'Race' and white privilege influenced our respective journeys through the same doctoral programme at the University of Georgia. Our brief stories demonstrate these differences.

Lisa's story

> I submitted my admissions materials and was interviewed by telephone by the doctoral admissions committee in the spring of 1996 in anticipation of matriculating in the fall. I was somewhat anxious about the interview but my

nervousness dissipated when a committee member commented favourably about my work in Japan teaching English at a private English conversation school for adults. The committee inquired about my research interests, interest in the programme, and my experiences teaching adults. When I expressed concern that I had not seen many advertisements for adult educators in *The Chronicle of Higher Education* (a newspaper for academics), a committee member assured me that a doctorate would provide more opportunities for employment in the field.

As a full-time, out-of-state student, I needed an assistantship[1] in order to afford to attend the University of Georgia. I had taken a GRE General Test preparation course to raise my scores because I assumed they were heavily weighted when awarding graduate assistantships. In late May, I received an acceptance letter and learned that I received a graduate assistantship for the 1996–1997 academic year that meant I would receive a small stipend and tuition waiver. I was ecstatic. I did not consider 'race' as a factor in my admission.

Juanita's story

I applied to the doctoral programme in Adult Education at University of Georgia in 1988. My application was rejected and the reason given was that my grade point average was too low. The required GPA was 3.5 and mine was 3.49. I was emboldened to launch a protest by a black sorority sister who had the same experience at the university. She explained that being rejected especially did not make sense in her case because she had graduated from the University of Georgia and had already completed one graduate degree in education before she applied there to pursue her second graduate degree. So I appealed my denial and explained during my interview before a panel of three professors and Dean of the Graduate School that I was very proud of my 3.49, given that I completed my undergraduate degree in three years instead of the usual four and had finished with honours. After a successful appeal, I began the adult education programme in January of 1989. It was almost a decade later, when I came to the university following another faculty appointment, when I found out that it was the norm for the department to send a faculty representative to a graduate school appeals hearing to support the applicant if the programme wanted the applicant to be admitted. I had sat alone at the opposite end of the table, unaccompanied in my solitary defence.

In the weeks before I entered school there were never any meetings with faculty members to plan my petition, to advise me or to orient me to the programme. As a first generation college student, I never even knew that assistantships existed and during my four years as a student. I never learned how one obtained the coveted assistantship prizes. Until I selected a major professor during my third year in the programme, my advisement consisted of another black student, who was a year ahead of me, telling me which classes to take and which professors black students should avoid. In one of my last courses, I remember a participatory class exercise where students likened their graduate school residence to a being like a garden – there had been weeds but there were mostly flowers. My analogous simile was graduate school was like skipping barefoot over broken glass, some days there were bigger chunks of glass than on other days.

After matriculation: factors affecting retention

Clearly, more people of colour are enrolling in higher education in the United States; however, completion rates for whites outpace those of people of colour (Bell, 2008; Snyder, Dillow and Hoffman, 2009). This is largely due to institutional factors, classroom interactions with peers and faculty, and the support received by individuals (Turner and Thompson, 1993; Daniel, 2007). In this section, we explore how racism and white privilege interact to influence the experiences of students enrolled in higher education. Again, we will conclude by briefly delineating our experiences as doctoral students in the same doctoral programme at the University of Georgia.

Higher education's 'hidden curriculum' is defined as 'the tacit teaching of social and economic norms and expectations to students in schools' (Apple and King, 1977: 29), and it is also twofold, with 'strong' and 'weak' manifestations. The 'weak' form of the hidden curriculum involves a subtle socialisation process of individuals whilst the 'strong' form means overt actions intended on 'preserving the existing social privilege, interests, and knowledge, of one element of the population at the expense of less powerful groups' (Apple and King, 1977: 34).

Margolis and Romero's (1998) study, concerning the experiences of 'women of color enrolled in PhD sociology programs' (paragraph 1), clearly demonstrates how the hidden curriculum influences socialisation. The reproduction of faculty identity is accomplished through 'department culture . . . mentoring or apprentice relationships, the informal or formal allocation system for teaching and research assistantships, the selection of courses for teaching assistants to teach' (paragraph 28). Therefore, the women of colour were encouraged to teach courses on 'race' or gender, an assignment that signalled their place as 'experts' of the 'other' knowledge. The professional socialisation in sociology involved competition for grades, resources, graduate assistantships, faculty attention and sponsorship, rewarding assertiveness, confidence and independence, while discouraging cooperation (Margolis and Romero). Women of colour who wanted to work cooperatively were defying departmental norms and received no mentoring or opportunities to assist them in professionalisation. Social experiences such as relationships with professors, feedback on assignments, and opportunities to work with faculty acculturate students to the educational culture. An absence of such encounters has been reported to negatively affect the persistence of blacks in graduate school (Lovitts, 2001; Herzig, 2002; Golde, 2000).

The 'strong' form of the hidden curriculum involves reproducing inequality. This is accomplished through stigmatisation, such as whites' belief that the admission of people of colour is due solely to affirmative action rather than academic credentials (Margolis and Romero, 1998; Murakami-Ramhalo, Piert and Militello, 2008). Another way to reproduce inequality is to blame the victim (Margolis and Romero, 1998) by looking specifically rather than systemically, and thereby insisting that individual minority ethnicities are the problem rather than the institutional racism inherent in higher education. In addition, stereotyping reproduces inequality because often blacks and Latino/as are labelled as less intelligent by society in general than their white counterparts, which in some cases causes blacks and Latino/as to doubt their own abilities (Margolis and Romero, 1998; Murakami-Ramhalo, Piert and Militello, 2008; Johnson-Bailey et al., 2009). This bleak cycle of negative predictive assumptions is then compounded by white faculty who perceive those from minority ethnicities as less intelligent and grade them using different standards, either more harsh if they rely on the deficit model or less harsh if they are influenced by white guilt or paternalism (Allen, 1988; DJani, 1993; Brookfield, in press, a, b).

Racist treatment, where blacks are considered suspect and intellectually inferior, is part of the strong hidden curriculum that advantages whites and disadvantages people of colour (Johnson-Bailey and Cervero 2004). It has been shown that a negative campus climate can affect the experiences of black students (Foster, 2005). In a study on the racial experiences of black students at a PWI, Foster (2005) found that black students were asked to identify themselves when they entered their residence, whilst white students, even those who were visitors, were not. In this same study, African American students reported being advised to enrol in remedial maths courses, despite their completion of advanced placement courses in high school. In addition, black students often must cope with blatant racism in the classroom, as demonstrated by the account given by Sheila, an African American woman who returned to a predominantly white institution to complete her undergraduate degree after a 14-year hiatus (Johnson-Bailey, 2001). This re-entry black woman's psychology professor would tell embarrassing stories that demonstrated blacks' deviancy and 'then challenge her black students with, "Now if I'm wrong about ya'll, speak up and defend yourselves"' (p. 107).

Schools based their curricula on white norms and knowledge and this transmission of cultural capital serves to further oppress and reproduce inequities. 'The very fact that certain traditions and normative "content" are construed as school knowledge is prima facie evidence of perceived legitimacy' (Apple and King, 1977: 30). The frequent relegation of the knowledge of people of colour to the periphery rather than to the centre demonstrates the devaluing of their contributions (Margolis and Romero, 1998). Primarily, the occasional inclusion of diverse course readings is instructor-dependent rather than institutionally mandated across the curriculum (Gasman, Hirschfeld and Vultaggio, 2008).

Another reproduction of the hidden curriculum is the isolation that minority students face on PWI (Margolis and Romero, 1998; Golde, 2000; Carter, 2001;

Gasman et al., 2008; Johnson-Bailey, Hirschfeld and Vultaggio, 2009). This isolation typically consists of black students being ignored in class, excluded from informal social organisations such as study groups, and formal formative experiences such as teaching and research opportunities (Taylor and Anthony 2000; Schwartz et al., 2003; Gasman, Hirschfeld and Vultaggio, 2008; Johnson-Bailey et al., 2009). In a study examining the social experiences of African American graduate students at a PWI, the students reported forced social isolation and discrimination (Johnson-Bailey et al., 2009). Whilst the treatment diminished in the faculty/student relationship over the 40-year period examined, 1963 to 2003, this circumstance did not lessen in the student/student relationship, but instead, discrimination by white students increased (Johnson-Bailey et al., 2009).

As our stories demonstrate, white privilege and racism affected our respective experiences in the doctoral programme at the University of Georgia after we were admitted.

Lisa's story

> Similar to many adults returning to school after a hiatus, I initially doubted my ability to complete graduate level work. However, after the first year of study, I gained confidence in my academic abilities as I received positive comments about my work from professors. As a graduate student and research assistant, I was socialised into a community of practice through a steady stream of opportunities. During my first year, I found out how to perform literature searches and edit manuscripts for publication. The next year, my major professor invited me to co-edit a text. This experience demystified the world of publishing as I learned how to write a book proposal, selected text materials, gained copyright permissions and wrote introductory material for several sections of the text. Later that year, I joined a research team composed of a doctoral candidate, two professors and myself. I learned how to conduct interviews, code data, produce an article for publication and how to respond to reviewers' comments. Another professor invited me to assist with the publication of her book. My final year, I presented research at a national conference with the research team, co-taught a graduate-level course with my major professor, and served as a frequent guest lecturer in another professor's course.
>
> In short, I was taught how to think, act and behave like a professor and socialised into the profession. Moreover, the conversations concerning the field of adult education and mentoring during my co-teaching and guest lecture experiences regarding grading, pacing of course material, dealing with challenging students and syllabus construction prepared me for teaching graduate level courses. I was socialised into a profession where people looked like me. When I entered the field of adult education in 1996, white women were plentiful in the profession. The scholarship of white women was included in the curriculum and the knowledge of white people was valued.

Juanita's story

> Of course I experienced the imposter syndrome that so many female graduate students go through. However, there was little during my years at the university to make me believe differently. In addition, I also carried the burdensome childhood memory of witnessing the student violence and faculty apathy that occurred during the desegregation of my new institution a mere twenty years before when my new school desegregated when I was a child.
>
> Since I was not a part of the student network in the department, I did not know that other students were working with the professors on research and writing projects. So certainly, it did not occur to me to seek such opportunities. On occasion, I was often queried by some classmates, especially international students, about my fit: Why did you choose UGA? Did you attend a black undergraduate college? Did you do okay on that assignment? Although most of my exchanges with adult education students were pleasant, it was the occasional difficult interactions that kept me guarded, such as the Asian student who, when returning graded papers for the professor, told me that my paper was too short and then referred to my work as substandard; or the two white women students who, during a class exercise, characterised my ongoing dissertation research on black women as reverse racism.
>
> From my observations, the professors in the adult education programme never seemed to doubt my ability nor did they treat me any differently. Then again, when I ventured outside of the shelter to other departments I ran into racism head on: a statistics professor made jokes about the z scores being low because the group probably included black athletes; a professor who gave me a final grade of 'C' in a class when my lowest graded paper was an 'A–'; a professor who told me that my writing was 'muddy' like me.

If not for my major professor encouraging me to present at the first African American Adult Education Preconference and inviting me on to a writing project shortly before finishing my coursework, I would have exited academia and never returned. Buoyed by a publication and a conference presentation, I searched campus-wide to find and take a class from a black woman professor so that I could be certain that such a person existed. It was during her class that I began to feel that maybe there was the faint possibility of potential academic membership for me as a professor.

Emotions and learning

As the research and our personal stories demonstrate, emotions reside at the core of adult learners' higher education experiences. These emotions can enhance or detract from the learner's experience but 'emotion work' is always part of the meaning-making process (Clark and Dirkx, 2008: 94). In fact, adult students often pursue education as the result of an emotional event such as a divorce, death, or loss of a job (Kasworm, 2008). They enter higher education filled with excitement, self-doubt, fear, and happiness carrying the emotional experiences of a lifetime into the classroom (Johnson-Bailey, 2001; Kasworm, 2008).

Positive emotions such as enjoyment, hope, and pride enhance the motivation to learn, whilst boredom, hopelessness, anger, anxiety, and shame are negatively correlated with emotions (Pekrun et al., 2002). Positive emotions facilitate critical and creative thinking whilst negative emotions led to more 'rehearsal strategies' for learning (2002: 99). Likewise, 'positive emotions such as hope and pride predicted high achievement and negative emotions [such as hopelessness and boredom] predicted low academic achievement' (2002: 99). Negative academic emotions were more prevalent in people who withdrew from the university than in those who finished school. In short, emotions are tied not only to learning, but also to participation in higher education.

For students of colour, particularly African American students, the pervasiveness of institutional racism means that they must cope with racial microaggressions, intentional or unintentional momentary and frequent indignities, which convey racial hostility and degradation (Sue et al., 2007). Examples include being silenced in the classroom or alternatively asked to speak for one's 'race'; professors maintaining low expectations for African Americans in the classroom; and white students and professors believing that African Americans were admitted only due to affirmative action policies. Examples outside the classroom include not feeling welcome in social spaces such as the library and being questioned by campus police on a regular basis when entering and leaving campus buildings. These microaggressions increase feelings of self-doubt, frustration and isolation and the cumulative effect can impact students' physical and mental health (Solorzano, Ceja and Yoss, 2000). In short, racial microaggressions cause 'racial battle fatigue' which 'is the result of constant psychological, cultural, and emotional coping with racial microaggressions in less-than-ideal and racially hostile or unsupportive environments (campus or otherwise)' (Smith, Allen and Danley, 2007: 555). Students explain how tiring it is to deal with 'stereotype threat' (2007: 69), where whites have stereotypes of African Americans as intellectually inferior. This interferes with learning as students must constantly confront racism and deal with negative emotions on a daily basis becoming psychologically fatigued.

Recommendations for higher education

It is clear that the admissions and retention of students of colour is affected by racist policies that preserve the status quo and by behaviours that implicitly support the system. Some innovations in higher education regarding admissions requirements and strategies to retain minority ethnicities need to be successfully implemented. As a first step, institutions must reconsider how they evaluate applicants for admission. Because it is clear that standardised tests are biased, less emphasis on standardised test scores in the admissions process is warranted. Further, an institutional or departmental policy that mandates special attention to the recruitment of students and faculty of colour is recommended (Johnson-Bailey and Cervero, 2004; Quarterman, 2008).

Minority ethnicity students note that they are often enthusiastically recruited to programmes only to matriculate and feel invisible, disconnected from colleagues and professors and have their contributions to programmes go unrecognised (Malone and Barabino, 2009). Therefore, mentoring is essential to student success (Ellis, 2001; Johnson-Bailey, 2004; Mahtani, 2004; Quarterman, 2008). Students' mentoring needs might differ depending on their positionalities (e.g. race, class, and gender) and their unique life circumstances. For example, female students might need assistance balancing childcare needs with school demands (Maher, Ford and Thompson, 2004) and working class students might need support as they learn how to survive and thrive in an academic culture based on cultural codes with which they could be unfamiliar (Collier and Morgan, 2008). However, one thing is certain. A close relationship with a faculty mentor can provide advice that can help students navigate the institutional and departmental challenges as well as enhance provide opportunities that make students competitive for employment after graduation.

Peer support is also important to all students and vital to minority ethnciities (Johnson-Bailey and Cervero, 2004; Gasman, Hirschfeld and Vultaggio, 2008). This can be in the form of an official 'student-led and faculty advised group such as the Student of African Descent group that orients and welcomes new students that helps students cope with classroom and campus stress and hostility as well as helping them learn academic culture to increase 'opportunities for black student scholars' (Johnson-Bailey and Cervero, 2004: 86). Faculty advisors can also encourage individual students to seek each other out for support based on individual students' needs. More experienced students could be matched with less experienced students (Maher, Ford and Thompson, 2004).

Financial support is especially vital for successful degree completion for minority ethnicities and women (Maher, Ford and Thompson, 2004; Gasman, Hirschfeld and Vultaggio, 2008; Quarterman, 2008). Minority ethnicity fellowships and grants need to be readily available. Programmes such as the Diversifying Faculty in Illinois Higher Education Program provides fellowships to graduate students from minority ethnicities to increase 'the number of underrepresented faculty and staff in Illinois institutions of higher education and higher education governing boards' (Illinois Board of Higher Education, Diversifying Faculty in Illinois Higher Education Program, 2009, paragraph 1).

Faculty must recognise that Eurocentric knowledge is favoured in course curricula and must make a conscious effort to include knowledge produced by people of colour (Johnson-Bailey, 2004; Mahtani, 2004; Daniel, 2007). This effort must occur within courses and across the programme, department, college and university curriculum in order to create a classroom environment where voices from a variety of sectors are heard and valued (Johnson-Bailey et al., 2009).

In sum, only when we are deliberate in our efforts to make change will any transformation occur in higher education. Our efforts must be grounded on our understanding of the immense power of the status quo to be resistant and co-optive because of the nature of its hegemonic design. In addition, our new path is dependent on our understanding of how we have all contributed to the existing phenomena of racism in higher education, either actively or passively, with purpose or without intent or malice. But at present our pledge to create a different anti-racist higher education environment must be with purpose and with much forethought. Our efforts to eradicate racism in higher education must begin with self-examination of our personal beliefs and practices as educators and extend to our institution of higher learning and our community for true transformation to occur.

Note

1 An assistantship is 'a form of financial aid awarded to a student studying for a graduate degree at a college or university in which the student assists a professor, usually in academic or laboratory work' (http://www.assistantship.Dictionary.com, paragraph 1).

References

Allen, W. R. (1988), 'The education of black students on white college campuses: what quality the experience?' in Nettles, M. T. (ed.), (1988) *Toward Black Undergraduate Student Equality in American Higher Education*, Westport, CT: Greenwood Press, pp. 57–85.

Apple, M. W. and King, N. R. (1977), 'What do schools teach?' in Weller, R. H. (ed.), (1977) *Humanistic Education: Visions and realities*, Berkeley, CA: McCutchan Publishing Company, pp. 29–63.

Bell, N. E. (2008), 'Graduate enrollment and degrees: 1997–2007'; Washington, DC: Council of Graduate Schools. Retrieved on 15 March 2009 from http://www.cgsnet.org/portals/0/pdf/R_ED2007.pdf.

Brookfield, S. D. (in press, a), 'Introductory remarks', in Sheared, V., Johnson-Bailey, J., Colin III, S. A. J., Peterson, E., and Brookfield, S. D. and associates (eds), (in press) *The Handbook of Race in Adult Education*, San Francisco: Jossey-Bass.

Brookfield, S. D. (in press, b), 'Concluding remarks', in Sheared, V., Johnson-Bailey, J., Colin III, S. A. J., Peterson, E., and Brookfield, S. D. and associates (ed.), (in press) *The Handbook of Race in Adult Education*, San Francisco: Jossey-Bass.

Brug, P. (2006), 'The diversity challenge: the representation of ethnic minorities in the Dutch educational system', in Allen W. R., Bonous-Hammarth, M. and Teranishi, R. T. (eds), (2006) *Higher Education in a Global Society: Achieving diversity, equity and excellence: advances in education in diverse communities, research, policy and praxis* (Volume 5). London: Elsevier, pp. 149–158.

Carter, D. F. (2001), *A Dream Deferred: Studies in higher education*, New York: Routledge.

Clark, M. C. and Dirkx, J. M. (2008), 'The emotional self in adult learning' in Dirkx, J. M. (ed.), (2008) *Adult Learning and the Emotional Self*, San Francisco: Jossey Bass, pp. 89–95.

Collier, P. J. and Morgan, D. L. (2008), '"Is that paper really due today?" Differences in first-generation and traditional college students' understandings of faculty expectations', *Higher Education*, 55: 4, pp. 425–446.

Daniel, C. (2007), 'Outsiders-within: Critical Race theory, graduate education and barriers to professionalization', *Journal of Sociology and Social Welfare*, 34: 1, pp. 25–42.

Dirkx, J. (2008), 'The meaning and role of emotions in adult learning', in Dirkx, J. (ed.), (2008) *Adult Learning and the Emotional Self*, San Francisco: Jossey Bass, pp. 7–18.

DJani, K. (1993), 'Racism in higher education: its presence in the classroom and lives of psychology students', paper presented at the Annual Meeting of the American Psychological Association (101st, Toronto, Ontario, Canada, 23 August).

Ellis, E. M. (2001), 'The impact of race and gender on graduate school socialization, satisfaction with doctoral study, and commitment to degree completion.' *Western Journal of Black Studies*, 25: 1, pp. 30–45.

Freedle, R. O. (2003), 'Correcting the SATs ethnic and social class bias: a method for reestimating SAT scores', *Harvard Educational Review*, 73: 3, pp. 1–43.

Foster, K. M. (2005), 'Diet of disparagement: The racial experiences of black students in a predominantly white university', *International Journal of Qualitative Studies in Education*, 18: 4, pp. 489–505.

Gasman, M., Hirschfeld, A. and Vultaggio, J. (2008), '"Difficult yet rewarding": The experiences of African American graduate students in education at an Ivy League institution', *Journal of Diversity in Higher Education*, 1:2, pp. 126–138.

Golde, C. M. (2000), 'Should I stay or should I go? Student descriptions of the doctoral attrition process', *Review of Higher Education*, 23: 2, pp. 199–227.

Heiser, S. (2008), 'Completion rates differ by study demographics', (PhD) (press release 9 September 2008), Washington, DC: Council of Graduate Schools. Retrieved 1 May 2009 from: http://www.cgsnet.org/portals/0/pdf/N_pr_PhDC_bookII.pdf.

Herzig, A. H. (2002), 'Where have all the students gone? Participation of doctoral students in authentic mathematical activity as a necessary condition for persistence toward the Ph.D.' *Educational Studies in Mathematics*, 50: 2, pp. 177–212.

Illinois Board of Higher Education, Diversifying Faculty in Illinois Higher Education Program (2009), retrieved 5 August 2009 from http://www.ibhe.state.il.us/grants/grantPrg/DFI.htm.

Johnson-Bailey, J. (2001), *Sistahs in College: Makin' a Way out of No Way*, Malabar, FL: Krieger Publishing.

Johnson-Bailey, J. (2004), 'Hitting and climbing the proverbial wall: Participation and retention issues for black graduate women', *Race, Ethnicity and Education*, 7:1, pp. 331–349.

Johnson-Bailey, J. and Cervero, R. (2004), 'Widening access for the education of adults in the United States', in Osbourne, M., Gallacher, J. and Crossan B. (eds) *Researching Widening Access to Lifelong Learning: Issues and approaches to international research*, London: RoutledgeFalmer, pp. 77–90.

Johnson-Bailey, J., Valentine, T., Cervero, R. M. and Bowles, T. A. (2009), 'Rooted in the soil: The social experiences of black graduate students at a Southern research university', *Journal of Higher Education*, 80: 2, pp. 178–203.

Kasworm, C. E. (2008), 'Emotional challenges of adult learners in higher education', in Dirkx, J. M. (ed.) *Adult Learning and the Emotional Self, New Directions for Adult and Continuing Education*, (Volume 120). San Francisco: Jossey-Bass, pp. 27–34.

KewalRamani, A., Gilbertson, L., Fox, M. and Provasnik, S. (2007), *Status and Trends in the Education of Racial and Ethnic Minorities* (NCES 2007-039). Washington, DC: National Center for Educational Statistics.

Lovitts, B. E. (2001), *Leaving the Ivory Tower: The causes and consequences of departure from doctoral study*. Lanham, MD: Rowman & Littlefield.

Maher, M. A., Ford, M. E. and Thompson, C. M. (2004), 'Degree progress of women doctoral students: factors that constrain, facilitate and differentiate', *Review of Higher Education*, 27: 3, pp. 385–408.

Mahtani, M. (2004), 'Mapping race and gender in the Academy: the experiences of women of colour faculty and graduate students in Britain, the US and Canada', *Journal of Geography in Higher Education*, 28: 1, pp. 91–99.

Malone, K. R and Barabino, G. (2009), 'Narration of race in STEM research settings: Identity formation and discontents', *Science Education*, 93: 3, pp. 485–510.

Margolis, E. and Romero, M. (1998), '"The department is very male, very white, very old and very conservative": The functioning of the hidden curriculum in graduate sociology departments', *Harvard Educational Review*, 68:1, pp. 1–32.

McIntosh, P. (1992), 'White privilege and male privilege: a personal account of coming to see correspondences through work in women's studies', in Anderson, M. and Hill-Collins, P. (eds) *Race, Class and Gender: An Anthology*, Belmont, CA: Wadsworth, pp. 70–81.

Micceri, T. (2007, February), 'How we justify the white, male academic status quo through the use of biased college admissions requirements', *Technical Report*, University of South Florida, Office of the Provost.

Mupinga, E. E. and Mupinga, D. M. (2005), 'Perception of international students toward the graduate record examination', *College Student Journal*, 39: 2, pp. 402–408.

Murakami-Ramalho, E., Piert, J. and Militello, M. (2008), 'The wanderer, the chameleon, and the warrior: experiences of doctoral students of color developing a research identity in educational administration', *Qualitative Inquiry*, 14: 5, pp. 806–834.

Pekrun, R., Goetz, T., Titz, W. and Perry, R. P. (2002), 'Academic emotions in students' self-regulated learning and achievement: a program of qualitative and quantitative studies', *Educational Psychologist*, 37: 2, pp. 91–105.

Quarterman, J. (2008), 'An assessment of barriers and strategies for recruitment and retention of a diverse graduate student population', *College Student Journal*, 42: 4, pp. 947–967.

Ratcliffe, P. (2006), 'Higher education, "race" and the inclusive society', in Allen, W. R., Bonous-Hammarth, M. and Teranishi, R. T. (eds) *Higher Education in a Global Society: Achieving diversity, equity and excellence: Advances in education in diverse communities, research, policy and praxis* (Volume 5). London: Elsevier, pp. 131–148.

Sacks, P. (2000), *Standardized Minds: The high price of America's testing culture and what we can do to change it*, Cambridge, MA: Perseus Publishing.

Schwartz, R. A., Bower, B. L., Rice D. C. and Washington, C. M. (2003), '"Ain't I a Woman Too?": Tracing the experiences of African American women in graduate school', *Journal of Negro Education*, 72: 3, pp. 252–268.

Sensoy, O., and DiAngelo, R. (2009), 'Developing social justice literacy', in *Phi Delta Kappan*, 90: 5, pp. 345–352

Shavit, Y., Ayalon, H., Chachashvili-Bolotin, S. and Menahem, G. (2007), 'Israel: diversification, expansion, and inequality in higher education', in Shavit, Y., Arum, R., Gamoran, A. with Menahem, G (eds) *Stratification in Higher Education: A comparative study*, Standford, CA: Stanford University Press, pp. 39–62.

Smith, W. A., Allen, W. R., and Danley, L. L. (2007), '"Assume the position . . . you fit the description": Psychological experiences and racial battle fatigue among African American male college students', *American Behavioral Scientist,* 51: 4, pp. 551–578.

Snyder, T. D., Dillow, S.A. and Hoffman, C. M. (2009). *Digest of Education Statistics 2008* (NCES 2009-020). National Center for Education Statistics, Institute of Education Sciences, US. Department of Education. Washington, DC.

Solorzano, D., Ceja, M. and Yosso, T. (2000), 'Critical race theory, racial microaggressions, and campus racial climate: the experiences of African American college students', *Journal of Negro Education,* 69: 1/2, pp. 60–73.

Spencer, B. and Castano, E. (2007), 'Social class is dead. Long live social class! Stereotype threat among low socioeconomic status individuals', *Social Justice Research,* 20: 4, pp. 418–432.

Sue, D. W., Capodilupo, C. M., Torino, G. C., Bucceri, J. M., Hoder, A. M. B., Nadal, K. L. et al. (2007), 'Racial microaggressions in everyday life: implications for clinical practice', *American Psychologist,* 62: 4, pp. 271–286.

Taylor, P. (1998), 'An overview of blacks in British Higher Education', *Journal of Blacks in Higher Education,* 19, pp. 130–131.

Taylor, E. and Anthony, J. S. (2000), 'Stereotype threat reduction and wise schooling: towards the successful socialization of African American doctoral students in education', *Journal of Negro Education,* 69: 3, pp. 184–198.

Test Score Optional List (2009), retrieved 12 April 2009 from http://www.fairtest.org/university/optional.

Turner, C. S. V. and Thompson, J. R. (1993), 'Socializing women doctoral students: Minority and majority experiences', *Review of Higher Education,* 16: 3, pp. 355–370.

US Department of Education, National Centre for Education Statistics (2007–2008), Integrated Postsecondary Education Data System (IPEDS), Fall 2007 (Table prepared July 2008). Retrieved 12 June 2009 from: http://nces.ed.gov/programs/digest/d08/tables/dt08_266.asp.

Zwick, R. (2002), *Fair Game: The use of standardized admission tests in higher education.* New York: RoutledgeFalmer.

Chapter 7

Senior learners and the university

Aims, learning and 'research' in the Third Age

Keith Percy and Fiona Frank

Introduction

In Lancaster University in the UK there has been for 30 years a fascination with issues concerning older people and learning. There has been the opportunity not only to debate and to undertake research and but also to experiment and to construct educational innovations from which it might be possible to glean further insights into the processes and content of learning for older people. There has also been interest in the question of whether a university – a particular kind of environment in which reflection, enquiry and learning co-exist – has something special to offer in making a connection with the experience of older people which is 'a prime under-used educational resource in our society' (Percy, 1990, p. 238).

There is not room in this chapter to reflect on the whole of this thirty-year process. After some discussion of a theoretical approach to older people and learning, in the context of universities, and a brief resume of relevant developments at Lancaster since the early 1980s, the chapter focuses upon a recent innovation, the Senior Learners' Programme. Then, because that Programme is multi-layered, a closer concentration is given to a core element, the Research Circle, which has been the object of research by some of its own participants. The chapter concludes by asking how this recent innovation might develop, what we need further to understand about it and whether it might have any lasting applicability.

Senior learners

The United Kingdom shares with other industrialised countries the phenomenon of an increasing proportion of older people in its population. It was projected that in 2007 the population of pensioners in the UK, for the first time ever, would have exceeded the population of children under 16 years. In 1951 11 per cent of the population of the UK was aged 65 years or over; in 1981 it was 15 per cent; in 2006 it was 16 per cent – being a rise of 1.2 million people in 25 years. Statistical estimates suggest that the proportional rate of increase in the ageing population will escalate and that by 2031, 22 per cent of the population will be 65 years or over (while only 18 per cent will be under 16 years). Moreover, centenarians are the fastest growing section of the population. In 2006 there were 10,000 people aged 100 years or more; in 2031, the figure is estimated to reach 59,000 (Office of National Statistics, 2007, p. 13).

The United Kingdom is in no way unique in these demographic shifts. Lynch, for example, reflects that between 1990 and 2025 the proportion of the population over 65 as a fraction of those aged 20–64 'will rise substantially in all of the G7 countries', with increases 'anywhere from 40 per cent to 160 per cent, and the largest growth in Japan'. Lynch's particular concern is with the age distribution of the workforce. Throughout the G7 countries, she suggests, the impact of an 'ageing workforce' will be 'profound' (Lynch, 2002, p. 63).

It is a small step from observing these clear population and social trends to considering the relationship between older people and the provision of learning opportunities in our society. Most recent surveys suggest that older people participate in learning or 'learning activities' less than younger adults. Thus, a recent Government report on the 'well-being' of older people suggested that 75 per cent of people aged 16–49 participated in learning in 2004–2005, while only 48 per cent of those over 50 years did so (HM Government 2006). The annual NIACE participation in adult learning survey shows a similar contrast and also claims that older adult participation in learning is currently falling year on year (Aldridge and Tuckett, 2007). Of course, such statistics and claims have to be approached very cautiously. For example, it is has to be understood in each case what 'learning activities' are being counted – often different menus of 'non-formal' and 'informal' learning are being included. Moreover, such generalised statistics hide a heterogeneity of differences between social sub-groups.

But if older people are participating less in learning activity than younger people, and if participation declines with age (and might also be declining year on year through, for example, government fiscal policies), most commentators regard these phenomena as a matter of concern. The concern is held to be all the greater in the context of the ageing population. The reasons advanced for concern are various. Participation in learning by older people below pensionable age is argued to enhance their chances of remaining in, or regaining, employment (Department of Work and Pensions, 2005); and the amount of takeup of learning opportunities by older people, particularly those who are retired, is held to be an indicator of well-being (HM Government, 2006) and a cause of continued good health and delayed ageing (Withnall et al., 2004). Learning and education have been asserted to be a *right* for older people – earned, perhaps, by the simple fact of growing older, working hard and having paid a lifetime of taxes, (Laslett, 1984). Participation in learning has been described as ' the liberation of the elders', that is, a means for older people to develop the critical and advocacy skills necessary to counter-act the social and financial disadvantages of many that are exaggerated or caused by older age (Glendenning and Battersby, 1990).

It is possible that such discourse misses the point. The statistics on so-called 'participation' in 'learning' are largely unreliable and are not comparable. The arguments for greater participation in learning by older people are mainly calls for greater expenditure from the public purse. There is an element of (no doubt unintended) condescension in some of this discourse which comes close to problematising older age and stigmatising older people.

This chapter will assume that the reasons why older people should participate in learning activity are the same as those for people of any age. Thus, from a humanist point of view on learning, one can argue that 'to be fully human, to exploit the potential of being alive . . . one has to be continuously a learner and the proper society would make this possible' (Percy, 1990, p. 236). A key set of questions arises, not about whether there should be learning opportunities for older people, but about whether the *process* and *content* of learning might be different for them. Educational gerontologists have debated for decades about the life 'experience' of older people and whether and how this experience should affect the teaching and learning opportunities that are offered to them. The content of learning could be made more meaningful, some say, if it takes account of this 'experience'. Teaching and learning would become more immediate, it is urged, if that experience were incorporated into the structure and delivery of learning (Withnall and Percy, 1994). Moreover, there is the possibility of a blurring of the line between teachers and learners: the notion of older people as the 'wise elders' – 'older people as teachers, facilitators of learning, role models, educational resources, repositories of wisdom' (Percy 1990, p. 237) is potentially a fruitful one.

The education and learning of older people (at least in the UK) suffer from terminological confusion and a superfluity of descriptors. Henceforward, in this chapter, the discourse of 'senior learners' is borrowed from the Programme and used as appropriate.

Senior learners and universities

Despite the fact that the number of universities in the UK has more than tripled since the early 1960s, universities have retained a potent symbolism and a special legitimacy, representing a supposedly symbiotic relationship between teaching and research, between critical reflection and dispassionate enquiry, between new knowledge and innovation. Access by senior learners to this powerful concoction has been, and is, limited. Tiny minorities of British undergraduates and postgraduates (including those at the Open University) are over 45 years old. Senior learners are represented much more strongly in the continuing education programmes of those universities that still provide them, but these programmes in most senses are, as the classic expression has it, 'outside the walls'.

It is certainly possible that, in the next few decades, British universities will try to recruit many more students who are senior learners. As the reservoirs of younger students recede and the population ages, it would be a logical recruitment strategy for universities to position themselves to do this. But what would and how would these new and older students study? It seems unlikely that the curricula and teaching approaches of universities would remain unchanged.

Issues and questions about the process and content of learning seem to stand out with particular clarity when one considers what universities can contribute to education of senior learners.

Evidently increases in the proportion of older people in the population, improvements in their health and increases in their life expectancy cannot be regarded as isolated, ring-fenced, quantitative phenomena. They have existential dimensions, and it is to these dimensions that universities would have to respond. These quantitative phenomena are actually about people. People act and react; they see changes in the world around them and seek to interact with them, aspiring to make sense of them; they reconstruct and interpret their worlds to give them meaning and value. Blaikie writes of the changes in 'work, leisure, family life and consumerism', which will touch older people more or less closely but of all of which they will have to make sense. He comments that, amid these changes, older people will have 'to make their own cultures' (Blaikie, 1999, p. 131). Thus, being *alive* for a senior learner today, compared to being alive several generations ago, will mean something different – there is a different set of questions with different assumptions behind them. Any educational situation set up for older people that does not attempt to assist them to find answers to those different questions is missing the opportunity for a very real engagement in people's changing lives.

Phillipson and Biggs (1999, p. 162) are pessimistic about the situation of the elderly in today's society. They identify the 'problem of social marginality among the old' in the present society and find it to be a fundamental problem. 'For the young and able-bodied, increased fluidity of identity, uncertainty and [the] risk associated with these trends may appear liberating.' But the life situation of older people may mean that a world of 'increased indeterminacy' has the opposite effect upon them. 'The risks and hazards surrounding the maintenance of a stable framework make identity more rather than less problematic. Established frameworks, which used to promise security and continuity of identity have been degraded' (1999: pp. 165–166). Following Phillipson and Biggs a need for the restoration of a sense of identity implies a role for the educator. In a world of 'increased indeterminacy', they say, 'there is no credible place . . . [for the older person] in which to make a stand, no arena in which one's voice can genuinely be heard'. This chapter argues that the university can be one 'credible place' in this analysis.

Moody (1990) is also interested in the *locus* where the restoration of older people's self-identity might be engineered, despite the swirling society around them. Influenced by Jung, Moody (1990, pp. 34–39) recognises the multiple experiences which senior learners bring to an educational situation but dismisses them as, in effect, meaningless unless the senior learner passes beyond them, glimpsing 'in experience itself something unsatisfied, something unknown', and extracting from experience meaning that is formative. 'My past is finished, but it is also unfinished because its meaning is never exhausted', he says. Moody describes the process as 'transcendence' – a process both unique to, and crucial for, the senior learner. 'Transcendence means overcoming one's previous role and definitions of the self; it means recovering them *in order* to let them go . . . This educational enterprise is immensely important; it is serious, and above all, it is *difficult.*' Letting go of past experience, re-configuring it, reflecting upon its relevance to current life and then going forward into the future with a new self, a new identity and a new set of understandings is both necessary and an essentially educational process, even a *higher* educational process.

We think that it is these kinds of ideas that a university, wishing to increase significantly its intake of senior learners, would have to consider. As Dickerson et al. (1990, p. 307, p. 315) write, rather grandiloquently, there could be an 'emergence of the "new" older person with remarkable potential for continuing personal growth' . . . 'and an ability to provide significant intellectual contributions . . . throughout the intellectual life of the . . . university'. But in the UK we are a long way from universities realising the potential of senior learners both as objects of analysis but more especially as the rationale for a new educational mission. Experimentation, pilot programmes, evaluations and risk-taking will be necessary, though economic factors, of course, come into consideration and universities are increasingly having to decide between their commitment to people in their travel-to-learn area against their commitment to their international, research-led presence. The developments and innovations at Lancaster, to which this chapter now turns, may be one contribution to the debate; in terms of setting out how a university Continuing Education department has, in a relatively idiosyncratic manner, provided a route by which older adults have been able to access university level learning opportunities.

Senior learners at Lancaster University

The first research publication on education and senior learners from the Department of Continuing Education at Lancaster University (actually from the small unit which was one of its institutional antecedents), in 1977, was very much of its time. It identified a 'pragmatic concern . . . to discover the extent to which educators could help an ageing population to be both happy and socially useful for as long as possible'. It promised that 'in Lancaster itself we anticipate . . . attempts to promote further inter-service co-operation in support of the elderly and other small-scale research into educational provision for the elderly' (Percy, 1977, pp. 2–3).

There were modest developments in the 1980s. The Department pioneered a form of community 'open lecture' provision, which brought into the University hundreds of senior learners; was active in supporting the emergence of the University of the Third Age movement in the United Kingdom; and worked with Age Concern Lancashire to research and to promote training and opportunities for older volunteers (Percy, 1985, 1988). In the 1990s, the Department increased the scale of its work with senior learners. It experimented with distance learning provision for senior learners (Percy and Withnall, 1992); researched self-directed learning among senior learners and considered implications for formal providers of learning (Percy et al., 1995a; Percy et al., 1995b); and developed a large regional programme of accredited and non-accredited university certificates and courses in which a significant proportion of the thousands of students *per annum* were senior learners. In the 2000s, the Department looked to build on its experience and to blend together these various strands of research, innovation and provision by the creation of the University of Later Life and of the Certificate in Research Methods for Older People.

The University of Later Life runs annually and is a weeklong opportunity for thirty to fifty senior learners to explore on campus what a university has to offer them. It involves participants in the different forms of university teaching, it confronts them with a wide range of areas of university study and research, it encourages them – in the course of one week – to explore at least one new intellectual interest and it provides advice and guidance on possibilities of future higher education study. The Certificate in Research Methods for Older People started as a joint venture between the Departments of Continuing Education and Applied Social Studies at Lancaster University. The Department of Applied Social Studies wanted to use trained older people as field researchers in a research project on housing choices by older people; the Department of Continuing Education, therefore, developed and delivered a University Certificate programme of training that contained theoretical content as well as practical experience of, and reflection upon, fieldwork research and which (at the time) was open only to those 60 years and over (Clough et al., 2004). After the completion of the research project the Certificate in Research Methods continued to run with a student body, which, at first, was wholly (and more recently mostly) made up of those over 50 years. A group of the earliest cohort of senior learners emerging from the Certificate programme set themselves up as a successful independent research consultancy.

With this experience behind it, the Department moved to a more ambitious innovation, which has tried to implement the philosophical approach outlined in the previous section of this chapter. The Senior Learners' Programme was launched by the Department of Continuing Education in October 2006. It was perceived as the culmination of 20 years of experience, innovations and explorations in the provision of higher education to senior learners. The key questions that this substantial experience was judged to have raised were how should senior learners gain access to, and how could they use, a university to accomplish the sorts of personal transcendence of which Moody (1990) wrote?

Formally, in the University arena, the Senior Learners' Programme was based on the arguments that:

- a university is a repository of expertise and facilities in research, knowledge and opportunity for learning, mostly provided and maintained by public funds;
- this expertise and these facilities need not be confined to young adults but should, where possible, be set within a framework of learning throughout life and especially later life;

- ‘provision’ for senior learners could often be based on the model of the independent learner – a learner with maturity and life experience whose learning goals can pursued more easily outside conventional programmes of study which are normally time-bound and may be discipline-bound.

And finally that:

- the programme, as stated in its publicity, aims to ‘bring the University to the attention of senior learners and to bring senior learners to the attention of the University’.

More intrinsically, the Senior Learners’ Programme aimed to give senior learners space – space to learn about themselves and their past and space to transcend that past and to redesign a future. It was to place the resources of the University, in a modest way, at the disposal of senior learners and offer them the chance freely to examine the world around them and to make sense of it in the company of peers. It was not anticipated that participants would remain with the programme in an open-ended manner. Using Moody’s concepts, the Programme was to aim to create opportunities, through a variety of intellectual activity, for participants to rediscover themselves, to transcend ‘previous roles and definitions of self’ and to move on. ‘The enormous value of education in old age lies in the way in which each subject studied can illuminate an aspect of [the] unrecovered self’ (Moody, 1990, p. 37).

The Programme was planned as a weekly day-long learning opportunity throughout the University year. Monday was arbitrarily settled on as ‘senior learners’ day’ and that day has worked well – ‘it’s a great start to the week’, as one senior learner noted. The Programme seeks to introduce senior learners to the range of University study, to the expertise of its staff and to the University’s facilities.

Senior learners pay a termly or yearly composite fee; the Programme is expected to cover at least direct costs. A concessionary rate is available for people whose sole income is a state retirement pension or who are registered unemployed. Around one-third of the intake of students in the first year paid the concessionary rate. Students were also given the option of applying for a bursary ‘for those in a situation of financial hardship’; no applications were in fact received for this bursary in the first two years of the Programme.

The Programme was launched at almost the same time that the United Kingdom adopted the European directive that there should be no age discrimination in publicly provided courses of education. The Senior Learners’ Programme is therefore open to learners of all ages. In practice, most of the ninety or so participants (2006–2007) were aged over 50 years. Enrolments by women were four times higher than those by men, with nineteen men and seventy-four women enrolling in the first four terms of the programme (see Figure 7.1).

Each day includes a choice of short accredited and non-credit bearing courses, at level 4 (equivalent to first year undergraduate level); a plenary lunchtime

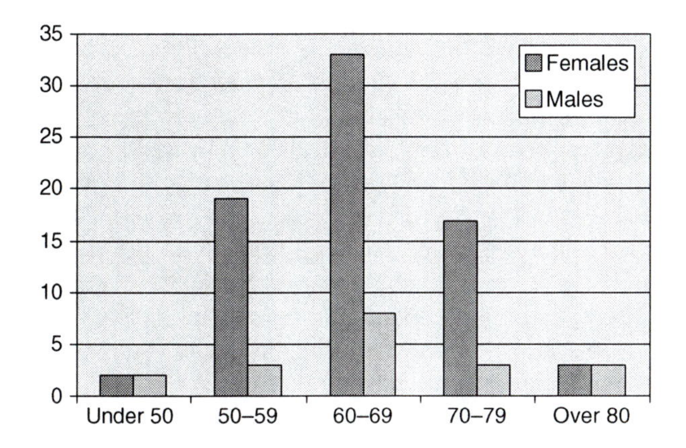

Figure 7.1 Students enrolled on Senior Learners' Programme, September 2006–December 2007, by age and gender

seminar/workshop led, each week, by a different (often senior) academic from any of the departments or faculties of the University; opportunities for one-to one tutorial sessions on learning methods and on personalised programmes of study and research; discussion time; a computer workshop led by a tutor but supported by student volunteers; and visits to different parts of the University. Each term, instead of a lunchtime seminar, one lunchtime would be given over to feedback from students from each of the courses reporting back on their learning.

A range of short formal courses emerged in the first four terms as one component of the Programme. These have included:

- Chinese language and culture
- Latin for beginners
- Alexander Technique
- Romantic Music in the Nineteenth Century
- 'Hard Times': Victorian Working Lives
- Pen, Ink and Wash in Art
- Starting a Small Business
- Coaching and Mentoring
- Introduction to Computer Animation
- Brush up your French
- Painting with Acrylics
- Discussion sessions on Books, Money, and Health.

This formal part of the programme has been demand-led and has been reconstructed from term to term. When lunchtime speakers proved to be particularly popular, they often agreed to deliver a taster course in their subject as part of the short course programme in the following term. This was the case with the Introduction to Coaching and Mentoring course organised by staff from the University Management School; with the Computer Animation course taught by staff from the Department of Communications Systems; with a course on 'Looking to the future: perspectives on death and dying' run by staff from the University's International Observatory on End-of-Life Care; and with a philosophy course 'What's it all about?' led by a lecturer from the Department of Philosophy.

In the second year, the format was changed slightly to include taster courses in the mornings where participants would try out new subjects – and 'workshop sessions' or 'learning circles' in the afternoons – where participants would bring their own ongoing projects in art, creative writing, history, or computing, for guidance from the tutor and mutual support from other learners.

Each Monday afternoon since the programme started, a Research Circle has featured as a core element of the Programme. The next section of this chapter focuses on the Research Circle.

The Senior Learners' Programme Research Circle

In the late 1980s, the Department of Continuing Education devised and ran what it called the 'Community Learners' Scheme'. This was based on early outcomes from the series of research projects undertaken at Lancaster into self-directed learning among adults (Percy, 1988; Percy et al., 1995a, 1995b). The research projects had, of course, been stimulated by the seminal work of Tough and his American and Canadian collaborators and successors (Tough, 1968; Candy, 1991). This body of research shows that a large proportion of adults, at least in western societies, are engaged independently in enquiry, improving knowledge and skills, satisfying curiosity, finding things out. These activities may be unsystematic, intermittent and varying in success. They are probably undertaken with reliance on the advice of friends, family and peers rather than on that of professionals. But they exist and the fundamental premise of the 'Community Learners' Scheme' was that a university should seek to engage with this body of activity and help where it could (Percy, 1988, p. 112). At Lancaster the Scheme ran for a couple of years and confirmed that there were independent learners in the community who would like to access university expertise but, hitherto, had not known how to do so. Many of them were older people who wanted to use the time made available by retirement to pursue enquiries on topics about which they had been curious for years. The Scheme sought to twin community learners with university academics who had relevant expertise and community commitment. Some successful programmes of university-assisted independent enquiry took place (e.g. on the history of sanitation, eastern religions and Egyptology). Perhaps unsurprisingly, however, the Scheme foundered within the University arena over questions of definition, boundaries and fees.

Nevertheless, the philosophy behind the 'Community Learners' Scheme' remained alive in continuing education programmes at Lancaster in the 1980s and 1990s (and combined with ideas fermented by Lancaster's unique School of Independent Studies – see Percy and Ramsden, 1980). Essential features of the philosophy were the questioning of the boundaries between 'research', enquiry and self-directed learning and the challenging, in particular, of the reified notion that all who want to be engaged in 'research' in a university environment have to be enrolled on a research or postgraduate degree or aiming for publication. On the other hand, remaining integral to the philosophy were the values and techniques of university research – respect for evidence, rigour, system, logic, testing of validity and the ethics of enquiry. Aspects of the philosophy were tested out in the University of Later Life and Certificate in Research Methods programmes, begun earlier in the 2000s. When the Senior Learners' Programme was devised, it was evident that these ideas should have a central role in it and, through the Research Circle, they did.

The Senior Learners' Programme Research Circle began in October 2006. By early 2007 it included eighteen participants. One participant could not attend physically during the second term, after an operation, but joined in discussions through a telephone link. Over half of the participants were over 60 years of age; most of the remainder were between 50 and 60 years. Two-thirds were female.

The aims of the Research Circle were to be inclusive and experimental. It was believed that some of the University's older MA and PhD students might want to participate in an informal support group. But equally the Circle was set up to attract, support and stimulate those senior learners who defined themselves as researchers or, at least, who engaged on self-directed projects of enquiry or who wanted to do so. It transpired that the Circle came to consist largely of the latter group, although during the year some of them began to consider if they might ultimately register as postgraduate students. It is true that one or two of the initial members signed up for the Circle because the afternoon Art class was full but they soon became committed and active participants of the Circle. As one of them wrote: 'I was doing stuff at home, but I didn't realise that what I was doing was research.'

The Research Circle was planned to run for two hours on Monday afternoons on a workshop basis. The key to its success would lie in the skills and experience of the facilitator who was seeking to integrate a group of individuals who, by definition, had different backgrounds, skills and goals and, initially, expectations. 'I was expecting formal research', wrote one, but it's 'completely different'. Wrote another, 'I didn't want a straitjacket, I wanted to flutter my wings'. The two hours were structured so that plenary time was interspersed with time for small group work. A priority was to give each member the opportunity weekly to contribute on his or her research activity, to comment constructively on the contributions or questions of others and/or to discuss common problems or issues. Each session was carefully structured to allow for: (1) discussion of best practice and relevant enquiry skills, (2) individual informal presentations, (3) focus groups on issues and problems.

The timetable was strictly adhered to by the facilitator, who used some of the principles of 'co-counselling' (New and Kauffman, 2004) to ensure that each member of the group would have equal time and attention within the session. The first five minutes was a time to talk informally with a neighbour about what each had been doing at the weekend. This was nothing to do with research, but a time to ensure that the group developed and maintained bonds of friendship as well as functioning to support each other as fellow researchers. A timer was used to ensure that each participant had equal time in the second part of the session to report back – this way no one student monopolised the time, and everyone knew that they would only have to speak for two minutes. They also knew that they would be required without fail to speak for two minutes about what they had done in their project during the previous week. This was an excellent motivator.

No interruptions were allowed in the 'report-back' session; so if participants had comments, questions or suggestions for their peers, they would save them for the next session – around 10 to 15 minutes of feedback by other students and the facilitator on what had come out of the reporting-back sessions. At this point students shared comments and suggestions on each other's work.

The next part of the session was a 20-to-30 minute input on some aspect of research methodology, delivered by the facilitator or an outside speaker. Occasionally this session was replaced by a presentation by one of the students on their own work; or a focus group discussion led by one of the students, or a pair of students working together. The 'methodology' sessions included topics such as:

- interviewing;
- designing questionnaires;
- advanced searches on Google and other internet search engines;
- using electronic journals;
- the use of a research journal;
- planning your time;
- making notes on books and journal articles;
- managing research paperwork.

After a refreshment break, small group discussions in threes or fours allowed each participant to focus in more depth on their own research topic and to get detailed feedback from others in the group. A final 'closing circle' provided a chance for individuals, if they wished, to commit to the whole group on something that they would do by the following week, a chance to appreciate the group itself and say what they had gained from the day.

In the second year, the daily timetable for the Senior Learners' Programme was changed. The morning sessions started later to allow people to use off-peak concessionary bus passes, it was decided to terminate the programme of end-of-day visits to University departments, and the afternoon sessions were increased from two hours to two-and-a-half hours. In the new extended timetable for the Research Circle, more time was devoted to the small group sessions; and an additional section was added to the programme, just before the refreshment break, in which participants spend five minutes on silent writing in their research journals.

Although most members of the Research Circle had very clear and formed ideas on what they were researching, two members had joined the group in early 2007 without clear ideas on a research topic, after hearing the positive reactions of other members of the course in one of the lunchtime course feedback sessions. These two members agreed, after a suggestion by the tutor, to carry out research on the group itself. They used a questionnaire (which was completed by all members) and a focus group. They presented their findings not only to the rest of the Senior Learners at a lunchtime discussion session, but also in a presentation to education professionals from 15 countries at an international conference in Scotland in May 2007.

Some of their findings are reported in what follows. For example, they asked members what they were, or wanted to begin 'researching'. The answers, listed below, show the wide range of interests present in the Research Circle:

What was being 'researched' by members of the Research Circle
Family history
Family networks
History of numbers
Witchcraft gender in the Cameroon
History of fairy tales
The life of Amy Johnson
Local geomorphology
Research into a local (18th century) African slave
Origins of life
Bertrand Russell on philosophy and religion
Cultural effects of religion
Pursuit of wisdom
Role of the housewife in the 1940s and 1950s
Evolution – individual thought and atheism
How to enjoy retirement
The life and times of Cecil Rhodes
Undecided
(*'but really enjoying the dynamics of the Research Circle'*)

In fact, the dynamics of the Circle worked very positively. Despite the disparate nature of the topics, members began to show a deep interest in their fellow members' work. They started to find references for each other and to report on relevant exhibitions, books, magazine articles and radio programmes which they had come across or looked for which related to another member's research interest. A sort of 'research market-place' or 'research co-operative' came into being. Members' topics became fluid and merged into one another. Two members ran a focus group on attitudes to religion, and another Circle member, who had originally joined the group to research ways of marketing the children's book she had written, was so transformed by that discussion that she began researching and writing about the origin of the universe. As indicated above, one woman, housebound in the second term after a serious operation, rejoined the group by participating in the weekly discussions on a speakerphone. Other Circle members borrowed library books for her so she could continue her research.

In their responses to their colleagues' questionnaire, members argued that the Research Circle was a source of motivation and inspiration. What were perceived as its 'innovative ways to learn' helped to 'renew enthusiasm'. The activities of the Circle 'generate[d] inspiration' and confidence. They had learned that 'it doesn't matter how slowly you go, as long as you don't stop'.

Members wrote that the diversity of the Circle was in itself stimulating; that the facilitation and the excellent group dynamics of the Circle gave them confidence to contribute; that the weekly meetings disciplined study and helped with progress and focus. They wrote of the benefits of participation in the Circle as being 'Learning . . . Personal . . . and Health'. Personal benefits included 'new friendships', 'peer support'; health benefits were expressed in terms of' a stress reliever', 'contact with others', 'increased brain activity', 'a time for me'.

Members were asked about the intended outcome of their research activity. How would it be used? They responded variously in terms, for example, of making 'presentations, 'writing a novel', communicating 'family history', 'putting together a handbook', ' full-time course', 'placing information on the internet', and 'disseminating information locally'.

As the Senior Learners' Programme moved into its second year (2007–2008), it became clear that it might become a victim of its own success. New members wanted to enrol but most existing members showed no inclination to leave. Within a year, then, the Programme had reached a crossroads. Was it to grow or not? If the point was to attempt to establish a presence within the University, to create a dynamic, the Programme had to grow. If the point was simply to experiment, to show that it was possible make a provision for senior learners that flowed from in the cycle of reflection, research and development ongoing at Lancaster over a long time period, then growth was not imperative. The decision was taken to grow.

The future of an innovation

The Senior Learners' Programme development has been presented here as a quasi-logical extension of research, provision, innovation and theoretical reflection which has taken place at Lancaster University over a period of almost 30 years. Yet it is too early to seek to evaluate an innovation after only one full year of delivery although all the indicators are that the Programme has begun with format and contents that are successful. Of course, there have been unplanned developments and unexpected consequences. Senior Learners have independently created a students' association, which organises events outside the Programme and has affiliated to the University Student Union. The Programme has been awarded small grants from external sources for equipment.

University departments have identified the Programme as a ready source of older people to be either the objects of research or (as formerly in the Certificate in Research Methods) as fieldwork research assistants or co-researchers. The International Observatory in End of Life Care, for example, has worked with three members of the Senior Learners' Programme throughout the year, inviting them to conferences nationwide and consulting with them on the development of their work. The Department of Educational Research has recently established a collaborative research project with a group of around ten members of the programme who will chart the changing technologies associated with reading and writing and how older people are engaging with these technologies. A European project looking at older people and volunteering will be working with a small group of Senior Learners to ensure that their project reflects their views. And a group of the Senior Learners are working with an evaluation team looking at the responsiveness of a project designed to improve services for older people in the Lancaster and Morecambe District (in the Northwest of England).

There is a sense in which the creation of the Programme has created a new capacity, and released a new dynamism, within the Department of Continuing Education, and even within Lancaster University, which was not there before and of which the potential is unknown.

However, the realpolitik of a twenty-first-century British university has to be taken into account. Lancaster University is one of those pre-1992 universities that sees itself as international in recruitment and excellent in research. It competes well in all of the university-sector league tables. Undergraduate students are mostly full-time, young and with high 'A' level entry qualifications. Senior Learners do not figure in the University's Mission Statement, Strategic Plan or widening participation targets. As a small programme it is sufficient for the direct costs to be covered by composite student fees. If it is to establish a presence in the University by becoming significantly larger, it will have to cover (or come close to covering) indirect costs and overheads.

Already the thinking about the future of the Programme is turning to the notion of self-help by the Senior Learners, albeit within the framework of guidance, learning resources, standards and training which a university can provide. If the Research Circle is to be replicated, if there are to be similar groupings using similar approaches around other activities and areas of study, then many more expert facilitators will be required. They could be University staff who may need to be trained for this new and specific context. But they could also be Senior Learners themselves, working to a pattern and format appropriate to the Senior Learners' Programme and within the support structure which it would provide. This may be a more economical means of expansion as well as having intrinsic justification.

Would the Programme then have transformed itself into a University of the Third Age? Probably not, and certainly not to the U3A model that has been adopted in the UK (e.g. Midwinter, 1985). In a sense the British U3A model rejected close association with publicly chartered universities – the early protagonists had somewhat idealised visions of mediaeval peripatetic universities of senior learners springing up in every town. Although there have been accommodations subsequently between public universities and the voluntary 'universities' of third age learners (see for example the alliance between the national U3A and the Open University), the British U3A is not primarily concerned with accessing public university resources of people, expertise and learning resources and facilities. In a sense, then, the future development of the Senior Learners' Programme at Lancaster may be closer to the original continental Universities of the Third Age of the late 1970s and early 1980s, such as those at the Universities of Toulouse and Geneva, which grew up alongside, or on, a university campus. But the parallel will not be too close. The Universities of the Third Age largely did not, and do not, rely to the same extent as the Senior Learners' Programme on experimentation, freedom and diversity in teaching and learning methods.

There may lie the lasting contribution of the Senior Learners' Programme. The experience of the Programme to date (particularly of the Research Circle) lends significant support to the findings of enquiries into self-directed learning among adults, specifically older adults. The Research Circle has provided an exciting demonstration of the 'research' interests of 'ordinary' older people and of how a university context can give extra meaning and direction to those interests. Individual and group learning paths spring up naturally from the intellectual ferment, and opportunities for transcendence and new identities, which a well-facilitated learning environment such as the Circle can generate. What this chapter suggests (and which may be of significance theoretically and in terms of directions for research) is that it may be time with regard to the learning of older adults to move beyond the restrictions of the dichotomous terminology of teaching and learning, of directed and self-directed learning, of formal, non formal and informal learning, of theoretical and experiential learning. It is not so much that we need a new paradigm; it is rather that we need a more extended and sophisticated paradigm that has no unnecessary barriers and that sets free the energy, capacity, experience and curiosity of senior learners and assists them to transcend the past and to make progress in the search for new understandings, identities and futures.

References

Aldridge, F. and Tuckett, A. (2007), *The Road to Nowhere? NIACE survey on adult participation 2007*, Leicester: NIACE.

Blaikie, A. (1999), 'Can there be a cultural sociology of ageing?', *Education and Ageing*, 14, 2, 127–2.140.

Candy, P. C. (1991), *Self Direction for Lifelong Learning*, San Francisco: Jossey-Bass.

Clough, R., Leamy, M. and Miller, V. (2004), *Housing Decisions in Later Life*, Basingstoke: Palgrave Macmillan.

Department of Work and Pensions (2005), *Opportunity Age: Meeting the challenges of ageing in the 21st century*, London: Stationery Office, Cm6466i.

Dickerson, B. E, Myers, D. R., Seelbach, W. C., Johnson-Dietz, S. (1990), 'A 21st century challenge to higher education integrating the older person into academia', in Sherron,

R. S. and Lumsden, D. B. (eds) *Introduction to Educational Gerontology*, 3rd edn, New York, Hemisphere Publishing.

Glendenning, F. and Battersby, D. (1990), 'Why we need educational gerontology and education for older adults: A statement of first principles', in Glendenning, F. and Percy, K. (eds) *Ageing, Education and Society: Readings in educational gerontology*, Keele: Association of Educational Gerontology.

HM Government (2006), *Independence and Well-being of Older People: Baseline report*, Corporate Document Services.

Laslett, P. (1984), 'The education of the elderly in Britain', in Midwinter, E. (ed.) *Mutual-aid Universities*. London: Croom Helm.

Lynch, L. M. (2002), 'Too old to learn? Lifelong learning in the context of an ageing population', in Instance, D., Schuetze, H. G. and Schuller, T. *International Perspectives on Lifelong Learning: From recurrent education to the knowledge society*, Buckingham: Society for Research into Higher Education and Open University Press.

Midwinter, E. (ed.) (1984), *Mutual-Aid Universities*, London: Croom Helm

Moody, H. (1990) 'Education and the life cycle: A philosophy of aging', in Sherron, R. S. and Lumsden, D. B. (eds) *Introduction to Educational Gerontology*, 3rd edn, New York, Hemisphere Publishing.

New, C. and Kauffman, K. (2004), *Co-Counselling: The theory and practice of re-evaluation counselling*, New York: Brunner-Routledge.

Office of National Statistics (2007), *Population Trends*, 130, Winter.

Percy, K. (1977), 'Education and the elderly in Lancaster: A local investigation', in Percy, K. and Adams, J. (eds) *Education and the Elderly*, Lancaster, Institute for Research and Development in Post-Compulsory Education, University of Lancaster.

Percy K. (1988), 'Opening access to a modern university', in Eggins, Heather (ed.) *Restructuring Higher Education*, Milton Keynes: Society for Research into Higher Education and Croom Helm.

Percy, K. (1990), 'The future of educational gerontology: A second statement of first principles', in Glendenning, F. and Percy, K. (eds) *Ageing, Education and Society: Readings in educational gerontology*, Keele, Association of Educational Gerontology.

Percy, K., Burton, D. and Withnall, A. (1995a), *Self-directed Learning among Adults: The challenge for continuing educators*, Leeds, Association for Lifelong Learning.

Percy, K, Burton, D. and Withnall, A. (1995b), *Self-directed Learning among Adults: Empirical studies of community carers and disabled adults*, Lancaster: Lancaster University Department of Continuing Education.

Percy, K. and Ramsden P. (1980), *Independent Study: Two examples from English higher education*. Surrey: Society for Research into Higher Education.

Percy, K. and Withnall, A. (1992), 'An examination of the motivation and experience of British elderly people when learning at a distance', *Gerontology and Geriatrics Education*, 13, 1–2, 57–70.

Phillipson, C. and Biggs, S. (1999), 'Population ageing: Critical gerontology and the sociological tradition', *Education and Ageing*, 14, 2, 159–170.

Tough, A. M. (1968) *Why Adults Learn: A study of the major reasons for beginning and continuing a learning project*, Toronto, Ontario Institute for Studies in Education.

Withnall, A., McGivney, V. and Soulsby, J. (2004), *Older People Learning: Myths and realities*, Leicester: National Institute of Adult Continuing Education.

Withnall, A. and Percy, K. (1994), *Good Practice in the Education and Training of Older Adults*, London: Arena Ashgate Publishing.

Chapter 8

Counting me in and getting on

The contribution of adult literacy and numeracy in informal and formal learning

Yvonne Hillier

There is a danger that we do not know how our professional practice has developed out of innovations from the past. We are continually asked to adopt the newest form of technology, 'enter cyberspace' and reach out to people who do not yet know that they are expected to be learning in a more formal way. We are constantly exhorted to reach more learners, engage their employers and deliver the ultimate goals of creating an economically successful, world-class workforce (Hillier and Jameson, 2003; Hillier, 2006). What lessons can we learn from earlier developments and from practitioners who were being creative in earlier decades? Second, what kinds of learning have practitioners been fostering?

Whilst there is a core infrastructure of learning opportunities formally organised through the learning and skills and higher education sectors, most people today constantly learn through watching television, using the internet, talking to friends and colleagues and trying out things for themselves. I would argue that this wealth of learning is what we should celebrate. A recent consultation by the former Department for Innovation, University and Skills, DIUS, is asking how far informal learning should be supported by government and, if so, how (DIUS, 2008). I am not convinced this kind of learning should be integrated into the remit of the institutions currently funded by government in England and the UK today. However, it is clear that of the £4.8 billion spent on adult learning by DIUS, a percentage does support learning that is not taking place formally and is recognised as contributing 'immeasurably to the well-being and health of our society' (DIUS, 2008: 2)

In this chapter, I briefly examine the ways in which adult learning has been influenced at policy level over the past three decades before using one area of adult learning, adult literacy and numeracy, to show how innovations in informal learning have developed and subsequently influenced mainstream adult learning.

Informal learning

My definition of informal learning, like Smith and Spurling below, suggests its defining characteristic is that it is always occurring. It may be unplanned, it may be a result of serendipity. It is *prevalent* but often unrecognised. People would not be able to use mobile phones, find their way in strange cities or use new foods without learning informally how to do so.

> Informal learning tends to be unplanned, even opportunistic, such as reading before sleep; watching an interesting programme on the television; looking over someone's shoulder at work; or dropping into a museum. Such learning can be anything but casual, and its impact is much understated. It can be the predominant element in learning lives.
>
> (Smith and Spurling, 1999: 4)

The recent DIUS consultation acknowledges that there is no formal definition of informal adult learning used by government departments but there is an agreed understanding that informal adult learning involves structured or non-structured part time, non-vocational learning which does not lead to qualifications or if it does, it is coincidental.

McGivney (2001) identifies three categories of informal learning, non-course based activities, planned short courses delivered in informal ways and settings, and learning taking place outside dedicated learning environments, which is often not recognised as learning. An example of the latter is the book club, where approximately 50,000 groups of people meet to read and discuss books. These have partly been stimulated by television, for example the 'Richard and Judy' books. Richard and Judy are the first names of the presenters of a particular daytime television programme and it is claimed that many more people are engaging with books and discussion about them because of their promotion of books, which have been enthusiastically read by viewers.

One section of funded provision that recognises the value of different kinds of learning is adult education, now commonly known as adult and community learning (ACL). Here, the reasons why people engage are not viewed through economic lenses but through social and 'liberal' discourses (Griffin, 1987). People are not expected to make a journey of progression through a qualification system. They can dip in and out of provision, their journeys can be 'untidy' (DIUS, 2008: 21) and they can decide for themselves when they want to progress to new activities rather than being expected to follow a set curriculum. The large numbers of people who have engaged and continue to engage in this kind of learning, McGivney's second category, do so to 'follow a common human impulse to satisfy their curiosity and thirst for knowledge' (DIUS, 2008: 31).

This provision has developed and been sustained over centuries. Adult learning has a long history in England, and has arisen from independent action by committed individuals as well as from government policy. This includes the creation of public libraries in the nineteenth century, alongside the mechanics institutes and settlements set up by local activists. In the twentieth century, the resettlement following the First World War and the development of adult education during the Second World War contributed to informing adults of current affairs as well as providing relief from the exigencies of war. The post-war influence of television and radio further developed informal learning by adults and government was aware by the early 1970s that it needed to understand and develop such learning. To do so, it commissioned a major report on adult learning published in 1973, the Russell report, with its counterpart the Alexander Report in Scotland (HMSO, 1975). It set out a detailed account of what adult learning could achieve and in many ways influences how we view adult learning today.

Government policy on adult learning

During the past three decades, there has been an increasing focus on those who are not 'learning', ie those who are not engaged in formal adult learning provision. The overwhelming message from government is that lack of learning has serious financial implications both personally and economically. Smith and Spurling (1999) argued that this lack of learning related to the places in which it was taking place, i.e. in the formal institutions:

> The current learning scene is stark. Too little learning of any kind is being done; a large section of society is doing none at all; and a large proportion of those who have no intention of doing any in the future. The profile of learning falls off far too sharply with increasing poverty and increasing age. The population is under-qualified by international comparison, particularly at the craft and technician level. A major culture shift is required to change all this . . . there is widespread claustrophobia in the UK learning system, where learning is often confined to special spaces.
>
> (Smith and Spurling, 1999: 213)

Given the wealth of informal learning occurring, it is something of a paradox to be told that people are not doing enough. This is partly because informal learning is 'pervasive and low profile' (DIUS, 2008: 13). Yet governments in England and more generally in the countries of Organisation for Economic Co-operation and Development (OECD), claim there are groups of people who are not doing anything after their initial, compulsory education.

> The number of lifelong learners actively learning today is likely to be small, perhaps very small; and there is a sizeable body of non-learners who are doing very little learning after initial education, if any at all. These people have in effect switched off from learning – or they have been switched off.
>
> (Smith and Spurling, 1999: 21)

Such groups are often defined as being poor, working class, ethnic minority and low skilled. In addition to not participating in learning, these groups are also seen to be economically underperforming or not contributing fully to society. Even if they do watch daytime television and know how to use mobile phones and DVDs, they are not seen to be doing the right kind of learning, even though this is informal learning as I outlined above. There are, it seems, certain activities that 'count', that equate to learning that is valued, that is funded, desired and can lead to financial and social benefits. A skim through current government policy in England leaves us in no doubt that learning should be focused on knowledge and skills for the workforce, so that we truly become 'world class' (Leitch, 2006) and competitive.

Why has government become so concerned about lack of formal adult learning? One way to understand this is to trace how government has supported adult learning in the past and to identify the aims of such provision through the funding provided. We can see how adult learning has been portrayed through the government reports and acts throughout the past three decades. The range of papers, reports and acts over the past three decades provides important clues to how adult learning is conceived, portrayed and funded. The following list represents the major documents relating to adult learning with a very rapid growth of these from 1997 onwards:

- 1973 Russell Report;
- 1982 ACACE report;
- 1986 DES White Paper Working Together: Education and Training;
- 1993 Further and Higher Education Act: Schedule 2 and Non-Schedule 2;
- 1997 Kennedy Learning Works;
- 1997 Fryer Report (NACGELL);
- 1998 The Learning Age;
- 1999 Learning to Succeed;
- 1999 Moser Report;
- 2001 Learning and Skills Act;
- 2002 Success for All;
- 2005 Foster;
- 2006 Leitch;
- 2007 Further Education and Training Act;
- 2008 Adult Informal Learning consultation.

This list is not exhaustive but as I have previously noted (Hillier, 2006), by the time you read anything about policy in education, it will be out of date because government machinery constantly tinkers with the system, resulting in initiatives overload, something Jill Jameson and I called 'raining policy' (Hillier and Jameson, 2003). The major change over time has been of narrowing the focus of adult learning to a vocationally oriented, economically focused provision, which leads to qualifications as a proxy for identifying learning and skills. The Department for Business, Innovation and Skills, DBIS (formerly DIUS) continues to argue that their priority is for the development of skills and qualifications for those of working age and this limits the resources available for informal education (DIUS, 2008: 8). Yet the importance of adult education *was* recognised thirty years ago when the government commissioned the Russell Report examined in the following section.

The Russell Report: champion of adult learning

The idea of adult education in 1973 was firmly rooted in the notion of 'education permanente' a European concept that envisaged

> a society in which the whole life-long learning needs of all citizens would be taken as the field with which the national education system is concerned in its basic planning structures and expenditure . . . it would meet people's life-long but *discontinuous* needs which might recur in *personal, social, academic or vocational* life and make calls for adaptation and fresh educational resources.
>
> (Russell, 1973: para. 50; my italics)

It is clear that Russell has anticipated the need for adults to keep abreast of developments but that he also understood that such needs would come and go. He also recognised that people had personal and social reasons for learning and that their requirements would also affect the ways in which they could learn. He anticipated the need for learning providers to be innovative.

I really admire the way in which Russell approached adult learning. He argued that education was in direct contrast to any concept of 'failure' and that education was not to be seen as a 'finalisation of any kind'. In other words, he anticipated the restructuring of concepts of adult learning or indeed, any form of education, into one that was characterised by continual evolution, where adults would from time to time update their skills and knowledge as their unfolding lives demanded.

A discourse 'lens' helps show ways in which phenomena are named and applied. Russell talked about *permanent education*, in the 1980s we used the term *adult education*, European definitions included the term *education permanente* (see above) whereas today we talk about *lifelong learning*. These terms are not synonymous and convey meaning in particular ways. If we contrast the way in which Russell is written compared with, for example, the Leitch Report (2006), there is a depth of engagement with what adult learning is, rather than the following series of bullet-pointed exhortary statements that Leitch uses:

> 'Economically valuable skills' is our mantra. Institutional change and simplification are necessary
>
> To reach our goals, we as a society must invest more, It is clear who will pay. It is all of us – it is the State, employers and individuals. But this will be the best investment we could ever make.
>
> (Leitch, 2006: 2)

One exhortation that is contained in Russell, though, makes sobering reading:

> Although permanent education is as much concerned with infants as with adults, it has marked implications for adult education, staking a claim for it

> as an integral part of total provision, not as something for the less fortunate or more studious, but as something to be expected and experienced by the whole nation, 'permanent education' is a long-term concept and *we have not time to wait for it.*
>
> (Russell, 1973: para. 50; my italics)

Russell envisaged numerous means by which adults would engage in learning. The use of television to broadcast formal education opportunities had been recently boosted by the creation of the Open University in the late 1960s. However, it was clear that these means could also lead to formal outcomes, and in particular qualifications were deemed to be the destination upon the 'road' that adult learners travelled.

> There would be available for all adults as a road, at any time, to academic and professional qualification as well as towards personal competence and development. At the same time there would be open courses at colleges, universities and other centres, and radio, TV, correspondence courses which could be taken by people in their leisure. Courses of all kinds, sandwich, release and leisure would, through graduated stages, subject to assessment, lead to all forms of recognised qualification including degrees.
>
> (Russell, 1973: para. 50)

Today, Leitch noted, 'the most common measures of skills are qualifications' (Leitch, 2006: 6). Accreditation has become so central to our notion of learning, that it is hard to remember that it was not the main focus of activity for most post-compulsory provision thirty years ago. As Mary Hamilton and I have noted (Hamilton and Hillier, 2006) funding fashions provision and one of the crucial components of learning today is that funding is directed at accredited programmes, thus skewing the type of learning on offer at affordable fees. The whole industry of qualifications is based on what Hodgson and Spours (2003) argue are contested sites of credit frameworks. Three decades ago, Russell clearly set out the framework that he anticipated would 'work' for adult learning.

> And the whole complex of provision would be arranged on a cumulative credit basis with free movement between courses and stages, regardless of intervening drop-out.
>
> (Russell, 1973: para. 50)

One of the great tragedies in the history of English adult education is that most of the recommendations of Russell were not implemented. One reason for this is that, as Russell noted, adult education was seen as a luxury, something that middle-class folk did as a pass-time and therefore expendable in times of economic squeeze.

> At times, especially where economies were being sought, there has been a tendency, even in official pronouncements, to depreciate many [subjects] as recreational and therefore of little educational value; to assume that people go for social intercourse rather than to learn and to dismiss certain kinds of activity (like classes in bridge, golf and entertaining in the home) as pandering to petit-bourgeois aspirations.
>
> (Russell, 1973: para. 13)

Russell noted the following activities exemplified adult learning: arts and crafts, painting and the plastic arts, music, dance, drama and movement, speech and creative writing, office skills, physical skills and games, languages (including English), general education and intellectual and humane studies (Russell, 1973: para. 13). Many of these subjects continue to be offered in adult and community learning environments today with, of course, the addition of numerous technology courses, health and complementary medicine activities and self-management programmes. Some of the terminology has changed, for example, office skills have been replaced by use of technology, and physical skills and games has been extended into 'self-help' courses and personal development. In fact, looking through prospectuses from adult education institutions over the past three decades one can see evidence of how our society has evolved, where the workplace needs are identified, where language has changed and where new groups of learners are being encouraged to participate.

Creating spaces and places of learning

Much formal learning takes place within adult education institutions, community and voluntary organisations, higher education, the workplace and further education colleges. One of the criticisms of the further education (FE) system in England is that is has become so dispersed in its activities that it has lost its way (Foster, 2005). This system originally offered vocational provision for young people and adults in technical colleges but over the past three decades this has expanded to include vocational provision for school age pupils from 14 years onwards, adult education, professional development and workplace learning. Learners can be any age from 14 to old age, they can learn during the day or evening, in the workplace, in colleges, at home, through face-to-face or online means. This range of provision has not happened in an unplanned way. In both higher education and further education, there are more mature adults than young people, even though current government policy is primarily aimed at those aged 14–19 in further education and 18–21-year-olds in higher education. Colleges are overwhelmingly adult institutions, and the majority of FE students are over the age of 26. FE colleges have become more flexible in delivery and the curriculum, and more diversified in provision for all age groups. As Hyland and Merrill note, FE has been moved along a skills-based vocational road by government policy, although some colleges have struggled to maintain a community focus in their philosophy and practice (Hyland and Merrill, 2003: 50–51).

Making provision more open, and more accessible physically and temporally has been a key component of adult education discourse and policy. For example, in the 1980s, when there was huge rises in unemployment amongst adults and young people at a time when technology was beginning to afford opportunities to learn outside the institutional classroom, the then Council for Adult Continuing Education, ACACE, published its review of adult education. This Council had been created by the Secretary of State for Education to advise on matters relating to provision for adults in England and Wales. Amongst its recommendations were:

- The development of open access systems, including both distance and independent learning, could be one of the most important education innovations over the next twenty years (ACACE, 1982: para. 8.38).
- All major establishments of further and higher education should provide resource centres open to independent learners (ACACE, 1982: para. 8.40).
- [this] varied approach to learning offers adults greater flexibility in their patterns of study. With very few limitations people can study when, where and at a pace convenient to themselves – a considerable advantage to those many adults who are often unable to make a regular commitment to other forms of study . . . while more adults can be expected to choose to continue their education through distance learning, many will still want to benefit from face-to-face tuition (ACACE, 1982: para. 4.32).

Learning in an increasing technological age

ACACE identified a number of approaches, some of which were fleeting (Open Tech) and others have become central to current educational practice (flexi-study). The main areas identified at the time were: distance learning (e.g. Open University), individualised learning (for example Independent Learning offered at the then North East London Polytechnic, NELP), flexi-study, open learning (Open Tech, BBC), correspondence courses (National Extension College, NEC), independent learning (TV, radio, library) and self-help. ACACE argued that new modes of learning should be rapidly developed to overcome the limitations of physical attendance at set times in particular places (ACACE, 1982: para. 13.18).

The link between innovation and technology was clearly anticipated by the ACACE report:

> These developments within existing provision could be complemented by the exploitation of new technologies to provide new opportunities; Open access systems, including both distance learning and independent learning could be among the most important education innovations in the next twenty years; the growth of independent study facilities and self-help groups should therefore be encouraged.
>
> (ACACE, 1982: para. 13.18)

However, to ensure that such innovations could be introduced, ACACE recognised that the staff who work with adult learners need to develop their practice.

In other words, there was a staff development implication for introducing more accessible and innovative ways to learn.

> The main aim [of staff development] must be the effective provision and management of a wide variety of teaching systems to meet the needs of adult learners.
>
> (ACACE, 1982: para. 11.12).

A reader may be forgiven for assuming that such encouragement to innovate was smoothly taken up by providers, despite the increasing influence of technology on everyday life. Yet adult learning has not enjoyed the focus or the accompanying funding that further and higher education received over this period of time and was not able to introduce technology on the same scale. In further education, for example, there was funding not only to purchase and use computers but also to help the staff develop their knowledge and use of technology. Adult education was particularly vulnerable to funding cuts, not least because it was often seen as a luxury compared to the vocational focus of further education, which contained economically driven reasons for its funding to be maintained in times of budget constraints.

> Despite the advances of the post-war years what had emerged was a highly uneven provision that varied substantially from one locality to another. Legislation had been permissive, allowing LEAs wide scope for interpretation.
>
> (Green and Lucas, 1999: 20)

Today, we have so many opportunities to use technology that it is truly hard to keep abreast of developments. People can use wikis, blogs and interact through a variety of social networks using Web2 technology. An estimated 7.7 million people use Google, with 6.5 million people using Youtube, and Wikipedia counting 6.4 million users (DIUS, 2008: 11). People use podcasts from a variety of sources and prestigious institutions such as the Royal Institution enable people with broadband to download their annual science lectures in addition to viewing them on television. The sheer pace of change means that people do not need to rely on particular places such as adult education institutions for their learning and in addition, staff who work in these institutions need to be able to make use of the new forms of technology to engage and interact with their learners.

Adult learning has played an important part in the UK government's desire to ensure that adults can contribute to the economic well being of the country, along with a view that adult education needs to keep up with the times, meet people's changing needs and embrace the new technologies as they are created, constantly needing to innovate and react to whatever demands are placed on it. How has this constant need for innovation affected the practice of adult education? The following section outlines research that identified one part of adult learning, adult literacy, language and numeracy, where innovation played a central role.

A study of innovation in adult learning: adult literacy, language and numeracy

Mary Hamilton and I undertook a critical history of adult literacy, language and numeracy (ALLN) to examine how policy and practice had evolved from 1970–2000, the Changing Faces Project (Hamilton and Hillier, 2006, 2007). We conducted nearly 200 interviews with key policy makers, practitioners, volunteers and learners and examined documentary evidence. We created an archive of materials, documents, policy texts and memorabilia donated by practitioners and policy makers. We adopted a deliberative policy analysis (Hajer and Wagenaar, 2003) where we used five lenses as a guiding framework for their research: chronology, discourse, agency, tension and deliberative spaces. From the wealth of materials and interview data, it is possible to trace how practice has evolved, providing evidence for the innovatory approaches that I would argue have influenced mainstream adult and further education today.

Chronology is the primary lens to examine how practice developed in ALLN. It is important to remember that in 1970, very few people undertook any kind of formal adult education if they needed help with their literacy, language or numeracy. It was only when the BBC became involved in the 'Right to Read' campaign being spearheaded by the British Association of Settlements (BAS) that the general public became aware of adults who had not developed basic literacy skills and who needed help to do so. As a result a series of 26 ten-minute programmes called 'On the Move' was broadcast on Sunday evenings. The very first helpline used by the BBC was introduced in the series and people swamped the service with either offers from volunteers or from people finally finding somewhere they could turn to for help.

The problem was that an approach to teaching adult literacy had not yet been fully developed, although in a parallel context, recruits in the army had been given such assistance for years (White, 1963; Hamilton and Hillier, 2006). Learners were taught initially on a one-to-one basis with a volunteer. Volunteers were supported by tutor organisers, who were often working on hourly paid contracts and who themselves were only a little further forward in their literacy practice. The organisers began to develop the practice of volunteers through training but resources were not initially available for this to be extensive:

> I mean God knows that in those days they took me on and I hadn't got any training at all except for a few weeks of experience as a literacy volunteer. I think I had an introductory week course or something that you used to get in those days. So I mean looking back I think it was really shocking.
>
> (Literacy organiser)

From the initial one-to-one pairings, gradually resources were found to provide group sessions with paid tutors and by the 1980s, the standard provision was to be found in adult education institutions, with paid tutors, supported by volunteers and managed by a basic education organiser.

The first requirement, though, was to find resources from everyday materials and make up approaches individually:

> But all the variety, all the books that you might need, all the large bits of paper you needed to do things, printing things off, there just wasn't that, that wasn't available. In fact the volunteers used a lot of their own equipment. People just went about it in their own way – you would go to the public library and get something out that they thought their students were interested in and used that. They did manage quite well.
>
> (ESOL organiser)

There was little appropriate material for adults wishing to improve their literacy, numeracy and language. Indeed, in a survey of provision for adult 'illiteracy' in England in 1972, Haviland identified that 70 per cent of the literacy provision used children's books, and 80 per cent used material for 'backward readers'. He even listed the popular teaching materials, and they are all children-focused (Haviland, 1973). This practice obviously managed to continue into the later part of the 1970s as this comment shows:

> One organiser discovered 'Old Lob' being used in which I think is a phonic reading scheme dated from the 1950's (*sic*). I found 'Clumsy Charlie', 'Sound Sense', 'The Royal Road Readers'. These are reading schemes that don't even have much credibility with children let alone with adults. And when I walked into what was my office a beautiful medieval warehouse, there in vast piles were Ladybird books.
>
> (Basic skills organiser)

How did practitioners deal with this dearth of material suitable for adults?

> We would make materials or find (realia) and use that to structure our lessons, made lots and lots of worksheets and things, and had folders and folders full of stuff where you would develop all sorts of approaches with people. And we used to run specific things like 10 week spelling courses and develop all sorts, and they were quite a hit actually, people used to really quite like those.
>
> (Literacy tutor)

The teaching in group sessions was even beginning to be standardised as this tutor remembered:

> We started with something that the group did together, inspired by a newspaper article . . . I think it is probably typical having to start classes like that . . . and then move on to differentiated exercises which people would work at individually.
>
> (Literacy tutor)

Newspapers played an important part in literacy teaching. Not only were they sources of themes, triggers for discussion and used for more in depth writing and reading skills such as audience and genre, they were an important part of the social practice of literacy, and related to the learners' definitions of what they thought being successful was:

> We wouldn't accept 'I just want to learn to read', we would say well 'what do you want to read?' . . . one student I remember said 'I want to learn to read the Sun' [national tabloid] and I wanted to say to him 'don't read the Sun'. He worked at Fords factory and at lunch time they would get out their sandwich boxes and the blokes would all open the Sun and he wanted to be able to.
>
> (Literacy tutor)

For language learners, the use of everyday objects could be quite creative. One ESOL tutor fondly remembered using tops from sweet packets:

> I can remember us saving anything like the tops of plastic, Smartie tubes, [sweet containers] you know those little plastic tops? Well of course they are wonderful little counters, you can teach colours and they'd got letters on and you can carry them around as they are so light. And fir cones or marbles, things one might have at home. Those were typical examples of the material we used and we made.
>
> (ESOL tutor)

Throughout this early period, tutors and volunteers gave up personal time to foster their practice. There was financial support for running training provided by the then Adult Literacy and Basic Skills Unit (ALBSU) now the Basic Skills Agency. Much of the training centred around bringing practitioners together to share their ideas, sometimes to create materials that would then be disseminated regionally and eventually nationally. To help create materials specifically aimed at adult learners with basic levels of literacy to draw upon, the field created these 'from scratch'. This was achieved through a process of regional professional development activities, which at the time were undertaken voluntarily and without pay:

> But we used to have these training days where you would come in on a Saturday and you would learn from practitioners particular things and they were brilliant.
>
> We used to go without pay. You used to go on a Saturday and just go to learn so that you could do your job better.
>
> (Literacy tutor)

A feature of the approach developed for adult literacy was that of the language experience approach. Essentially, this started with using learners' own language, and from there led to writing in their own words and helping them to read, write and spell their own language, rather than the formal language seen in books:

> And we always made a point at focusing on the language experience approach. It took us a while to really grasp the concept of a language experience approach, that you used the language and the experience of the learner and that phonics and all the other kind of techniques should be a part of that. It took us about a year before it dawned on us all that it wasn't an optional extra, it was the absolute way to do it, there was only one approach and that all the other methods had to fit into that.
>
> (Basic skills organiser)

Something happened to the spontaneous, creative practices during the late 1980s and into the 1990s. As provision became more settled, more integrated into adult and further education, so began a drive to create a more coherent and national approach to this practice. It was during this time, particularly influenced by widespread adult and youth unemployment that government became aware of the need to improve basic literacy and numeracy amongst the workforce and the unemployed:

> We tend to channel them down certain paths now and . . . there's less emphasis on. . . . just learning for learning's sake and writing for writing's sake. . . . it's more about skills. . . . It's more sort of skills for work, skills for . . . life and things like that.
>
> (Basic skills organiser)

As practice developed, so did the resources available. Tutors were able to draw upon resource banks of worksheets that others had created that had been tried and tested. Eventually, such resources were published, either by community groups or eventually through commercial publishers. Whilst these resources were reliable, the need to update and keep abreast of the increasing demands for a professional 'look' to materials continued:

> So it's no longer good enough to provide worksheets and sit somebody down, or a tape, that's not enough. I think resources have to be appropriate.
>
> (Basic skills organiser)

The learners were encouraged in a variety of settings, not just adult education institutions. Literacy was taught through a range of contexts, initially known as 'linked skills' where people could learn for example, cookery and improve their literacy and numeracy at the same time. This approach has now become mainstreamed into 'embedded skills' but the principle is the same, to teach literacy or numeracy through a focus on other knowledge and skills. One example that has been particularly successful with parents is known as family literacy and here innovation makes use of traditional sources of materials and approaches that *are* used with children but which are not inappropriate for the adults:

> The work that they do in the parent family literacy class is all done with resources that they could find in a home with limited financial means. They make things out of bits of material, out of magazines, they use things from the kitchen, bottle tops and there's nothing that would need expensive art materials. Everything they use, corrugated paper, cardboard boxes, a bit Blue Peter style! We do the same with survival cookery and do-it-yourself, '101 ways with mince' but at least through that you can do the weighing, the measuring and so on and it's practical.
>
> (Family literacy tutor)

Student writing

Perhaps the clearest example of the interplay between teaching grammar, phonics and functional approaches to literacy compared with the language experience approach can be seen in the student writing movement. This has a long association with the literacy approaches developed from the 1970s, but actually can be seen in practices from the army's preliminary education centres and from activities in the Settlements. However, the finest example of a movement relating to student writing is the *Write First Time* publications, which comprised broadsheet size newspaper style publications containing writing entirely produced by learners (although these were edited by practitioners). This innovation in writing drew upon a longer tradition of community writing projects, but as part of adult literacy it was phenomenally successful in giving learners a voice and showing them that they could produce the written words that others would be interested in reading:

> I remember that poetry writing is prolific in prisons and we collected and made a book, and again, I taught grammar through it by getting the students within the education team to correct and look up and check spellings – no such things as computers in those days and spell checks – so if they weren't convinced the way a word was spelled, they used the dictionary, they used the thesaurus and we produced a wonderful booklet of poetry which was in itself an English exercise to produce. They could all have a copy and send it out to the children, 'now I wrote this, it's got my name on'. So, things had to be relevant, things had to mean something and have a transferable skill.
>
> (Literacy tutor)

Today projects continue to foster innovation. One of these is the LEIS project (2006) which examined how non-text based ways can help foster literacy and in this particular case, help build peace across two countries, Northern Ireland and Eire. The project team examined 'ways into writing' and worked with local groups to use such examples as ghost stories, fairytales, poetry, telling stories, community writing, visual and creative activities (Literacy and Equality in Irish Society (LEIS) project, Weir, 2006)

Although the main focus of basic skills was literacy, numeracy began to become part of provision and again, it was clear to practitioners that they needed to find meaningful ways to make basic maths sessions relevant and engaging for their learners:

> Well I discovered very quickly when I first started trying to teach fractions in isolation to a group of women, was a waste of time, because it meant nothing to them. As soon as you started to convert it to decimals and put a pound sign in front of it then 'oh yes I understand it'. This was in the days before computers were mainstreamed, even before calculators were considered an every day thing that was ok to use. I would do things like get them to talk about how many children they have got and then add them up together . . . then the ages of the children, and all the children added together and then what is the average age, so I would link it very much into the things that were important to them.
>
> (Numeracy organiser)

Doing maths requires a commitment to using activities that would normally be found 'the real world'. However, one enterprising maths tutor made use of the local environment to teach trigonometry:

> We would go out to the pond and measure, using trigonometry using the tree and the shadows. It was wonderful, it really was.
>
> (Numeracy tutor)

Another important project funded by the Inner London Education Authority (ILEA) centred around working with women returners who wanted to become teachers but needed a qualification in maths. This approach not only took account of what they needed to learn mathematically and how to do so in non-threatening ways, it also undertook to give them control over what they learned:

> We had a lot of games in the pack and if they liked playing games they might go through until they found a game to play. And we kept on telling them that we expected them to be independent learners in the sense that they had to decide what they needed, it was no use them coming to us and saying 'what should I do next?' We would just look at them blankly and say 'how the hell do you expect us to know, you're the learner, you have got to be in charge of what's going on'.
>
> (Numeracy tutor)

Games were an important way in for many adult learners. It is difficult to strike the right balance between activities that are not patronising or insulting if they are associated with children and yet without them, teaching certain topics would be very dry indeed:

> We spent hours and hours with paper and cardboard making materials . . . We made endless games of bingo. I got to the stage where I could teach anything through bingo!
>
> (ESOL tutor)

The story of innovation in ALLN would not be complete without mentioning technology! Initially, technology involved reproducing handwritten or typed materials through something called a 'banda machine'. This used a drum that has certain chemicals that coloured the text or diagrams and would be rotated to produce copies of the worksheet. This was always mentioned with fondness, irony and humour!

> I have this pack of human rights materials which was all produced by hand on a banda machine, okay, these rather faded tatty looking work sheets that we produced. And there was a mixture of some quite political things about human rights and some very practical things like, I can't quite remember how we fitted reading the gas meter in with human rights (laughs) but things like that we did.
>
> (Literacy tutor)

Technology does not have to be very grand to be useful. One organiser gained funding to buy resources and at the time, the most important resource was something that is standard today, a photocopier:

> One of my first ever projects was to buy a photocopier because there was always a problem about the photocopier, how much paper you used and how much access you had to it. And the most liberating thing for a group of part-time tutors would be to have their own photocopier with nobody asking questions about how many copies you were doing.
>
> (Basic skills organiser)

As technology improved in mainstream education tutors began to adopt it for ALLN.

One development used both in schools and in adult language classes was the Language Master, a piece of equipment that helped particularly with language teaching. It comprised a card with a strip of tape on it with a record word, phrase or sentence. There was room on the card to write the sentence. When fed through the card reader learners heard it and saw it at the same time. There could be a picture attached. This early innovation soon became replaced by video, cassette players and sometimes overhead projectors (OHPs) and eventually computers and today laptops. All have their benefits and challenges, particularly for tutors who have to work in outreach centres such as village halls, where technical support is available.

Early use of computers involved trundling BBC computers, for example, on trolleys from one room to another, as institutions rarely had enough funds to purchase enough to be permanently located in classrooms. The introduction of computers meant that tutors needed to innovate again, and unsurprisingly, early champions of technology jumped at the chance to create resources that could be disseminated to their peers and used with sometimes different groups of learners, i.e. those that wanted to be able to use technology and by stealth, would also be able to improve their basic skills.

A fairly recent innovation throughout adult learning, but particularly for ALLN has been the way in which the BBC and other terrestrial television have supported literacy and numeracy. As noted earlier, the original 'Right to Read' campaign gained immense support from the BBC and this was followed by a number of initiatives aimed at helping people improve their writing, spelling and maths. The use of 'issues' in soap operas such as *Eastenders* and *Brookside* began different means to raise awareness of the impact of low levels of literacy and maths. The BBC has been a particularly important source of educational support through involvement in specific initiatives such as the basic skills initiative (BSAI) in the early 1990s, and ITV has today become a cornerstone of government policy with the 'Get On' campaign and use of gremlins to entice (or frighten!) people into doing something about their basic skills.

The BBC has long had an education component to its programme, especially given that its original aims were to inform, entertain and educate. Today, it is clear that in using interactive websites, being able to download programmes, music and play these anytime, almost anywhere, the education role of the BBC has extended but also dissipated. As one producer interviewed for Changing Faces noted:

> I think it's too simplistic to say that the internet came along so the education burden was transferred from air time to the internet. So it's now quite possible for a mainstream programme like Blue Planet to be classed as an educational success – it has educational wrap around on the internet. I would argue that that kind of support has always been part of the BBC package, it would just have been delivered in print. What is new is internet learning resources that go out independent of broadcasts, this is a medium in its own right and is scheduled for it. This is happening more and more.
>
> (BBC education manager)

Impact of policy

In our study of ALLN, we were able to identify key moments that had occurred as a direct result of policymaking. For example, cuts to adult education budgets had impacted hard on provision and many tutors recalled how they and their students had fought against the cuts. A major impact of government policy was on accreditation of learning, which had been highly controversial in the practice of adult basic skills where the emphasis had been on encouragement and development and if anything, assessment was an anathema to practitioners. They were particularly concerned that their learners who had experienced failure in the past would be put off by accreditation. At the same time, there was a tension within this view as they also recognised that gaining a qualification for the first time was immensely important to learners and gave them confidence and enthusiasm to pursue their studies. Indeed, some tutors recognised on hindsight that their reluctance to engage with accreditation was more about their views than those of their learners:

> When I came back to basic education in 1994 I was really aware of how the teaching, the teachers were different, they had a different attitude . . . by then we had to have accreditation, it was a good thing, the students wanted it, we were beginning to realise that we should think about progression and progress and measuring distance of travel. What I realised was that teachers had become almost acclimatised, almost habituated to accreditation and there was a danger in that and there still is a danger in that. . . . I do think in the 1970s and 1980s we tended to work for ourselves and for our own pleasure rather than for the student.
>
> (Basic skills organiser)

The increasingly compliant culture that pervaded further education, in which ALLN primarily resided in the 1990s, meant that practitioners were expected to have consistent approaches to literacy and numeracy, and they were subject to inspections by the Further Education Funding Council (FEFC), and today by the Office for Standards in Education (Ofsted). Yet some older practices and resources continue to be used by tutors who developed their approaches from earlier times. This can lead to difficulties, as this organiser recalls:

> This poor woman let the side down by having resources that weren't [modern], so they had to come back and look at the resources again, and she was clinging onto this really tatty book and she said 'but I love it and I always use it'. 'But you can't, they've seen it, you've got to hide it' and she obviously thought it was terribly effective. So that seems a bit sad doesn't it?
>
> (Basic skills organiser)

Conclusion

The history of adult literacy and numeracy tells a story of innovation and creativity throughout. Practitioner commitment to the developing field has survived numerous attempts to diminish the work through funding cuts, or move it into more mainstream provision where aims differed, particularly focusing on employment rather than improving skills for personal benefit.

The influence of ALLN on mainstream adult provision is inestimable. One only need examine the curriculum in initial tutor training to see that the learner-centred approaches that were developed in this field are now set in the generic standards that all teachers and trainers must follow (LLUK, 2007). This is an important achievement. And for those who have been part of that history, there are clear reasons for their involvement:

> I think it's really exciting actually, that whole engagement of people who could not be a part of learning, even if you only got 5 out of 50 who have suddenly become learners and feel confident and comfortable where they can go. I think one of the things when I first started getting involved with basic skills was very much that empowerment, the whole politics of empowerment.
>
> (Literacy tutor)

I have argued, in this chapter, that informal learning is particularly apparent in adult learning and such learning has been influenced by a number of government policies. I have also argued that one key strand of adult learning, adult literacy, language and numeracy, has been a fertile area in which practice has been creatively developed and where tutors have been innovative. The importance of this practice can be seen in its influence in more mainstream adult learning practice. Ultimately, I do not want to see the informal and more democratic forms of learning become part of government remit as I believe there is a danger that it, as other more formal types of provision, becomes drawn into the compliance and accountability culture that pervades much of education currently. This is not to argue against the need for funding and for recognition of the value of informal learning. But its inherent characteristic of being amorphous, flexible, unstructured and spontaneous can only continue if left to those activitists and committed people who notice and engage with new issues, new challenges and new interests.

Last word

Perhaps the last word should rest with a tutor who described how she turned a fairly standard session of literature into a very moving and unusual event. This is how innovation has been sustained in the field of ALLN and I hope will endure elsewhere:

> We were studying *Pride and Prejudice* and people really enjoyed it. We did all the analytical stuff and literary theory stuff, all totally serious. And then there was the bit about Darcy and Elizabeth, that there was going to be the proposal. In their own lives and indeed in mine we have never had proposals, some of us weren't married and all of us had children but the dream of somebody proposing to us formally and asking us to marry them was still around and why shouldn't it be? We had all the kinds of ironies and cynicisms about that. Anyway we decided we would keep this for next week, somebody brought in a bottle of sparkling wine, somebody else brought in cream cakes

and when we got to that bit a roar broke out in that room of shouting and cheering like you have never heard, a bottle popped and we ate cream cakes. And of course we all knew that we would probably never have a Darcy that would propose to us and take us off to a stately home to live in riches for the rest of our lives but the fun and the dream of it were great.

References

Advisory Council for Adult and Continuing Education (1982) *Continuing Education: From policies to practice*, Leicester: ACACE.

Department for Innovation, Universities and Skills (2008) *Informal Adult Learning – Shaping the Way Ahead*, London: DIUS.

Foster, A. (2005) *Realising the Potential: A review of the future role of further education colleges*, Annesley: DfES Publications.

Green, A. and Lucas, N. (1999) *FE and Lifelong Learning: Realigning the sector for the twenty-first century*, University of London: Institute of Education.

Griffin, C. M. (1987) *Adult Education as Social Policy*, London: Croom Helm.

Hamilton, M. and Hillier, Y. (2006) *The Changing Face of Adult Literacy, Language and Numeracy*, Stoke-on-Trent: Trentham Books.

Hajer, M. and Wagenaar, H. (2003) (eds) *Deliberative Policy Analysis: Understanding Government in the Network Society*, Cambridge: Cambridge University Press.

Hamilton, M. and Hillier, Y. (2007) 'Deliberative policy analysis: adult literacy assessment and the politics of change', *Journal of Education Policy*, 22 (5) 573–594.

Haviland, R., (1973) Survey of Provision for Adult Illiteracy in England, Reading: Centre for the Teaching of Reading, Reading University.

HMSO (1975) *Adult Education: The challenge of change* (The Alexander Report), Edinburgh.

Hillier, Y. (2006) *Everything You Need to Know about FE Policy*, London: Continuum.

Hillier, Y. and Jameson, J. (2003) *Empowering Researchers in Further Education*, Stoke-on-Trent: Trentham.

Hodgson, A. and Spurs, K. (2003) *Beyond A Levels: Curriculum 2000 and the reform of 14–19 Qualifications*, London: Kogan Page.

Hyland, T. and Merrill, B. (2003) *The Changing Face of Further Education: Lifelong learning, inclusion and community values in Further Education*, London: RoutledgeFalmer.

Leitch, S. (2006) *Prosperity for All in the Global Economy: World class skills*, final report, London: HM Treasury.

Lifelong Learning UK (2007) http://www.lluk.org/national-occupational-standards.htm (accessed August 2009).

McGivney, V. (2001) *Fixing or Changing the Pattern? Reflections on Widening Adult Participation in Learning*, Leicester: NIACE.

Russell Report on Adult Education: *A Plan for Development* (1973) Department for Education and Science, London: HMSO.

Smith, J. and Spurling, A. (1999) *Lifelong Learning: Riding the tiger*, London: Cassell.

Weir, L. (2006) *LEIS Project*, Belfast: Queen's University of Belfast.

White, A. (1963) *The Story of Army Education 1643–1963*, London: Harrap.

Part II: Conclusions

Sue Jackson

This part has been concerned to explain 'participation' and critique current understandings of 'non-participation' to point to more innovative practices in lifelong learning. The chapters challenge current complacencies that suggest that diversity or structural inequalities no longer matter, and that non-participation is based in individual deficit and lack. The authors of these chapters have shown the resistances to being classified as non-participatory that come from learners and from teachers. They have also challenged current policy definitions of non-participation. The chapter authors demonstrate how people participate in both informal and formal learning in myriad ways and, as Hillier (Chapter 8) argues in her conclusion, there is much practice in lifelong learning that has told, and continues to tell, stories of innovative creativity.

As the next part will go on to show, some of the resistances, challenges and creative innovations outlined in this section have developed through work-based learning and learning through work.

Part III

Work-based learning and learning through work

Introduction

Sue Jackson

The final Part of the book turns to an area of ever-growing debate, challenge and innovation in lifelong learning: work-based learning and learning through work. In doing so, it draws on issues of diversity, participation and non-participation already explored in earlier Parts. For example, Gemma Piercy (Chapter 9) shows how participation rates still reflect broader social inequalities, including employment. She demonstrates how the current global economic recession has led to cuts in education/lifelong learning budgets, noting (as do other authors in this Part) the development of a skills and vocational focus on lifelong learning, with participation (in education and the workplace) linked to particular qualifications. As Jacqueline McManus shows (Chapter 12), work-based learning and learning at work evolve through complex and inter-related constellations of individual, economic and social goals. It is context, rather than content, which becomes the key organising principle (Portwood, 2007).

Mary V. Alfred (Chapter 11) explores ways in which the terrain of workplaces are changing with the global increases in ethnic and otherwise diverse workplace communities (see also Chapter 10 in this Part, and Chapter 1 in the first Part). Like Etienne and Jackson in Part I, Alfred shows how communities of practice (Wenger, 1998) can on the one hand enable participation but can also, on the other hand, marginalise others through the exercise of power of dominant groups. The complex and variable ways in which power is exercised and resisted – the politics of 'power in action' – forms much of Jon Talbot's discussion in Chapter 10, as it does in greater or lesser ways for other authors in this volume. For example, Piercy (Chapter 9) shows how the Māori renaissance and other political movements have exercised power. As have several other authors in this book (see Part I for example), Alfred explores intersectionality: here the intersections of ethnicity, race, identity and perceptions of place.

As all the authors in this Part show, work-based learning and learning through work is political, contested and inseparable from discussions of learning communities and participation and non-participation (see Parts II and III). Situated in New Zealand, Chapter 9 begins the Part with a broad overview of lifelong learning policies over the last decade or so, moving on to discuss some specific projects on learning in the workplace. The chapter critically evaluates the ability of such projects to genuinely innovate and improve participation in lifelong learning. Piercy examines the efforts of New Zealand's Labour-led coalition government to continue the previously established emphasis on increasing levels of educational achievement and participation during times of social, political and institutional change.

She sets the scene by elaborating on ideological tensions between government and other stakeholder and end-user groups in relation to learning in the workplace, and briefly introduces the initiatives put in place over the last decade. The chapter moves on to discuss some specific case studies: jointly run projects focused on learning in the workplace. These include 'Skill New Zealand', managed by the Industry Training Federation, the New Zealand Council of Trade Unions and Business New Zealand and funded by the Tertiary Education Commission; and the 'Workplace Productivity' initiative run by the Department of Labour, which places a high level of importance on increasing skill levels in the New Zealand workforce and has run a number of workplace literacy case studies (and thus returns to some of the issues raised by Hillier in Part II). The chapter concludes by critically evaluating the ability of these projects to genuinely improve participation in lifelong learning, determining the strength of legacy left by the values of access and equity.

In Chapter 10, Jon Talbot presents a case study through integrative projects, this time of a work-based and integrative studies programme located within a university setting. He explores the changing power relations on work-based learning programmes, which struggle to meet sometimes competing needs of learners, employers and tutors. He does so through a discussion of innovative learning programmes that straddle higher education institutions and the workplace. Talbot argues that the newer forms of higher education involve a negotiations and re-negotiations through the borders between new and existing stakeholders, including employers, learners and universities. The chapter discusses some of the implications for the role of university tutors and the centrality of educational objectives where there is a cultural shift towards meeting the needs of learners and employers. The case study is used to examine changing power relations on work-based learning programmes between tutors, learners and employers. Talbot argues that the newer forms of higher education involve a negotiation of relationships between tutors and new stakeholders (including employers and learning technologists) and a re-negotiation with existing ones (learners and the university). He concludes that whilst in some circumstances this can lead to a positive exchange of power, in others there are undoubted tensions and contestations.

Extending the arguments of the first two chapters, Chapter 11 calls for a deeper understanding of workplace learning, one that expands from the narrow conceptualisation of learning in terms of literacy, skills building and corporate training (Billett, 2002) to a more global view informed by culture, diversity and the movement of people across national borders. Chapter 11 is concerned with other sorts of borders, those across national boundaries, examining learning and work among women of the diaspora. Its author calls for a deeper and global understanding of workplace learning, informed by culture, diversity and the movement of people across borders. Using narratives of women of the diaspora, Alfred highlights the shifting notions of identity and place as they inform the realities of learning and work among both voluntary and involuntary immigrants. She argues that immigrant women's perceptions of themselves and their experiences within the workplace culture influence what is learned, how it is learned, and how that knowledge is used to leverage position within the workplace. It concludes that workplace learning must be understood within the broader concepts of social and identity capital, diaspora and migration, and place and the politics of location.

In what is not only the concluding chapter to Part III, but also to the book, Chapter 12 continues the issues raised elsewhere in this Part and explores ways in which capacity can be developed for learners in the workplace (Mitchell and Sackney, 2001), arguing for more holistic and global approaches to understanding and re-positioning lifelong learning. Drawing on reports from the Organisation for Economic Co-operation and Development, the European Centre for the Development of Vocational Training and the European Union, McManus argues that there is an over-regulation and formalisation of competence-based training and skills development in lifelong learning policies, and calls for the (re-)development of capacity-building for worker/learners as a necessary condition for successful and lifelong learning in the workplace and beyond. McManus argues for the return of a focus on UNESCO's (1972) core lifelong learning theme of self-awareness, redeveloped through the concept of capacity-development, encapsulating agency and identity in holistic ways. She outlines ways in which capacity can be developed in worker/learners, showing how workers and their environment interact and impact on each other. The chapter concludes that developing capacity is a pre-condition for successful and lifelong learning in the workplace. Like Avoseh in Chapter 2, McManus argues for broader and more holistic conceptions of learning, with an inter-relatedness that is currently missing from most Western conceptualisations.

References

Billet, S. (2002) 'Critiquing workplace learning discourses: Participation and continuity at work', *Studies in the Education of Adults*, 34: 1, pp. 56–66.

Mitchell, C. and Sackney L. (2001) 'Profound improvement: Building capacity for a learning community', *Journal of Educational Change*, 2: 4, pp. 356–368.

Portwood, D. (2001), 'Towards an epistemology of work-based learning: Eliciting clues from work-based learning projects', in Young, D. and Garnett, J. (eds), *Workbased learning futures*, Bolton: University Vocational Awards Council, pp. 8–20.

Wenger, E. (1998) *Communities of Practice: Learning, meaning and identity*, Cambridge: Cambridge University Press.

Chapter 9

Access and equity in Aotearoa[1]/New Zealand

Increasing participation via policy and practice

Gemma Piercy

Introduction

The words 'access' and 'equity' convey a very strong social justice message that taps adult education's deep, democratic impulse, re-affirmed in the 1970s when UNESCO championed its emancipatory vision of lifelong learning (Faure et al., 1972). At the heart of that vision was a determination, through education, to transform cultural, economic, political and social inequality. In practice, of course, government policies concerning adult education are shaped and moulded not just by visions but by the prevailing ideology of the times (Law, 2005). Thus the emergence of neo-liberalism as the dominant ideology of the late twentieth century (King, 1987) inevitably challenged the emancipatory essence of the UNESCO vision. But, it can be argued, not entirely. For although the last quarter-century has seen the notion of 'lifelong learning' substantially refocused towards labour market priorities, other forces in society continue to press for a more democratic educational agenda.

This chapter focuses on how the values of access and equity have continued to have a role in Aotearoa/New Zealand over the last ten years (1999 to 2008). At one level, its purpose is to provide an overview of lifelong learning policies in a small democracy during the term of a Labour-led Coalition Government. But at a deeper level, it also seeks to illustrate the resilience of the emancipatory vision of lifelong learning in a national context that has been dominated, since the late 1980s, in a similar fashion to other western nations, by a neo-liberal notion of labour force training (Law, 1998). In the face of continued domination of neo-liberal ideas internationally in education and training this case study serves to illustrate how social justice values can be renewed and revived with the assistance of policy and practice. This is particularly in relation to the calls from Government officials in New Zealand and elsewhere for increased participation and innovative solutions to increase productivity in the pursuit of a human capital theory-driven vision of international competitiveness.

The chapter begins by describing the New Zealand context. Second, the origins of New Zealand's lifelong learning policies are briefly described in order to identify the tensions between the underlying political ideologies. Third, the chapter provides an overview of the lifelong learning policy over the last ten years, examining the efforts of the New Zealand's Labour-led coalition government on increasing levels of educational achievement and participation. This will be achieved by examining some of their key post-compulsory education and training (PCET) policies and their practices by focusing on some specific projects related to work-based learning. These projects include the *Skill New Zealand* (SkillNZ) campaign, jointly managed by the New Zealand Industry Training Federation (ITF), the New Zealand Council of Trade Unions (NZCTU) and Business New Zealand (BusNZ), funded by the Tertiary Education Commission (TEC); and the 'Workplace Productivity' initiative run by the Department of Labour (DoL) also in conjunction with the aforementioned stakeholders. By highlighting the policy and practice under the previous Labour Government the chapter makes connections to some of the themes of this book, for example, participation and diversity through the emphasis on access and equity. Innovation and vocational learning are addressed through the focus on the projects outlined above.

The New Zealand context

New Zealand is a small former British colony located in the South Pacific. Its society is shaped by the following factors: the Treaty of Waitangi, recognised by the indigenous Māori population and the State; its history and location; and its economy, which is driven by primary sector exports such as timber, milk powder, wool, lamb and beef, and service sector industries such as tourism.

In many respects New Zealand is no different from the other former British settler colonies such as Australia and Canada. Its dominant culture is western; it belongs to organisations such as the Organisation for Economic Co-operation and Development (OECD); it is important to note however, that the Treaty has placed an emphasis on creating a bi-cultural society.[2] When compared with other western nations, the Treaty and the subsequent commitment to bi-culturalism is a significant difference in how this country responds to the growing needs of an increasingly diverse and multi-cultural citizenry.

New Zealand's current population is approximately 68 per cent Pakeha or European; 15 per cent Māori; 9 per cent Asian; and 7 per cent Pacific peoples (Statistics New Zealand, 2009). These population differences demonstrate that New Zealand must carefully balance the needs of bi-culturalism with the other minority groups present in our society. This is especially true when considering participation rates in industry training.

The three phases of change

In order to tell the story of lifelong learning in New Zealand policy changes will be highlighted by focusing on three key phases in the recent history of industry training (Cochrane et al., 2008). The first phase is 1984–1989 and the second phase is 1990–1999. The last phase, 1999–2008, will receive the most attention, as it is the primary focus of this chapter.

Phase one: calls for reform

The second half of the 1980s heralded a period of intense social, political and institutional change. Prior to this point New Zealand had continued to operate as a relatively static colony with many regulations dating back to the previous century (Russell, 1996). Calls for change were prompted for various reasons from the 1970s. The Māori renaissance and the women's movement (the second wave of feminism) were particularly powerful, as were more general social movements such as the fight to end apartheid, represented most vividly in the reaction to the 1981 Springbok rugby tour[3] when the government of that time was challenged to do things differently (Cheyne et al., 2008; King, 2003; Walker, 1990). The union movement was also part of these struggles and some unions, specifically the Engineers' Union,[4] started to re-examine their attitudes particularly towards the role that education could play in enhancing workers' lives (Law, 1994; Piercy, 1999; Law and Piercy, 2000). These groups fought not only for acknowledgement but also for ways to improve their participation rates in the workforce and in education.

The Fourth Labour Government (1984–1990) responded to these calls for economic and social change but once elected pursued instead a range of reforms that deregulated the labour market and substantially altered, and in many parts reduced, the role of the state. These changes were for the most part consistent with the neo-liberal policies promoted by the Thatcher and Reagan governments in the UK and USA respectively from the late 1970s. However, given the social pressures that led to Labour's electoral victory some ministerial portfolios continued to have a residual social democratic emphasis. The education portfolio with its accompanying policy and practice was the clearest example of this mixed level of commitment to neo-liberal reform (Law and Piercy, 2000; Piercy, 1999). This was also the portfolio that acknowledged and embraced the values of access and equity in a social democratic sense – the words regularly appearing in policy documents.

The policy documents *Learning for Life I and II* (Department of Education, 1988; 1989) demonstrated how this mixed commitment would be enacted. The recommendations from these reports, in conjunction with others (such as the Hawke (1989) and Picot (1988) reports), resulted in the Education Amendment Act 1990, which radically altered how the key stakeholders facilitated and organised PCET (Piercy, 1999). Polytechnics which functioned as regionally based community colleges began to offer degree qualifications, placing them in competition with universities for students; facilitating the introduction of a market model but also opening up opportunities for degree study outside of the main cities. Fees were introduced but were means-tested and still very low, indicating an early but mixed buy-in by the government of neo-liberal human capital theory. Significantly for Māori, the policy facilitated the formal recognition of *wānangas* or tertiary education organisations (TEO) designed to provide education shaped by indigenous cultural practices and language in mind (McCarthy, 1996). Unionists were also given their own TEO – the Trade Union Educational Authority (TUEA) (Law, 1997). Industry training was expanded to include new types of work, for example the service sector, in order to better meet the needs of women (Piercy, 1999). Despite this attention participation rates in industry training fell markedly during this time period due to economic upheavals such as the 1987 Wall Street crash and the corporatisation of government departments.

Another example of this mixed approach can be seen in how policy officials and social groups used human capital theory, particularly the drive to increase educational achievement levels at a societal level, to change PCET in order to open it up to adults and increase the levels of participation/qualifications attained. For example, entry criteria were removed for those over the age of 20 and a graduated system of criterion-referenced assessment or competency-based training was introduced. This system was designed to provide portable education units of achievement that would allow adults and youth to earn building blocks towards nationally recognised qualifications. This shift was significant as it heralded the movement away from national exams that used norm-referenced assessment in order to push low achievers into the labour market, an exam system that effectively blocked many workers from being able to participate in lifelong learning (Piercy, 1999).

Phase two: benign neglect

Most of the changes proposed in Phase One were not fully in place when Labour lost the 1990 election. As such it was the neo-liberal National government (1990–1999) that implemented these reforms, which they did with only a few specific changes (Cochrane et al., 2008). This uncompromising neo-liberal era brought in a new (quasi) TEO as provided by the Industry Training Act 1992 (ITA), Industry Training Organisations (ITOs). These institutions were designed to replace the previous centrally run, tripartite structures, which regulated training in the workplace and designed trade based qualifications. ITOs are responsible for designing qualifications and selecting tertiary institutions to provide them. ITOs are also responsible for monitoring trainees' progress through their training programmes (Green et al., 2003; Murray, 2001; Piercy, 1999). Under the National government, funding for industry training increased but due to increasing levels of participation it was inadequate. The market model assumed that employers and, increasingly, learners would pay for much of the training. The introduction of a student loan scheme and high fees was linked to a neo-liberal or 'new' human capital perspective that viewed the acquisition of skills as a private good (Cochrane et al., 2008; Marginson, 1993, 1997; Piercy, 1999, 2005).

It is important to note that the foundation for these reforms was located in the first phase where, in line with the values of access and equity, policy makers wished to extend industry training beyond the traditional trades and by doing so enable workers outside of those trades to access learning on-the-job, including women and Māori, up-skilling all workers. However, the 1990s was a wasted decade for industry education and training. Framed by a market model of educational demand and deliver, National's ITA 1992 was hampered by a voluntaristic approach and the impact of the 1991 Employment Contracts Act (ECA) led to unions being, to varying degrees, steadily sidelined, even in industries such as dairy manufacturing, that had remained substantially unionised (Cochrane et al., 2008, Law, 1998, 2003a; Law and Piercy, 2000, 2004; Piercy, 2003a, 2005). The market approach allowed the *Whare Wānangas* (there are three: *Te Wānanga o Aotearoa*, *Te Whare Wānanga o Awanuiārangi*, and *Te Wānanga o Raukawa*[5]) to survive and even thrive but they were not funded consistently with other state institutions (McCarthy, 1996). The claim that women would be able to participate in greater numbers was also only a partial success; whilst numbers participating in formal full-time study grew, women continued to choose traditional female-dominated areas. As a result gender disparities in participation rates actually grew between the new areas of vocational training and the traditionally male dominated trades and industries. It should be noted though that participation rates in industry training grew steadily throughout this period but participation was uneven with younger workers, women and Pacific Islanders all under-represented and with Māori rates increasing but only in certain industries (Curson et al., 2004: Piercy, 2003b; Piercy, Murray and Abernethy, 2006).

These different participation rates and the inequalities they reflected, alongside the identified funding shortfall and inconsistent coverage of ITOs, lead to a consensus by the end of the decade that the market model was failing (Doyle, 1999; Green et al., 2003; Cochrane et al., 2008). This was captured in Labour's 1999 election manifesto, which foreshadowed a more 'hands-on' approach to industry training, and this is dealt with in the next part of the chapter.

Phase three: revival of social rights

Labour's manifesto document, *21st Century Skills: Building Skills for Jobs and Growth* (New Zealand Labour Party, 1999) was critical of National's market-based approach. The document's general direction was inclined towards a more legislative, semi-regulatory approach, coupled with a more pronounced third way notion of partnership (Law, 2003a; Law and Piercy, 2004; Piercy, 2003a). The central theme that threaded through the document was the view that education and employment/industry/economy had to be brought together. Furthermore, Labour's alternative approach favoured a third way[6] shift to the use of targets, partnership and networks in order to co-ordinate and encourage collaboration while still trying to retain the neo-liberal, market model's funder/provider split (Law and Piercy, 2004; Piercy, 2003a; Powell, 2003).

One of the new government's first initiatives from the manifesto was the enactment of the Modern Apprenticeship Act 2000. While this legislation did not challenge the current system directly, it did provide a pathway to access learning for younger members of the labour market who had previously been marginalised (Piercy, 2003b; Murray and Piercy, 2003; Murray 2005). The second major government initiative was to set up a tertiary education advisory committee (TEAC). Its task was to review and evaluate the entire area of PCET provision in New Zealand.

Several very important policy changes resulted from the broader TEAC exercise. First, the role of the state was enhanced with the establishment of a Tertiary Education Commission (TEC): 'a single comprehensive, central steering body for the whole education system' (TEAC, 2001a, p. xvi). One of the Commission's first actions was to implement the first tertiary education strategy (TES) – a five-year plan (2002–2007). The TES is a third way device that allows for the setting of targets and for investigations into how specific parts of PCET can be regulated in order to better meet the needs of society and the economy. This is significant as it highlights how third way policy makers do not want to return to the high levels of prescription characterised by social democratic governments, yet still want to intervene in situations of either perceived market failure or social exclusion.

The intention of the TES is to provide a mechanism that assists the government to steer the PCET system towards contributing to six national goals, linking education more explicitly to broader needs of society and the economy. This linking is to be achieved through six corresponding strategies, which aim to:

- strengthen system capability and quality;
- contribute to the achievement of Māori development aspirations;
- raise foundation skills so that all people can participate in our Knowledge Society;
- develop the skills New Zealanders need for our Knowledge Society;
- educate for Pacific Peoples' (sic) development and success; and
- strengthen research, knowledge creation and uptake for our Knowledge Society. (Ministry of Education, 2002a, p. 2)

The government enshrined many of the TES aims and provided for the creation and implementation of a Statement of Tertiary Educational Priorities (STEP) in its Education (Tertiary Reform) Amendment Act 2002. Each STEP, which was to be published at least every three years but in practice published between every 12 to 18 months, outlined the priorities needed to work towards the six strategies and set dates for when the priorities were to be implemented (Ministry of Education, 2002a).

The first STEP (2002–2003) outlined how the market model was to be retained in order to ensure responsiveness by Tertiary Education Organisations (TEOs). However, clear future statements provided by both the first STEP and subsequent STEPs were intended to provide a more certain and supportive policy climate in order to promote collaboration between key stakeholders, including unions (Ministry of Education, 2002b). For example, the first STEP suggested that the initial changes would be driven by TEOs through a Charter and Profile exercise, the purpose of which was to guide each TEO in how they could contribute to the achievement of both the TES and the six national goals. The STEP also outlined how the Charter and Profile exercise would be used to assess the need, suitability and extent of funding for the TEOs. This demonstrated another type of central planning that was imbued with neo-liberal notions of accountability especially as non-compliance led to threats of cuts to funding, such as the funding freeze to private training establishments that was put in place at this time.

Key priorities for the second STEP (2003–2004) were to articulate better the role of the Tertiary Education Commission and continue the development of the infrastructure and processes that supported the new system, such as the funding model outlined previously (Ministry of Education, 2003a). The most significant priority was, however, promoting a greater leadership role to be taken in and by industry training and its stakeholders, ITOs, employers and unions (Ministry of Education, 2003b).

The third STEP (2005–2007) continued fine tuning the steering mechanisms, for example, the key priority was: 'Improving the quality and relevance of tertiary teaching, learning and research' (Ministry of Education, 2005, p. 1). This longer term STEP 'focuses on securing the shifts that the education reforms were designed to bring about by reiterating more firmly how funding via the profile process would be linked to an organisation's ability to provide relevant courses' (Tertiary Education Commission, 2005, p. 1). Throughout this period participation levels in industry training increased with the targets set by the government through the STEP process not only being met but often exceeded.

The fourth STEP 2008–2010 was embedded in the TES 2008–2012. This second TES set out new targets, shifting away from the six national goals in order to build on the work of the previous five years and address the problems outlined above. The intention was to map out more specifically what the government wanted each TEO to provide, in turn outlining what each TEO's distinctive contribution to PCET should be, then relating this change of emphasis to new areas of focus. While this tactic was designed to continue the promise of certainty specified in the first TES, the message of distinctive contributions was also one of accountability. The TES provided three broad areas of focus to back up these messages:

- Success for all New Zealanders through Lifelong Learning.
- Creating and Applying Knowledge to Drive Innovation.
- Strong Connections between Tertiary Education Organisations and the Communities They Serve. (Office for the Minister of Tertiary Education, 2006, p. 5)

The first area of focus is a clear reiteration of the more traditional social democratic values associated with access and equity. The universal message of lifelong learning for all suggests a commitment to addressing the uneven participation trends in PCET.

More specific goals were set out in the STEP, which identified areas of priority as:

- increasing educational success for young New Zealanders – more achieving qualifications at level four and above by age 25;
- increasing literacy, numeracy and language levels for the workforce;
- increasing the achievement of advanced trade, technical and professional qualifications to meet regional and national industry needs;
- improving research connections and linkages to create economic opportunities.

The emphasis on the issues of non-completion threads its way through both the areas of focus and the STEP's goals with the use of success in achievement. Given the clear relationship of priorities to the industry training sector and its shortfalls in achieving them, the development of a *Skills Strategy: Action Plan 2008* (DoL, 2008) followed the release of the TES and STEP. Significantly this was the first one to be developed since 1991. The *Skills Strategy* was jointly developed by the Industry Training Federation, the New Zealand Council of Trade Unions, Business New Zealand, and government through the Department of Labour, as well as other key agencies such as TEC but also the 'Ministry of Education, Te Puni Kōkiri, Ministry of Pacific Island Affairs, ACC, and the Ministry of Social Development' (DoL, 2008, p. 19). It is this type of consultative tripartite relationship that is the focus of the next section.

The changes to PCET policy outlined above did not happen in isolation. There were also substantial, related changes to employment or industrial relations legislation. Law (2003a, 2003b) argued that a very significant effect of the Employment Relations Act, 2000 (ERA) and related industrial relations legislation had been the return of unions as the collective voice of organised workers and as significant social partners. This notion of partnership was reflected in the re-involvement of unions in policy formation such as the skills action plan. Another example was the reform of the Health and Safety in Employment 2000 legislation, which enshrined the place of the union movement in the provision of health and safety education by making them part of the policy implementation. The Department of Labour (DoL) has been an important driver of learning at work directly through employment relations and health and safety legislation and also through their best practice partnership and productivity programmes. *The Workplace Productivity Challenge* and the 'Skill New Zealand' brand are two examples of this type of policy in practice discussed below.

The marketing brand *SkillNZ* is a tripartite initiative, involving the ITF, NZCTU, BusinessNZ, with some support from the government provided by the TEC (BusinessNZ, 2002). The branding exercise was established prior to the TES to promote work-based learning in order to help facilitate the introduction of the recent changes, such as Modern Apprenticeship, and also to rebuild an industry training culture in New Zealand workplaces. For example the brand is used to identify and address 'barriers in specific industries that have low participation rates. Barriers are currently being addressed in the retail, hospitality, tourism and furniture industries' (DoL, 2008: 73). The type of activities pursued under this umbrella include such programmes as the state funded workplace learning representative initiative conducted by the Council of Trade Unions (2005). The Workplace Learning Representative (http://www.learningreps.org.nz/) was imported from Britain but has been adapted in ways that reflect a more social democratic tinge. For example, the policy programme has maintained a much more explicit link with the New Zealand union movement than its British counterpart, being implemented alongside other workplace training programmes such as the Health and Safety training and Employment Relations Leave, all of which are driven by the leadership of the NZCTU. Workplace Learning Representatives alongside the other programmes incorporates notions of partnership not just between government and unions but also with employers. In this sense it, along with the wider *SkillNZ* project, marks something of a return to the tripartism (government, employers, and unions) that preceded 1990s neo-liberalism. However, the project is 'British third way' in that an important part of a workplace learning representative's role is to promote the various learning opportunities that workers can access that are closely tied to labour market considerations. But the learning brief is much wider than just work-based learning and given the project is union-led there is a distinctively New Zealand, residual social democratic echo of a broader tradition of worker education (Law, 1994, 2005).

The *SkillNZ* brand has provided a successful platform for the tripartite stakeholders to work together effectively. This is demonstrated by the 'buy in' from the stakeholders. Business New Zealand, NZCTU and the ITF all provided visible support based on statements made in their press releases, as well as their contribution to the policy process. This included the three groups attending meetings, providing workplace contacts for research, and often leading different aspects of the policy development and deployment such as the learning reps programme referred to above. Another example of this effective tripartite relationship in the area of industry training is the workplace productivity project. The workplace productivity working group (WPWG) began meeting in 2004 and 'was established to determine ways that improved workplace productivity can deliver a high wage, high value economy for the benefit of all New Zealanders' (DoL, 2005, p. 8).

The working group's purpose was to assess current workplace productivity practices in a range of New Zealand workplaces in order to identify good practice. The group was also asked to determine whether or not policy promoted workplace productivity and to identify future policy options for lifting productivity. The first outcome from this process was the identification of seven drivers of workplace productivity, coupled with four types of actions. The seven drivers are:

- Building better leadership and management.
- Creating productive workplace culture.

- Encouraging innovation and the use of technology.
- Investing in people and skills.
- Organising work.
- Networking and collaborating.
- Measuring what matters. (DoL, 2005, pp. 9–12)

The four actions are:

- Raising Awareness – of what workplace productivity means and the actions that can lead to improvements.
- Diagnostic Tools – to assist firms in identifying how effectively they are performing and to identify where the firm may need to improve its business practices or performance.
- Implementation – assistance and support for firms to decide what specific actions to take and the best way to put these in place.
- Research and Evaluation – collecting and developing the knowledge base about workplace productivity and what business practices are successful. (DoL, 2005, p. 8)

The group's findings were based around the seven drivers, which included illustrative case studies. While the report on *The Workplace Productivity Challenge* (2005) only highlighted seven, the Department of Labour conducted 18 case studies in order to demonstrate one or more of the drivers and actions. There were five in manufacturing, six in the service sector, three in the not-for-profit, and four in the state sector. None of the case studies explored all seven drivers but instead were assessed in relation to the drivers that the case studies most typified. Due to this book's focus on lifelong learning, only the four case studies that focused on the driver *Investing in people and skills* will be discussed here. There were two from the manufacturing sector Rotaform, a plastics manufacturer (2009a) and Cottonsoft a paper manufacturer (2009b); one from the service sector Kapiti Island Alive tourism venture (2009c); and one from the not-for-profit sector Outward Bound personal development courses (2009d).

The two manufacturing case studies had broad trends in common. Both firms had decided to move to high value production and in order to make this transition successful both firms had to use techniques associated with high performance workplace systems (hpws). The firms also worked on lifting literacy and numeracy in the workplace, Rotaform had a programme in place but it was expanded. These training programmes were implemented in the case of Rotaform in response to change in legislation (the Health and Safety Act 2002) and the other, Cottonsoft, in response to changes in work environment with the introduction of automation.

The response to these changes required a number of initiatives in addition to the training. The firms had to increase pay in order to retain staff and chose to link their reward system to workers' adaptation to the change in production methods and professional development (skill-based pay). Workers were given greater flexibility in their work hours so they could attend off-the-job training courses. The firms also moved to a flatter organisational structure, with the workers taking on a greater level of responsibility of day-to-day problem solving. This left the upper management to be more future-focused on strategic decision and longer-term problem solving boosting creative thinking and innovation for the firms. These changes resulted in lower reject rates, increasing quality. The literacy programmes in particular also contributed to increases in effective and professional reporting and communication techniques between staff members and management. These case studies demonstrated good practice techniques of rewarding knowledge and providing paid time off to learn, both of which required large investment from the companies and were seen as worthwhile given the productivity and quality gains associated with the move to high-value production.

The other two case studies come from the service sector and demonstrate that these kinds of high performance practices are just as valuable outside of a factory context. The two firms on the surface faced very different problems – one organisation, Kapiti Alive, had outgrown its original low key family-run structure whereas the other organisation, Outward Bound, had stagnated around problems of disparate worksites and poor communication. Both however chose to solve their problems by committing to structured training for all their employees, including those hired on a seasonal basis. Outward Bound specifically identified the importance of frontline staff being well trained as they are the face of the organisation on which success or failure of the courses they offer depend. But both identified the role of qualified staff in the provision of better and more informed customer service. This was not just in terms of face-to-face communication but rather a broader understanding of who their clients were, leading to better idea generation and awareness of associated issues such as more appropriate marketing. The firms also changed their organisational structures that allowed for better information flow from all directions incorporating the consultative aspect of hpws where all workers are informed about all aspects of the organisation in regular meetings accompanied by feedback mechanisms where workers' ideas can be put into place as often as management's. This style of more obviously valuing the views of staff is beneficial because workers take pride in their work and identify their success as being part of the organisation's success. What these case studies also had in common with the manufacturing ones was that by providing higher-level training, workers were able to complete a more diverse range of tasks, providing management with the ability to delegate key tasks and put in place different organisational systems.

All four case studies highlight how productivity gains can be attributed to higher investment in people and skills, or work-based learning (DoL, 2009a, 2009b, 2009c, 2009d). However, these are good practice stories designed to portray this kind of observation. As a result it is important to look at other research conducted as part of the workplace productivity programme.

A useful report that echoes the findings from the case studies and isolates their key good practice principles is *The Skills–Productivity Nexus* (Harvey and Harris,

2008). The themes from this report in conjunction with the work produced in *The Workplace Productivity Challenge* (DoL, 2005) also link well to the growing understanding that simply lifting achievement and skills levels is insufficient for addressing the broader problems of skills shortages and skills mismatches. This line of thinking is typified in the skill ecosystem work being deployed in Australia where John Buchanan and his team have argued that skills alone are not the answer (Buchanan et al., 2001). The skill ecosystem project argues for policy development to be on industry or regional lines. This allows for greater specificity in policy intervention. However, the framework developed in the project also suggests that a more holistic focus on the skills formation situation is needed in order to determine where the problem is really occurring, as the problem area may not be in the provision of skills but managerial practice or industry structure (Department of Education, Science and Training, 2005). This kind of broader contextual understanding is also reflected in the New Zealand report. For example, Harvey and Harris argue that: 'Research has confirmed that the highest productivity gains are found when complementary changes are made in skills, innovation, workplace organisation, management capability and employee engagement and motivation' (2008, p. 8).

Harvey and Harris go on to argue that the role of ITOs needs to change. They claim that given the policy changes and the findings of the workplace productivity group ITOs need to move to a different way of working to a new model where:

> the focus of the emergent model is on the needs of the overall business. This includes but is not limited to its need for skills and how they might be applied and integrated in to the overall mix of factors contributing to performance. The 'trick' for ITOs lies in being able to respond to both.
>
> (2008, p. 31)

This report, when taken in conjunction with the *Skills Action Plan 2008* and the other workplace productivity reports, argues for a change in role for employers, workers, ITOs and also for the State. This explicitly reflects the acknowledgement that government intervention is required to achieve social and economic well being for its citizens, even if it is just the creation of a platform to lift skill levels and living standards via productivity. If these views are taken on board, policy development in the area of industry training or vocational learning needs to acknowledge, firstly, the importance of the role of the state in providing leadership and funding and secondly, that a holistic approach must be taken in regard to the provision of PCET that embraces wider understandings of the organisation of work. This revived role for the State and their partners again reflects the residual social democratic present in the third way.

Afterword

In November 2008 a general election was held. The National Government won a narrow majority but moved swiftly to arrange coalition partners with a far right party, ACT, and a moderate Independent. These partners were followed by supply and confidence arrangements with the Māori Party, which holds all bar one of the Māori electorate seats[7] and later with the Green Party. Given the consultation and cross-party agreements that the Mixed Member Proportional (MMP[8]) electoral system encourages and the slow nature of their more detailed policy development it is not yet clear how far to the right New Zealand will swing. However, in May 2009 the budget was published (English, 2009) which has signalled a squeeze on government funding similar to the neo-liberal tactics of the 1990s and, in the case of Britain, of Margaret Thatcher.

The current economic recession is being used as an excuse for this wholesale budget cutting tactic; and while funding in some small instances has been increased, e.g. literacy training and front-line case workers, the areas of relevance to the provision of and more significantly research into lifelong learning and work-based learning have been substantially cut back. Industry Training funding, such as the leadership development fund for ITOs, has been cut, to the disappointment of key stakeholder groups (ITF, 2009; BusinessNZ, 2009). The research completed as part of the workplace productivity programme clearly demonstrated the business gains that can be achieved through greater investment in people and skills. Therefore it cannot be said that the current decision-making is based on pragmatic realities. Clearly neo-liberal, or more likely, neo-conservative thinking has had a greater influence on policy formation. This challenge to the residual social democratic impulse is also demonstrated by the 2009 Budget recommendation that 80 per cent of the funding for community night classes be cut, with the remaining 20 per cent to be re-invested into a smaller number of providers focused on literacy and numeracy training (TEC, 2009). Unless some kind of intervention occurs over the next few months, placing pressure on the government to reverse their thinking, the skills strategy action plan and the workplace productivity work will become, in a similar fashion to *Learning for Life I and II* (Department of Education, 1988, 1989), an echo from the past. Lifelong learning in New Zealand is once again at a crossroads – one can only hope that the social partners and the TEOs can come up with some innovative practices to ensure that the market model does not erode too much the values of access and equity.

Conclusions

The key themes of this book include participation, diversity, innovation and vocational learning. This chapter has been interested in these themes in its discussion of access (participation) and equity (diversity). In terms of the case studies through analysis of policy documents, such as the TES, the chapter has argued that lifelong learning needs to promote innovation and creativity. The previous section indicates that where innovation needs to occur is in the policy development and practice. The workplace productivity programme in New Zealand and the skill ecosystems programme in Australia demonstrate that policy development in relation to industry training cannot be developed in isolation. The third-way emphasis on joined up government needs to be fulfilled if lifelong vocational learning is to have the promised effect of improving people's participation in work and in society. The policy context cannot just be about the supply of skills. Their content, how they are used and where, also matter. As such the nature of the workplaces where learning occurs needs to be part of the intervention.

Policy also needs to develop further in its ability to address the needs of diversity, or in the case of New Zealand, bi-culturalism and multi-culturalism. The participation rate targets set by Government does seem to have made a difference in the participation of Māori and Pacific Island men in industry training but the gender and ethnic segregation that occurs in the New Zealand labour market must also be addressed. As such it will take strong leadership from the government in order to address how what work you do limits your opportunity to participate in education training. Workplaces also need to realise that they need to play a role as well and make changes to how their work is organised. Practices need to reflect the importance of linking learning to pay, and of assuming that space should be allocated for the purposes of professional development. The skills ecosystem approach could facilitate these types of measures.

That lifelong learning is now mainly considered as learning for the purposes of work means that the broader societal connotations articulated in the 1972 UNESCO report have been undermined and marginalised by the growing dominance of neo-liberal ideas. This limitation seems universal in light of EU benchmarks and the policy recommendations of the OECD on lifelong learning (EU, 2000, 2008, 2009; OECD, 2001, 2007). However, workers who have the opportunity to learn continue to take their learning with them back into their homes and into their communities. That work-based learning can include the development of more positive attitudes to self, life and family can have a constructive effect on family life outside the workplace. This was one of the findings of a study of high performance workplace systems in the New Zealand dairy industry (Cochrane et al., 2005a). Demonstrating that, even in a context like New Zealand where vocational learning is closely tied to workplace requirements and has limited generic content, the learning can still meet those wider social needs and help workers fulfil their broader potential. Even if the programmes are focused on the introduction of high performance work systems or practices the impact of greater confidence pays social dividends and does increase workers' ability to participate in community groups and other social structures (Cochrane et al., 2005b). Participation will keep on increasing given the rhetoric of investment in human capital. What is more difficult to claim is whether or not equitable access will also result from the current policy direction.

This chapter has focused on access and equity in Aotearoa/New Zealand over the last ten years (1999–2008) in order to provide a broad overview of lifelong learning policies in New Zealand. However, the chapter also sought to illustrate the resilience of the emancipatory vision of lifelong learning in this national context providing an example to other international contexts of how such ideas can be preserved in the face of internationally dominant neo-liberal ideas. The Labour-led government took great pains to make sure that a more social democratic version of lifelong learning was embedded, not only in the PCET sector, but also by using initiatives such as the workplace productivity programme and the skills action plan, in the world of work. By focusing on productivity gains the government did accept the neo-liberal argument of human capital theory pushing industry training to serve the needs of the workplace but it did so in a more traditional fashion where the employers are responsible for providing leadership, funding and working conditions that reward and allow for their workers to pursue training. This emphasis on the social and financial obligations of employers to their workers is very social democratic. Good employers and firms pursuing change will have noted this message and addressed their workplace practices.

Participation in industry training in New Zealand continues to grow. The recession for example has increased the numbers of full-time students enrolled in PCET. However, the key to determining whether or not access and equity are really being achieved is to look further into the patterns of participation. As demonstrated by the discussion through the three phases, these patterns in participation rates for the most part still reflect broader social inequalities, particularly of employment patterns. Perhaps this is to be expected, but the pursuit of social justice embedded into the original understanding of lifelong learning would argue that these inequalities be challenged. Social justice values are still important and the clear gender disparities that cut through class and ethnicity based trends are evidence of the continuing need to work towards them rather than accept that the policy changes are sufficient to achieve equality. This line of argument, however, requires government support; and it is no longer clear if the state will provide the kind of leadership that lifelong learning needs in order to deliver on the promise of greater, more equitable participation.

Notes

1 Aotearoa is the indigenous Māori term for New Zealand, literally translated as 'Land of the long white cloud'.
2 Bi-culturalism refers to the partnership between the government and the *tāngata whenua* or 'people of the land', the indigenous Māori population. The basis of this relationship is the Treaty of Waitangi, which since the second half of the 1980s has been integrated into all key social policy areas including education. The inclusion and emphasis on recognition of the principles of the Treaty of Waitangi shifted the policy focus for Māori away from assimilation to integration (King, 2003; Walker, 1990).
3 The widespread opposition to the 1981 Springbok rugby tour meant that the South African rugby team would never tour again in New Zealand till the end of the apartheid era. It is considered to be part of a number of moments in the early 1980s that led to substantial changes in New Zealand society and Government (King, 2003).
4 The widespread opposition to the 1981 Springbok rugby tour meant that the South African rugby team would never tour again in New Zealand till the end of the apartheid era. It is considered to be part of a number of moments in the early 1980s that led to substantial changes in New Zealand society and Government (King, 2003).

5 '[T]he distinctive contributions of *wānanga* is the premise that the iwi groups providing support to each *wānanga*, particularly the respective founding iwi, are well-placed for helping to ensure āhuatanga Māori and tikanga Māori are appropriately upheld within a wānanga context' (Office of the Minister for Tertiary Education, 2006, p. 16). The Reo or Māori language in this quote refers to Māori customs, traditions and practice.
6 This part of the chapter traces the third way policy development in post-compulsory education and training (PCET) during the Labour-led coalition government, 1999–2008. The New Zealand interpretation of the third way has its origins in the publication *The New Politics: A third way for New Zealand* (Chatterjee et al., 1999). This book imported many of the ideas popularised by Anthony Giddens and put in place by Blair's Labour Government in the UK (1995, 1998, 2000). The arguments presented in the New Zealand book sketched a way to pursue social democratic ideals in a (post?) neo-liberal landscape (Law, 2003b). But while the authors drew on much of the Blair Government's policies and practices, they did not do so uncritically. Significantly, the New Zealand authors advocated a much more active role for the state than did Giddens. This paved the way for an adaptation of 'third way' ideas rather than simply their adoption (Law and Piercy, 2004). In this sense, the 1999 volume can be seen as an important bridge between the policies of the 1990s and those of the 2000s. This change in emphasis was also reflected in Labour's 1999 manifesto documents and in its post-election policies (Law, 2002).
7 In New Zealand there are two electoral rolls, the general and the Māori, of which you must choose only one. The Māori roll is exclusively for the Māori electorate seats of which there are seven, six in the North Island split into regions and one for the South Island and nearby Islands.
8 Under MMP citizens get two votes, one an electorate vote attached to their geographic region and one a party vote for the political party of their choice. This system allows for Members of Parliament to be elected to a position based on either their electorate or from a Party list. The consequence of this system for New Zealand politics is that it is rare for one party to gain a clear majority of over 60 out of 120 positions and instead most ruling parties have done so in conjunction with minor parties with sympathetic ideological leanings. This system that requires multi-party agreement has fostered a form of consensus politics that the third way ideology present under the previous Labour Government entrenched (King, 2003).

References

Buchanan, J., Schofield, K., Briggs, C., Considine, G., Hager, P., Hawke, G., Kitay, J., Meagher, G., Macintyre, J., Mounier, A. and Ryan S. (2001), *Beyond Flexibility: Skills and work in the future*, Sydney, Australia: NSW Board of Vocational Education and Training.

Business New Zealand (2002), *Tripartite Initiative on Workplace Learning: Skill New Zealand*, retrieved 2 August 2003 from: http://www.businessnz.org.nz/doc/544/Tripartiteinitiativeonworkplacelearning.

Business New Zealand (2009), *Budget 2009: Key issues and outcomes*, retrieved 2 June 2009 from: http://www.businessnz.org.nz/file/1686/Business%20NZ%20Budget%20Summary%20-%202009.pdf.

Chatterjee, S., Conway, P., Dalziel, P., Eichbaum, C., Harris, P., Philpott, B. and Shaw, R. (1999), *The New Politics: A third way for New Zealand*, Palmerston North, New Zealand: Dunmore Press.

Cheyne, C., O'Brien, M. and Belgrave, M. (2008), *Social Policy in Aotearoa New Zealand* (4th edn), South Melbourne, Australia: Oxford University Press.

Cochrane, B., Dharmalingam, A., Harris, P., Law, M. and Piercy, G. (2005a), *Skill Needs and Worker Voice in High Performance Workplaces: A case study of the dairy industry*, Hamilton: Centre for Labour and Trade Union Studies, University of Waikato, retrieved 9 April 2009 from: http://www.waikato.ac.nz/wfass/subjects/societies-cultures/reports/litreview-july05.pdf.

Cochrane, W., Law, M. and Piercy, G. (2005b), 'Lean, but is it mean? Union members' views on a high performance workplace system', in Baird, M. Cooper, R. and Westcott, M. (eds), (2005) *Reworking work AIRAANZ2005: Proceedings of the 19th Conference of the Association of Industrial Relations Academics of Australia and New Zealand*, Volume 1. Refereed papers. Sydney: AIRAANZ, pp. 129–133.

Cochrane, B., Law, M. and Piercy, G. (2008), 'Industry training organisations in changing times: new research possibilities', *New Zealand Journal of Employment Relations*, 32: 3, pp. 40–56.

Council of Trade Unions (2005), *The CTU Guide to the Learning Representatives Programme*, Wellington, New Zealand: Council of Trade Unions/Skill New Zealand.

Curson, R., Green, N. and Hall, D. (2004), *Women in Industry Training 2000–2003*, retrieved 22 March 2009 from: http://www.itf.org.nz/documents/Publications/060404%20Women%20in%20Industry%20Training%20-%20final%20draft%20_web_rc.pdf.

Department of Education (1988), *Learning for Life I: Education and training beyond the age of 15*, Wellington: Author.

Department of Education (1989), *Learning for Life II: Education and training beyond the age of 15: Policy decision*, Wellington: Author.

Department of Education, Science and Training (2005), *Skillecoystem.net: Linking jobs and skills*, retrieved November 2008 from: http://www.skillecosystem.net/.

Department of Labour (DoL) (2005), *The Workplace Productivity Challenge: Report of the workplace productivity working group*, Wellington: Author.

Department of Labour (DoL) (2008), *The New Zealand Skills Strategy: Action plan 2008*, Wellington: Author.

Department of Labour (DoL) (2009a), 'Cottonsoft case study 10: automation and skills development go hand-in-hand', retrieved 15 May 2009 from: http://www.dol.govt.nz/workplaceproductivity/case-studies/cottonsoft.asp.

Department of Labour (DoL) (2009b), *Rotoform Case Study 1: An amazing transformation: A workplace literacy case study from Rotaform Plastics Ltd, an Auckland plastics manufacturer*, retrieved 15 May 2009 from: http://www.dol.govt.nz/workplaceproductivity/case-studies/rotaform-plastics-full.pdf.

Department of Labour (DoL) (2009c), 'Kapiti Island alive: Investing in people and skills: investing in people brings business alive', retrieved 15 May 2009 from: http://www.dol.govt.nz/workplaceproductivity/case-studies/kapiti-island-alive-full.asp.

Department of Labour (DoL) (2009d), 'Outward Bound case study 5: people make the difference', retrieved 15 May 2009 from: http://www.dol.govt.nz/workplaceproductivity/case-studies/outward-bound-full.pdf.

Doyle, S. (1999), 'Workers' organisations and private sector training: the New Zealand Council of Trade Union's strategy for a skilled workforce', paper presented to *ILO APSDEP Regional Seminar*, Chiba, Japan.

English, B. (2009), 'Minister's executive summary', *Overview of Budget 2009 – the road to recovery*, retrieved 2 June 2009 from: http://www.treasury.govt.nz/budget/2009/execsumm/01.htm.

EU (Commission of the European Communities) (2000), 'A memorandum on lifelong learning', *A Commission Staff Working Paper*, Brussels: Author.

EU (Council of European Communities) (2008), Draft 2008 joint progress report of the Council and the Commission on the implementation of the 'Education & Training 2010' work programme 'Delivering lifelong learning for knowledge, creativity and innovation', – Adoption, Brussels: Author.

EU (European Commission – Education and Training) (2009), *European strategy and co-operation in education and training,* retrieved 30 October 2009 from: http://ec.europa.eu/education/lifelong-learning-policy/doc28_en.htm.

Faure, E., Herrera, F., Kaddoura, A.-R., Lopes, H., Petrovsky, A. V., Rahnema, M. and Champion Ward, F. (1982 [1972]), *Learning to Be: The world of education today and tomorrow*, Paris: United Nations Educational, Scientific and Cultural Organisation (UNESCO).

Giddens, A. (1995), *Beyond Left and Right: The future of radical politics*, Oxford: Polity Press.

Giddens, A. (1998), *The Third Way*, Cambridge: Polity Press.

Giddens, A. (2000), *The Third Way and its Critics*, Cambridge: Polity Press.

Green, N., Hipkins, C., Williams, P. and Murdoch, C. (2003), *A Brief History of Government Funding for Industry Training 1989–2002*, Wellington, New Zealand: Industry Training Federation.

Harvey, O. and Harris, P. (2008), *The Skills–Productivity Nexus: Connecting industry training and performance*, retrieved 30 March 2009 from: http://www.dol.govt.nz/publications/research/nexus/.

Hawke, G. R. (Chair), (1988), *Report of the Working Group on Post-compulsory Education and Training*, Wellington: Prepared for the Cabinet Social Equity Committee.

Industry Training Federation (ITF) (28 May 2009), 'ITF Budget 2009 response', retrieved June 2009 from: http://www.itf.org.nz/media-releases.html.

King, D. S. (1987), *The New Right: Politics, Markets and Citizenship*, Basingstoke: Macmillian.

King, M. (2003), *The Penguin History of New Zealand*, Auckland: Penguin Books.

Law, M. (1994), 'Adult education and working people: a critical reappraisal', in *Conference Proceedings: Adult education and the labour market*, Ljubljana: European Society for Research on Adult Education, pp. 146–183.

Law, M. (1997), 'The TUEA experiment: trade union education on New Zealand 1986–1992', in Armstrong, P., Miller, N. and Zukas, M. (eds), *Crossing Borders, Breaking Boundaries: Research in the education of adults*, London: Birkbeck College, University of London, pp. 275–279.

Law, M. (1998), 'Market oriented policies and the learning society: the case of New Zealand', in Holford, J., Jarvis, P. and Griffen, C. (eds) *International perspectives on lifelong learning*, London: Kogan Page, pp. 168–179.

Law, M. (2003a), 'Unions and social policy: enhancing educational opportunities for workers', in Jorgensen, C. H. and Warring, N. (eds) *Adult Education and the Labour Market VII, Vol. A*, Roskilde, Denmark: Roskilde University Press, pp. 9–33.

Law, M. (2003b), 'Bringing the state back in: new directions in trade union education in a small democracy', in Flowers, D. et al. (eds) *Proceedings of the 44th Adult Education Research Conference*, San Francisco: San Francisco State University, pp. 235–240.

Law, M. (2005), 'Ideology', in L. English (ed.) *International encyclopaedia of adult education*, Houndsmill: Palgrave Macmillan, pp. 299–302.

Law, M. and Piercy, G. (2000), 'Unions and education and training reform: a neglected story', paper presented to the *New Zealand Association for Research in Education Conference*, Hamilton, New Zealand.

Law, M. and Piercy, G. (2004), 'The "knowledge society" or the "knowledge economy": Does it really matter?', paper presented to ESREA Network Conference: Learning Participation and Democracy, Barnham, Britain.

McCarthy, M. (1996), 'The baited trap', in Benseman, J. Findsen, B. and Scott, M. (eds), *The Fourth Sector: Adult and community education in Aotearoa/New Zealand*, Palmerston North: Dunmore Press, pp. 81–94.

Marginson, S. (1993), *Education and Public Policy in Australia*, Melbourne: Cambridge University Press.

Marginson, S. (1997), *Markets in Education*, Sydney: Allen & Unwin.

Ministry of Education (2002a), *Tertiary Education Strategy 2002/07*, Wellington: Author.

Ministry of Education (2002b), *Statement of Tertiary Education Priorities 2002/03*, Wellington: Author.

Ministry of Education (2003a), *Statement of Tertiary Education Priorities 2003/04*, Wellington: Author

Ministry of Education (2003b), *Statement of Tertiary Education Priorities 2003/04*, retrieved 10 September 2003 from: http://minedu.govt.nz/rint_doc.cfm?layout=documentid=7366&data=1&fromprint=y.

Ministry of Education (2005), *Statement of Tertiary Education Priorities 2005/07*, retrieved 6 July 2005 from: http://www.minedu.govt.nz/index. cfm?layout=document&documentid=10296&data=l.

Murray, N. (2001), 'A history of apprenticeship in New Zealand', unpublished Master's thesis, Lincoln University, Christchurch, New Zealand.

Murray, N. (2005), 'Who gets their hands dirty in the knowledge society? Training for the skilled trades in New Zealand', unpublished PhD thesis, Lincoln University, Christchurch, New Zealand.

Murray, N. and Piercy, G. (2003), 'Learning from the master? A comparison of "Modern Apprenticeships" in Britain and New Zealand', paper presented to the Fifth International Conference Researching Policy and Practice in Vocational Education and Training, University of Greenwich, London, 16–18 July.

New Zealand Labour Party (1999), *21st Century Skills: Building skills for jobs and growth*, retrieved 24 April 2002 from: http://www.liveupdater/com/labourparty/print.asp?ArtID=-2069458396.

OECD (2001), 'Lifelong learning for all: policy directions', *Education Policy Analysis*, Chapter 1, Paris: Author.

OECD (2007), *Qualifications Systems: Bridges to lifelong learning*, Paris: Author.

Office for the Minister of Tertiary Education (2006), *Tertiary Education Strategy*, retrieved June 2008 from: http://www.minedu.govt.nz/web/downloadable/dl11727_v1/tes-2007-12-incorp-step-2008-10.pdf.

Picot, B. (Chair), (1988), *Administering for Excellence: Effective administration in education: Report of the taskforce to review education administration*, Wellington, New Zealand: Taskforce to Review Education Administration.

Piercy, G. (1999), 'Strategy and vision: the influence of the AMWU on the NZEU 1987–1992 with respect to education and training reforms', unpublished Master's Thesis. Hamilton, New Zealand: University of Waikato.

Piercy, G. (2003a), 'A "third way" in industry training: New Zealand's adaptation of selected British policies', in Jorgensen C. H. and Warring N. (eds) (2003), *Adult Education and the Labour Market VII, Vol. A*, Roskilde, Denmark: Roskilde University Press, pp. 35–62.

Piercy, G. (2003b), 'Modern Apprenticeship: a third way in industry training?' [CD-ROM], *Reflections and New Directions: Association of Industrial Relations Academics Australia and New Zealand conference 2003*, Monash University, Melbourne: AIRAANZ, paper from: Volume 2, non-refereed papers File: Piercy Modern Apprenticeships Item at http://airaanzweb.weebly.com/2003-conference-main.html.

Piercy, G. (2005), 'Riding the knowledge wave: an examination of policy implemented by the Labour led coalition Government focussed on work-based learning', in Hager, P. and Hawke, G. *Conference Papers: 4th International Conference on Researching Work and Learning*, OVAL Research, UTS: Sydney, December, retrieved 26 January 2006 from http://www.projects.education.uts.edu.au/RWL4/conf_search.lasso.

Piercy, G., Murray, N. and Abernethy, G. (2006), 'Women's participation in education and training in New Zealand: is the "learn while you earn" option accessible to all?', *Journal of Vocational Education and Training*, 58: 4, 515–530.

Powell, M. (2003), 'The "third way", in Alcock, P., Erskine, A. and May, M. (eds) *The Student's Companion to Social Policy* (2nd edn), Melbourne: Blackwell Publishing, pp. 100–106.

Russell, M. (1996), *Revolution: New Zealand from fortress to free market*, Auckland: Hodder Moa Beckett Publishers Limited.

Statistics New Zealand (2009), *Cultural Identity*, retrieved 11 June 2009 from: http://www.stats.govt.nz/products-and-services/new-zealand-in-profile-2009/cultural-identity.htm.

Tertiary Education Advisory Committee (TEAC) (2001a), *Shaping the System*, Wellington: Author.

Tertiary Education Commission (2005), *Statement of Tertiary Education Priorities 2005/07*, retrieved 6 July 2005 from: http://tec.govt.nz/about_tec/ strategy/step/step.html.

Tertiary Education Commission (TEC) (2009), *Budget 2009 Adult and Community Education (ACE)*, retrieved 2 June 2009 from: http://www.tec.govt.nz/upload/downloads/Budget%202009%20Fact%20Sheet%20-%20ACE%20-%20FINAL.pdf.

Tertiary Education Commission (TEC) (2009), *Budget 2009 Industry Training Organisations (ITOs)*, retrieved 2 June 2009 from: http://www.tec.govt.nz/upload/downloads/Budget%202009%20Fact%20Sheet%20-%20ITOs%20-%20FINAL.pdf.

Walker, R. J. (1990), *Ka whawhai tonu matou: Struggle without end*, Auckland: Penguin.

Chapter 10

Changing power relations in work-based learning

Collaborative and contested relations between tutors, learners and employers

Jon Talbot

Introduction

This chapter discusses some of the implications for the role of university tutors and the centrality of educational objectives in circumstances where there is a 'cultural shift' towards meeting the needs of learners and employers. The Work-based and Integrative Studies (WBIS) programme at the University of Chester is used as a case study to examine the changing power relations between university tutors, learners, employers and the university, compared with relations on traditional programmes. WBIS is an example of a flexible work-based learning programme using e-learning methods, of which there are increasing numbers globally (Murdoch, 2004). Although programmes like WBIS are unfamiliar to most academic practitioners there are good reasons to suppose we will see many more like it in the near future (CIHE, 2006; SQW and Taylor Nelson Sofres, 2006).

Much of the literature in relation to innovative learning is focussed on pedagogical issues. By contrast the central theme explored here is the organisational context in which such programmes operate. The chapter draws heavily upon organisational literature and is poststructuralist in the sense that organisational rationality is not assumed and the analytical framework developed is explicitly from the perspective of tutors, who in this context are seen having no interest other than promoting learning (Jackson and Carter, 2007). It is also consistent with an approach to learning embedded in WBIS, which is derived from an academic discourse that deconstructs epistemology to assert there is no end to the interpretation of experience (Costley, 2000).

The contents are organised as follows. The WBIS framework and its application in work-based e-learning is described. The main body of the chapter is concerned with analysing where effective work-based learning is likely to occur, based upon an analytic model of power relations between tutors and other stakeholders. The chapter assumes that learning is maximised wherever tutor influence is strong, as I go on to show.

The main conclusions are that the balance of power between participants in the process is more complex, variable and explicitly contested than in traditional programmes. Newer forms of higher education such as WBIS require a negotiation of relationships between tutors and new stakeholders and renegotiation with existing ones, such as learners. In some circumstances this can lead to a positive exchange of power, in the sense that both parties are empowered but can also lead to conflict. As a result, learning may be compromised in ways not encountered on traditional programmes.

The WBIS framework

Chester is one of a number of UK universities delivering negotiable programmes of work-based learning. Other notable examples are at the Universities of Middlesex, Derby and Portsmouth (Nixon et al., 2006). The Work-based and Integrative Studies (WBIS) framework at the University of Chester accords with the main features of 'innovative' programmes developed by UK universities in recent years (Slowey, 2000). At time of writing there is no research on the varieties of work-based learning frameworks either in the UK or globally but indications from colleagues nationally and internationally are that WBIS is distinctive by virtue of the degree of flexibility it allows learners to define their own learning, means of learning and progression.

WBIS was developed by a team of tutors in the mid to late 1990s and has enrolled learners since 1998. It is informed by a variety of theoretical and political developments in the field of learning from the 1980s and 1990s. It is therefore the conscious product of a group of academic practitioners with a strong interest in learning and commitment to a set of social values rather than the traditional subject focus of many academics. Unlike many other work-based learning frameworks, WBIS has always been trans-disciplinary and incorporates a number of learning constructs. These include the theory of andragogy (Knowles et al., 1998), which holds that adult learning preferences are significantly different from children and young people. Other important constructs include situated learning theory, where knowledge for most learners is context bound (Lave and Wenger, 1991; Wenger, 1998) and *action learning*, which holds that learning stems from doing and experiencing that which happens around us (Weinstein, 1995). Other important elements include the various models of *reflection* and reflective practice, usefully summarised by Moon (2000) and a commitment to *lifelong learning* (Field, 2006). The emphasis on the application of *learning in the workplace* reflects the preoccupations of government and some educationalists from the late 1980s onwards (Billet, 2001; Department for Education and Employment, 1998; Eraut et al., 1998; Sutherland, 1998).

By its very nature WBIS represents a critique of traditional university programmes based upon a standard pedagogic approach for full time, neophyte undergraduates. Although almost all the original tutor team have moved on, the model developed nearly a decade ago has remained and the number of learners and pathways within WBIS multiplied. Within Fuller and Unwin's (2002) five models of work-based learning, it can perform in a variety of roles but is principally designed to bring formal instruction to social learning in the work place as the basis for reflective practice. Individual pathways of learning are constructed for all levels of learning in the context of higher education. In relation to other work-based learning frameworks it bears the closest resemblance to *Learning Through Work*, developed at the University of Derby (Minton, 2007).

There are currently about 1,000 learners on WBIS, all of whom are employed adults. Most of these are on individually determined pathways funded by employers, whilst others are on pathways where there is considerable employer input into pathway design. Examples of the latter include a Foundation Degree[1] developed for the Civil Service and a Certificate for Decision Makers in the Department for Work and Pensions. WBIS is also used to deliver learning for defined occupational groups such as regeneration and housing professionals. It is also used to accredit employer delivered learning. All recent pathways developed using the WBIS framework use e-learning methods to facilitate workplace delivery.

Within the broad WBIS framework, individual and group pathways are created, tailored to the needs of either individual learners or those of an employing organisation. Learners, provided they meet standard academic entry criteria, determine not only the content of their programme but also the title of the award they obtain. They can opt for a Higher Education Certificate, Professional Certificate, Foundation Degree/Diploma, Degree, Postgraduate Certificate, Diploma or Masters. The title of their award, whatever the level of achievement, is always Award Title, Name of Pathway (Work-based and Integrative Studies). Examples include BSc Clinical Governance (WBIS), MA Regeneration Practice (WBIS) and so on. All award titles must relate to professional practice.

Learners on the programme can study modules that have been developed specifically for WBIS or any other module in the university, provided they are relevant and at the appropriate level. Individual learning needs can be catered for through the use of project modules or, if there is sufficient demand, new modules are developed on request. There is a rolling programme of module accreditation to accommodate changing requirements. It is therefore possible to adapt constantly to the changing needs of learners without the requirement for time consuming validations. Learners enrol when they want and study at their own pace, within prescribed limits. A fundamental aspect of the programme is therefore that it is demand-led.

Another distinctive feature of the WBIS approach is the intimate connection with workplace practice. In a typical taught WBIS module, the learner is introduced to a body of theory and wider literature and then asked to interrogate their practice, in a way consistent with Gibbs' (1998) cycle of reflective practice. From the learners' perspective, the relationship with theory becomes much more immediate than is the case on conventional programmes. They select those theories/models that are relevant to their needs and use these as the basis for an internal dialogue, based upon their own practice and that of colleagues. This requires a degree of sensitisation to formal, reflective practice, which is usually embedded at the start of most WBIS pathways through a module entitled *Self Review and Negotiation of Learning*. In this way learners are encouraged to reflect upon their current practice as a means of improving performance. Learners are encouraged not simply to demonstrate knowledge but also to understand its application to future actions.

The distinctive nature of learning using the WBIS framework has created a correspondingly distinctive community of practice among tutors (Leonard and Talbot, 2009). To be able to facilitate learning in this way, WBIS requires tutors to cede power to learners to determine their individual curriculum and award title. The role of tutors is therefore changed from subject specialist to one where the role is to facilitate and assist the learning process and translate it into formal academic credit-bearing qualifications. One of the consequences of this shared, collective enterprise is that it makes it difficult to write about practice in the first person: what 'I' do as a WBIS tutor is what 'we' do. Not only does WBIS represent a new and innovative form of higher education but it also represents a different set of tutor attitudes, roles and beliefs.

The central contention of this chapter is that in such new and emerging forms of higher education, not only are roles transformed, but the traditional authority of tutors can no longer be assumed. Innovations in programme design and means of delivery requires a corresponding re-examination of the role of tutors. Only by understanding the changed world in which tutors work can we begin to comprehend the scope for promoting good educational practice and recognise when and where effective learning is likely to occur. The starting point for this analysis is the recognition of the legitimate (and possibly competing) interests of other stakeholders in the learning process. Some may find this kind of discussion distasteful because it involves acknowledging the changing politics of learning and as Trow (2005) notes, politics of any description (or at least, their public expression) is almost a taboo among UK academics. The view of this author is that tutors engaged on innovative programmes are forced to confront the same sort of issues as WBIS tutors and as more universities adopt such models, more will do so in future. In short, politics is inevitable.

The contested power domains of university tutors

It is widely acknowledged that contemporary university tutors, along with other professional groups, do not enjoy the same degree of respect, authority and autonomy as previous generations (O'Neil, 2002). Harris (2005) for example, describes how the internationalisation and creation of mass higher education has transformed it from being essentially welfarist and paternalist to something more market-oriented and consumerist. This has various consequences for the way in which tutors perform their role. There are concerns that economies of scale and massification have led to tutor de-skilling and hence disempowerment (Campion and Renner, 1992). At the same time, changed learner attitudes have resulted in a more instrumental approach and willingness to complain (Jones, 2006).

Unwin (2007) describes a growing culture of mistrust and suspicion of university tutors, manifest in the 'plethora of rules, targets, audits, accountability requirements, performance management and quality assurance requirements' (p. 297). Others, such Avis et al. (1996) and Gleeson and Keep (2004), decry the increasing influence of employers on higher education and the 'asymetric' power relationship between the two, as part of a broader social, economic and political shift towards markets and neo-liberalism. Within the context of work-based learning Onyx (2001, p. 138) has described how the role it imposes on tutors generates resistance: 'Their new roles are . . . unclear. The loss of traditional academic authority may be seen as a threat to professional standards. The discourse of the market place may be offensive to the academic values of autonomy and collegiate decision making.'

It is not the purpose of this chapter to explore these ideas further. For present purposes they are accepted as axiomatic; they are simply the world we live in. Instead the purpose is to focus much more on how relationships in the higher education landscape that we will increasingly inhabit are played out in practice and how tutors can and do adapt, drawing upon the experience of the WBIS tutor team.

Some basic concepts: power, authority, influence

One of the noticeable features of discussion in the literature about the power of academic tutors is the informal way in which the idea of power is referred to. The concept of 'power' is one of the most contested in social sciences. The contested definitions reflect its centrality in all social relationships. One of the simplest definitions is Bertrand Russell's: 'Power may be defined as the production of intended effects' (Russell, 1938, quoted in Lukes, 1986, p. 19). Two other oft-quoted definitions are provided by Weber (1947, p. 152) and Dahl (1957, p. 202) respectively:

> Power is the probability that one actor in a social relationship will be in a position to carry out his own will despite resistance regardless of the basis on which this possibility rests.

And:

> A has power over B to the extent that he can get B to do something that B would not otherwise do.

At its most simple, it is the ability to be able to effect a desired change. But power exists in many dimensions and many contexts (Wrong, 1979; Barnes, 1988; Lukes, 1993). There is no single, widely-agreed definition since the view we have of it ultimately depends upon our own ideological view (Rush, 1992).

Power relationships exist in a number of dimensions. *Domination* is the ability to exert complete control. Another form of power that is most useful in the present context is that of *authority.* Unlike coercion, authority implies the ability to influence or command others without recourse to force. Authority is the legitimate exercise of power and implies an acceptance or recognition of the power of others and is at root, consensual (Parsons, 1967). That is, the power that others exert over us is exercised because we allow it. In practice, coercion and authority often go hand in hand, since with coercive power comes a degree of authority. But authority can exist without formal power structures, in the sense that people can attain moral authority, subject authority or competence authority for example. That is, their authority is derived solely from personal actions, knowledge of a subject or the ability to take effective action. For tutors authority is essential to their role in facilitating learning.

A closely-related concept is that of *influence*, which describes the process of change in others as the result of the exercise of authority. The ability of tutors to influence learners is the often-unacknowledged mechanism that facilitates learning in students. Any reduction in tutor authority is likely to reduce tutor influence over learners and hence, learning.

A framework for the politics of learning

So far I have considered power in the abstract, defining some key terms. What we have to do now is consider how power is exercised between players, both in a contested sense and, as we shall see, cooperatively. Understanding how education works in practice involves not only an understanding of the formal rules and culture but also its politics. Politics in this sense is simply 'power in action' (Robbins, 1996, p. 477). Politics, like culture, occurs wherever there are groups of people because there are different sources of power, often with competing interests, values and aspirations. The identified actors in the present analysis are learners, the university, employers and tutors.

Most writers on organisational power agree that it is access to and control of resources that are the principal sources of power in organisations. Handy (1993, pp. 126–141) for example, lists physical power, resource power, position power and expert power as sources of authority. Similarly, Morgan (1989) lists formal authority and the control of scarce resources as being the most important sources of power in organisations. The starting point for many analyses of organisational power is the general theory of social power developed by French and Raven (1960). They characterise the exercise of power as the ability to change the beliefs, attitudes or behaviours of a *target*. For French and Raven, power is conventionally exercised non-coercively: in practical terms the power of individuals and groups in organisational settings is measured in terms of the ability to influence others. The ability to influence is strongly related to access to resources which are described as having five origins. These are:

- *Coercive power*: the ability to compel by dint of being able to inflict punishment for non compliance.
- *Reward power*: the ability to be able to give people what they want, whether it is money, status, position or other resources.

- *Legitimate power:* legitimacy is derived from the position a person occupies rather than their personal qualities. A superior commands a subordinate not because they are more charismatic or more insightful but because they occupy a senior position and the target accepts the exercise of power because it is believed to be rightfully exercised.
- *Referent power*: is derived from a person being liked, because people wish to emulate that person or because it is considered desirable to maintain a relationship with that person.
- *Expert power*: is conferred upon a person who has expertise or knowledge in a specified domain.

The sources of power described in the model have different origins, different ranges of applicability and different levels of effectiveness. The first three sources ('coercive', 'reward' and 'legitimate') are derived from the position an individual or group holds in an organisation, whereas 'expert' and 'referent' power are based upon more personal characteristics. As a result, they are also likely to have the greatest range and be applicable in many more situations since they are less contextually dependent. 'Legitimate' and 'expert' powers are thought to be especially effective because they are usually congruent with the internalised values of targets. Thus a tutor 'commands' a learner because s/he is ceded authority to teach in a subject of which s/he has specialised knowledge. Conversely, 'reward' and 'coercive' powers are likely to be the least effective because they depend upon a willingness to exercise power irrespective of the values of targets and as a result, may lead to a loss of authority (Backman et al., 1968; Shetty, 1978).

French and Raven's framework has been validated in many empirical studies, in many contexts. Thirty years after their original work appeared, Raven (1992) listed some of its applications – parents influencing children; husbands and wives influencing one another; children influencing each other; doctors influencing patients; salesmen influencing customers; supervisors influencing subordinates; political figures influencing one another and so on. There have also been a number of studies of the ways in tutors influence learners (Jamieson and Thomas, 1974; Tauber and Knouse, 1983; Tauber, 1985; Tauber, 1992; Nesler et al., 1993). Most of these studies have reported how influence has been exercised in a positive manner to secure beneficial learning outcomes but in one study of a child-care programme, Zeece (1996) identified abuses of power by principals and instructors. Beyond the tutor–learner relationships there have been few applications of the French and Raven model in educational settings, with the exception of Raven and Erchul's (1997) study of the way in which US High Schools consulted with parents and others.

The emphasis of researchers on the tutor–learner relationship is understandable for a number of reasons. First, it is simply easier to describe relationships between two sets of actors than multiple relationships between actors. It is also, from the tutor's perspective, the centrally defining relationship in terms of 'what we do and what we are here for'. For the majority of tutors most of the time, core business is about facilitating learning. Finally, it is the view here that until recently tutors existed in a world of relatively settled relationships where power relationships were known, accepted by all sides and therefore taken for granted. It is the contention here that these relationships in emerging, innovative forms of education are more complex; existing stakeholder relationships, such as with the learner, have to be renegotiated and relationships with new stakeholders may be contested. The previously settled role of the tutor requires adaptation in a number of ways.

While French and Raven's model provides important clues as to how power relationships are defined in the context of higher education, it is not in itself a model of the way in which power is exercised. Up until now we have implicitly assumed that power is always contested and is only obtained by one group at the expense of another loss of authority. This view of the exercise of power, as a kind of zero-sum game where power is conceived of as a pie to be divided up, we will call the *contested view* and is strongly associated with the work of Machiavelli (1513).

An alternative view of the way in which power is exercised, arguably based on a more common and positive experience, is contained in the writings of Mary Parker Follett (1924) and represents a *collaborative* view of the exercise of power. For Follett, power is not a finite resource to be divided up among competing interests, groups and individuals. Nor is power defined solely in terms of one person or group exercising power over another. According to her, there is a sense in which a power holder can enable a subordinate greater power so that the sum total of power is increased. As an example, an organisation that enables subordinates to freely contribute to discussions about how to improve any aspect of the organisation increases the sum power of the organisation itself. Similarly an authoritative tutor able to influence a learner is likely to increase the learner's own power. Follett believed that power could not be 'given' to the powerless but conditions could be created to enable subordinates to develop their own power. Power, according to Follett, is self-generating most of the time. For Follett, the point is not to exercise power over others but to enable others to acquire power. These two views of power relations, contested and collaborative are evident in all social relations including those between tutors and other stakeholders with access to organisational power.

The type of relationship that exists in practice is likely to be determined by the interests and motivations of the stakeholders. In the real world the nature of power relations are continually renegotiated. Even in contested relationships there will be elements of collaboration and vice versa. The model described below simplifies this but enables a clearer understanding of how relationships can be conceptualised.

Conceptualising power relations between WBIS tutors and other stakeholders

At the heart of WBIS is a collaborative view of power which aims to empower learners in the workplace by identifying and meeting their learning needs in ways which are meaningful to them and relevant to the needs of employing organisations. This was the intention of the tutors who originally devised WBIS and remains the driving preoccupation for the current tutor team. What was planned as an increase in collaborative power between tutors and learners has also led to a change in the traditional power balance with other stakeholders, with whom tutors have varying degrees of influence. The variety of power relationship is situation dependent. For example, with some employers tutors enjoy a high degree of influence but this is not the case with all of them. For the most part, tutors exert strong influence over learners, but again, there are exceptions.

The following sections explore these relationships in more detail by identifying situations where tutors enjoy a high degree of influence and those where it is less so, using a combination of French and Raven's model, evidence from the literature and our own experience. In each circumstance, influence is defined as being High, Low or Variable. In circumstances where tutors have strong influence, power is exercised collaboratively – that is, there are gains on both sides, since the object is to maximise learning. This can and does happen in relations with learners. By contrast, where power is contested, there may be winners and losers.

Tutor–learner power relations

In most situations with tutors and learners, it is the tutor who is dominant. The tutor has access to strong coercive power, 'reward' power, 'legitimate' power and 'expert' power. These sources of power can be further enhanced by 'referent' power – an especially charismatic and well-liked tutor is likely to even further enhance their ability to influence a learner. This imbalance in power is not necessarily detrimental to the learner: learning is a mutual exercise and greatly facilitated by collaborative power relations.

To some extent tutors' authority has diminished in recent years in respect of their students. The general erosion in trust in professionals referred to earlier has eaten away at 'expert' power; 'legitimate' power has been undermined by the development of more consumerist attitudes among students and the greater willingness of students to withhold assent to authority whilst 'coercive' and 'reward' power have to some extent been undermined by the introduction of complaints procedures, appeal mechanisms and independent quality assurance procedures such as anonymous learner evaluations of the learning experience. These changes may help explain why tutors may feel obliged to be better liked by their students, as 'referent' power, unaffected by these changes, assumes greater importance.

All learners on WBIS are adults and while the andragogical model of learning developed by Knowles and his colleagues has been challenged there is little dispute that adults have a more developed sense of their learning needs than younger people (Davenport, 1993). WBIS and work-based frameworks like it enables learners to design their own learning pathway, reflect on personal experiences and select information that is relevant to them. However, learners are dependent on tutors in new ways, because it is tutors who facilitate the process of learning in a far more active and involved way than on traditional programmes. In place of 'learning taken for granted' tutors sensitise learners to the process of learning itself and there is a lot to explain. Students used to traditional forms of instruction often find it hard, especially at the beginning of their studies, to think in terms of learning in relation to their own needs and not those of the academy. Or, even if they grasp the notion of situated learning, they make the transition from descriptive/world-taken-for-granted accounts to those that involve deeper, transformative analysis. Boud (1990) has written of the way in which work-based learning necessarily involves deeper learning and for many this is a considerable step that requires a great deal of tutor assistance.

Student dependency is also more pronounced in an institutional sense. Formal representation is difficult when learners are distant from the campus and do not know their peers. As a result learners rely on tutors to represent their interests, with employers and the university for example, to a far greater extent than learners on a traditional programme. This is especially the case when the rest of the university assumes its business is to be looking after full time undergraduates.

The extent of tutor power over learners is also modified by other factors, such as the willingness to engage in learning. For the most part WBIS learners are highly motivated but, to some extent, they are self-selected. As with all distance programmes progression is more problematic than on traditional programmes. Research indicates that progression is a function of both individual motivation and the degree to which the work environment is supportive of learning (Fuller and Unwin, 2004) and that personal motivation is mediated by family and social relations (Smith and Spurling, 2003). WBIS tutors also know from experience that changes at home such as changing address, the birth of children, separation and bereavement have a major impact on progress. Other factors, such as gender or preferred learning style do not appear to affect motivation and this is born out by research elsewhere (Walsh et al., 2003).

Research elsewhere underlines tutor experience in other ways. Allen and Lewis (2006) for example, highlight the importance of the support of line managers in facilitating learning. Bryson et al. (2006) have demonstrated that access to learning time is mediated by status in the organisation. Higher status individuals have a tendency to enjoy paid study time, which facilitates learning. In the experience of the WBIS tutor team, the level of workplace support for learners is hugely variable, even within an organisation. A change of line manager can result in the end of study leave and learners leaving a programme. A cohort of learners on a Foundation Degree, occupying fairly low level roles in an organisation, are at the mercy of those above them.

From these observations we can construct the following model of power relations between tutors and learners on distance learning WBIS programmes (Figure 10.1). Tutors have access to a number of sources of organisational derived power and therefore have considerable influence over learners. Influence and hence effective learning is mediated by a number of factors. Where learners are personally interested in learning, are developed autonomous learners, where

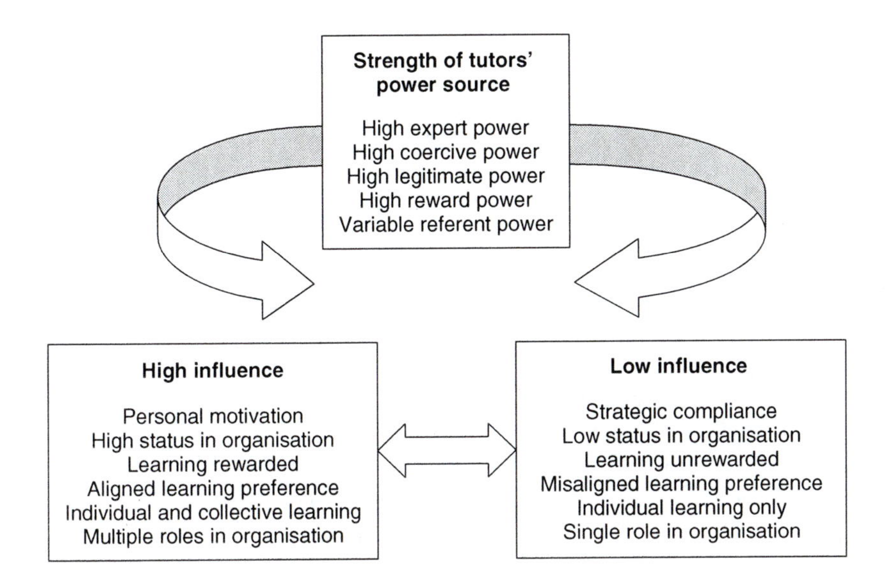

Figure 10.1 Tutor–learner influence on WBIS

they have relatively high status in the organisation and where the organisation both values learning and provides opportunities for its application in a wide variety of contexts, tutor influence will exert a powerful effect. Conversely, influence is low in situations where the learner feels compelled to study (perhaps out of fear of redundancy), occupies a lowly role in the organisation, feels uncomfortable with autonomous learning and where the organisation itself places little value on it. In these situations tutors have limited capacity to facilitate effective learning.

On WBIS there are two sets of relationships with employers. In most circumstances tutors deliver to learners who are employees and the employer pays. In other circumstances, the WBIS framework is used to accredit delivery of learning by an employing organisation – either to its own employees or to paying learners. In the latter situation, there are formal partnership agreements to ensure appropriate levelness and quality assurance. No discussion in this paper is included of power relations in these situations since the focus is on the changed power relations of university tutors.

In the experience of WBIS tutors, tutor–employer relations are highly variable. Most of these relationships are harmonious and in such circumstances tutors feel there is sufficient influence to facilitate effective workplace learning. Nonetheless it is striking how dependent this is on employers' voluntarily ceding influence. Employers have much greater power than learners and should they care to exercise it, greater power than tutors. In this respect, tutors have low 'coercive' power, low 'reward' power and even variable 'expert' power. In UK Foundation Degrees for example, there is a requirement for employers to determine curriculum, something unheard of on traditional programmes.

To understand some of the tensions that can arise it is important to appreciate the different motivations of tutors, learners and employers. For tutors the pursuit of learning is an unmitigated good; for employers that learning must be beneficial to the organisation; while for the learner motivation may be more complex and in some circumstances, unrelated to organisational goals. There is not the space here to explore learner–employer power relations but these issues are discussed by Costley (2001). Suffice it to say that employers may not view educational programmes, however tailored to their needs, in the same rosy light as tutors.

This is manifest in a number of ways. For example, tutors know that an over-reliance on e-learning methods is likely to affect the quality of the educational experience, progression and completion compared with a 'blended' approach involving more face-to-face delivery (Elliot, 2002; Garrison and Cleveland Innes, 2003; Garrison and Kanuaka, 2004; Singh, 2003; Hughes, 2007; Wheeler, 2007). Yet employers in some circumstances, for entirely understandable operational reasons, may insist on e-delivery only. Similarly, tutors advocate support for learning in the workplace because research and experience has demonstrated that paid study leave is essential in effective learning (Billet, 2004). Yet some employers may resist this. While it is easy to say from a tutor perspective that this should not be the case, it might be that the alternative is no educational programme at all.

Employers are also powerful in the sense they can take learning from a wide variety of providers. Tutors are aware that if an employer is unhappy they can go elsewhere. Employees and employers have many more means of meeting their learning needs than undergraduates. In some ways, tutors behave as supplicants with employers. They have to be courted and their needs addressed. While tutors are persuaded of the benefits of university education, employers may not be; at best 'legitimacy' power is variable.

The most important development in understanding the influence of employers on the learning experience is contained in the work of Evans (2006) and her colleagues. They hypothesise a continuum of expansive–restrictive approaches to workforce development among employers. There are many dimensions to the continuum and there is not space here to include all of them but Figure 10.2 below summarises some of the main parameters:

There are a couple of features worth commenting on the continuum. Not only does it help contextualise and explain a number of other empirical studies on workplace learning, it also has striking parallels with established organisational models, such as Burns and Stalker's (1961) mechanistic-organic continuum. Organisations near the head of the mechanistic scale tend to operate in relatively stable environments. They tend to be larger, more top down and bureaucratised with individuals performing prescribed roles. By contrast, organic organisations

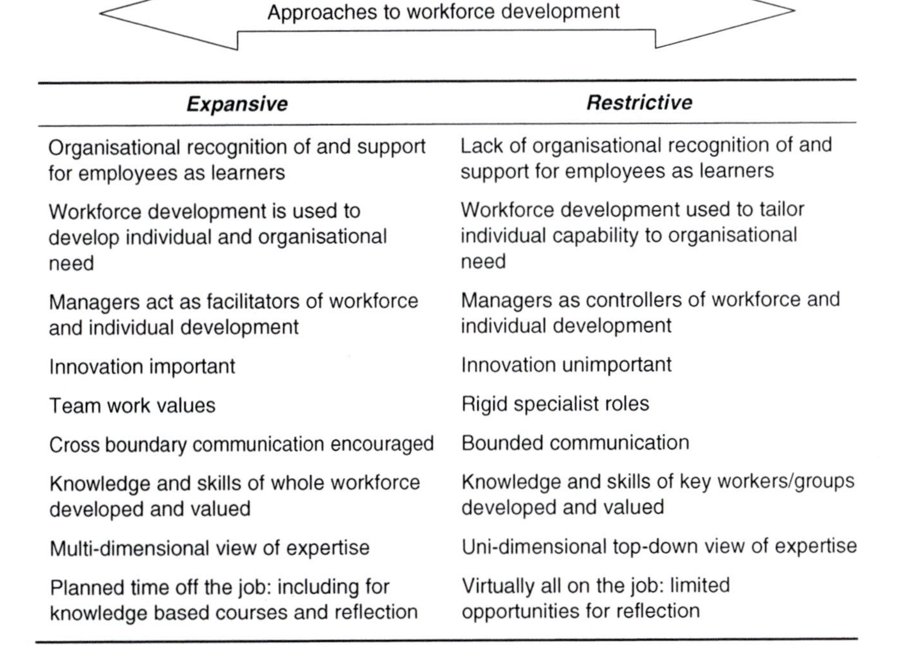

Expansive	***Restrictive***
Organisational recognition of and support for employees as learners	Lack of organisational recognition of and support for employees as learners
Workforce development is used to develop individual and organisational need	Workforce development used to tailor individual capability to organisational need
Managers act as facilitators of workforce and individual development	Managers as controllers of workforce and individual development
Innovation important	Innovation unimportant
Team work values	Rigid specialist roles
Cross boundary communication encouraged	Bounded communication
Knowledge and skills of whole workforce developed and valued	Knowledge and skills of key workers/groups developed and valued
Multi-dimensional view of expertise	Uni-dimensional top-down view of expertise
Planned time off the job: including for knowledge based courses and reflection	Virtually all on the job: limited opportunities for reflection

Figure 10.2 Approaches to workforce development – the expansive–restrictive continuum

Source: Based on Evans et al., 2006, pp. 40–41.

are less process-driven. They tend to operate in more uncertain environments, are flatter, innovative and far more flexible. Since their survival depends upon constant adaptation, it is not surprising that they place greater value on the skills and capacities of all their members and so place greater value on learning.

These observations accord with the experience of WBIS tutors. Organisations where greater value is placed on learning give greater support not just in terms of access to programmes but also time allocated for learning. By contrast, some of the largest organisations using WBIS are also those where tutor influence to maximise the educational experience of learners is the weakest. From these observations we can characterise a model of tutor–employer influence, as set out in Figure 10.3. Tutor influence and hence effective learning is likely to be strongest where the employer organisation is more organic with an expansive learning environment and support for learning embedded throughout the structure and culture of that organisation. Such organisations are likely to value staff more highly and seek to profit from their enhanced capacity. The relationship between tutor and employer in these kinds of circumstances are more likely to be based on trust.

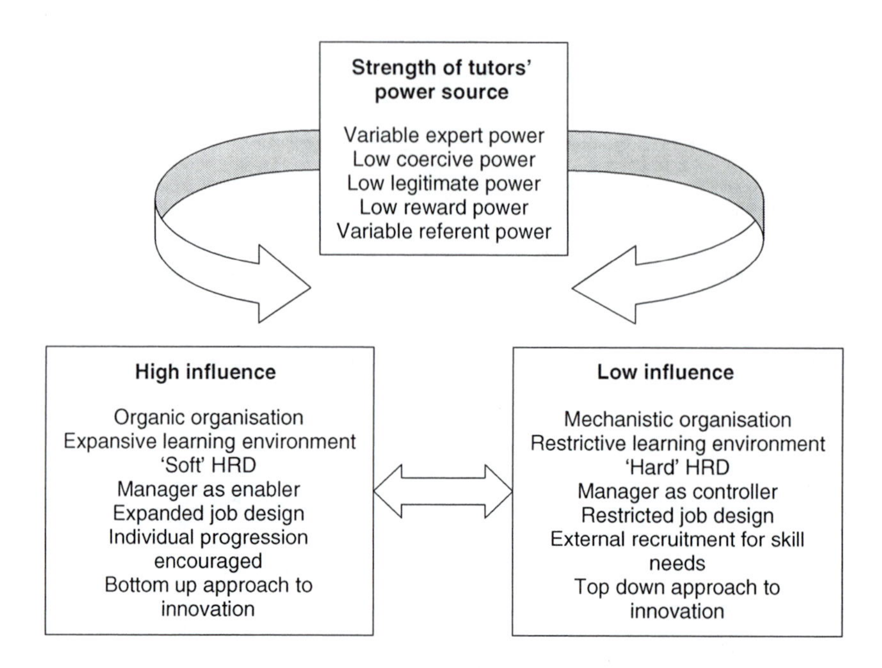

Figure 10.3 Tutor–employer influence on WBIS

Tutor–university power relations

The WBIS tutor team is not especially powerful in the institution in which it sits. They are powerful as 'experts' and the claim to expertise rests not just on subject knowledge but also pedagogical matters and e-learning. But they have low 'coercive' power in the sense that they are in a weak position to influence either the rest of the academic community or administration. They also have low 'reward' power, like all faculties, because resources are allocated centrally. Finally, they have low 'legitimate' power; legitimacy is derived from the university, not the faculty.

None of this is especially surprising about any university faculty. In the case of the WBIS tutor team the sense of powerlessness is exacerbated by cultural differences with the rest of the university. From the perspective of the WBIS tutor team, the rest of the university is an organisation principally designed to meet the needs of a traditional pedagogy and modus operandi. This does not appear to be something confined to Chester. In a national survey of the experiences of adult learners Callender (1997) found that universities are still largely catering for the needs of their traditional school leaver intake. More recently, Garnett (2007) has re-affirmed the 'lack of fit' between traditional university structures and distance, work-based learning. The majority of academic staff is still wedded to a traditional view of pedagogy where new technologies are seen as an adjunct to lectures, research and indeed the function of a university. The hostility of some university staff to innovative learning is rarely openly expressed (Smith and Webster, 1997) but WBIS tutors are certainly aware of it.

At a fundamental level, WBIS is a different kind of academic enterprise to that traditionally undertaken in higher education. Caley (2001, p. 118), in the context of discussing work-based learning programmes at Cambridge, identifies it as a different academic paradigm. In place of the 'scholarship of discovery' is an interest applying knowledge. Whereas traditional 'academic experience is founded on a recognised canon, work-based learning is founded on experience, problem solving and action based approaches'. Even where academics are sympathetic to the aims of lifelong learning, flexibility and putting the needs of learners first, in practice this can be seen as diluting academic standards and undermining the reputation of the institution.

One of the consequences of having a minority academic enterprise, in what can be termed a 'dual mode' institution is that it is likely to be regarded as having lower status than the dominant mode (Perry and Rumble, 1987). Past experience of innovative educational models has demonstrated the difficulty of integrating them within existing institutions. It is precisely because of institutional resistance to developing distance adult education that national, separate Open Universities have been established by central governments, first in the UK and then globally (Perry, 1976; Leibbrandt, 1997). At present there is no public debate on whether work-based learning requires new institutions although it is clear from experience other than Chester's that the lack of status afforded distance learning appears to be replicated in the case of work-based learning (Singh, 1979). If dual mode universities are to work effectively, Boud and Solomon (2001) observe that structures that embed innovative work-based practice in all academic departments and not in one, as at Chester and the majority of other institutions, may be important and suggests the need for research on organisational models that facilitate the wider diffusion of practice.

The differences in academic practice and culture of WBIS are one aspect of the differences with the rest of the university but there are also significant administrative and managerial cultural variances. In recent years, as in many other countries, all UK universities have been the subject to the same 'audit explosion' as has occurred in other public bodies (Power, 2007). This development, reflecting broader processes of centralising power, is not simply about tighter control of monies, in the traditional sense in which the term audit is used. It is also manifest in developments in quality assurance. Its effects have been documented in many sectors, including UK universities (Charlton and Andras, 2002). Conventional academics often find negotiating internal quality systems difficult and time consuming. These difficulties are compounded with something as non-standard as WBIS. WBIS tutors often find themselves having to explain WBIS and its attendant pedagogies to colleagues who do not really understand its purpose and objectives. This experience is replicated in other institutions with work-based learning frameworks where one colleague recently found herself shouting, 'I am not a deviant!' in response to a particularly tricky line of questioning.

In other areas, such as regulations, admissions, marketing, enrolment, finance and library services, the presence of a non-standard operating model also results in challenges. The tradition of academic autonomy creates practice and cultural diversity in any university (Sporn, 1996). From an institutional perspective, WBIS and its tutors represent one of a number of different cultural centres, whose needs have to somehow be accommodated within existing frameworks, rather than designing frameworks that suit WBIS and everyone else. The result is that WBIS administrators and tutors sometimes feel as if they are engaged in a battle with the rest of the university administration. One response has been the creation of a separate team of faculty-based specialist administrators, alongside the central administration systems. WBIS tutors have reported feeling like a 'University within a University'.

The difference in academic practice and administration creates a sense of difference and separation. If culture is 'what we do around here' (Drennan, 1992), the culture for those working with WBIS is radically different from the 'what we do around here' elsewhere in the organisation. This raises the issue as to whether the overall culture of any university, including Chester, is especially conducive or antithetical to innovative learning programmes like WBIS. The literature on university cultures is surprisingly sparse and marked by a lack of empirical research. One useful approach to characterising the culture of universities is that developed by Conole (2004), who highlights the differences between institutions arising from mission. She makes a fundamental distinction between more traditional research-driven institutions with those whose mission is widening participation. The latter, more focussed on learners and learning, are she implies, more likely to adopt innovative learning practices.

Another approach is that of McNay (1995, 1999), echoing the work of Handy (1993). He identifies four archetypal university cultures: 'Collegiate', 'Bureaucratic', 'Innovative' and 'Enterprise'. Collegiate culture is found in older universities with a research focus; Bureaucratic culture is common in technical colleges and new universities; Innovative cultures exist in some new institutions and subsets of older universities while Enterprise culture is found mostly in American institutions. While these typologies are useful, in the experience of this writer, all four cultures can exist within a single institution. This is also the experience of Sharpe (2005, p. 38) reflecting on experience of trying to deliver a multi-institution, innovative programme 'One of the key aspects,' he stated 'is that there are sub cultures within institutions and people have their own views within their own part of the organisation as to how things work'.

Lack of cultural fit and low levels of authority within the university are not just issues in their own right. What is less well understood is the way in which they can undermine learning. At one level this is a quantitative outcome. Like most universities, marketing is centralised and much of their effort goes into producing a prospectus, which is almost completely irrelevant for adults in work. The marketing and promotion of WBIS heavily relies upon tutor time and energy, with few resources. Fighting internal battles with systems designed for other purposes

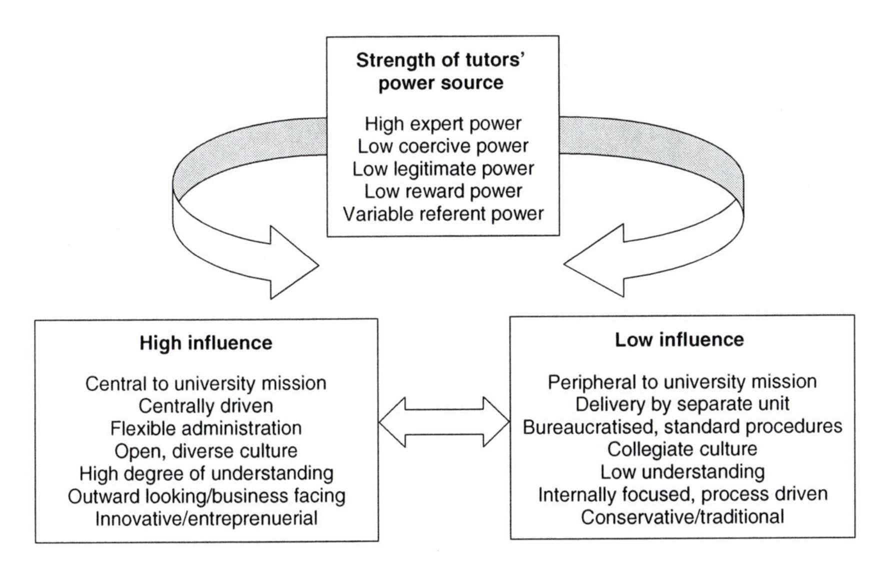

Figure 10.4 Tutor–university influence on WBIS

is not only time consuming, it is also exhausting and detracts from time spent facilitating learning.

From these observations we can begin to hypothesise situations where tutor influence with the university is likely to be strong and where it is likely to be weak (Figure 10.4). Influence for WBIS-type programmes is likely to be stronger where the university mission is understood to be centrally concerned with increased participation and vocational education. That influence will be stronger still when it is delivered from the centre but formally integrated with the faculties. Influence is enhanced further by the presence of an open and flexible system of administration rather than one heavily bureaucratised, which assumes all students are full time undergraduates. An open and diverse culture and a high degree of understanding is also likely to be associated with strong influence, as is a sense of the university being innovative and business facing.

Concluding comments

Although this chapter has focussed on experience with one programme in one university, others (see e.g. Harvey, 2007) have also begun to observe that with emerging forms of higher education, there is a change to the traditionally central role of tutors and their ability to effect the learning imperative can be compromised. Others, such as Sharpe (2005) have noted the institutional conservatism of universities when confronted with innovative learning models. Others, such as Conole et al. (2006), describing the failure of the UK E-University, have noted the power employers can wield to determine educational imperatives previously thought the preserve of academics. What this illustrates is that in the emerging landscape of higher education, control of the learning process will not automatically be ceded to tutors, as has been the case in the past, but that it is likely that it is tutors who will defend and promote it.

Despite the difficulties, WBIS tutors have not been passive: far from it. There is not space to fully elucidate all the complexities and fluxes in relationships but there is no doubt the university has in part at least been influenced by having a programme like WBIS. There has also been some conspicuous success with employers whose view of what it is gained from higher education has in some cases been transformed (Perrin et al., 2009). As WBIS becomes ever more embedded and popular with learners, many of the difficulties and tensions should be overcome.

In all circumstances power relations will continue to affect learning outcomes. If employers are to be an increasing part of the higher education landscape there will be tension with some and the learner's ability to engage will be mediated by their employing organisation and their role within it. What this chapter has attempted to do is set out a theoretical model of situations where tutors can expect to have influence and others where their influence is likely to be weaker, and suggest a direction for research into the institutional implications for new modes of delivery.

Note

1 A Foundation Degree is a UK qualification designed to meet the needs of employers and is therefore designed with them. In academic terms it is 240 credits at levels 4 and 5 – the equivalent of the first two years of a conventional Bachelor Degree programme.

References

Allen, B. and Lewis, D. (2006), 'Virtual learning communities as a vehicle for workplace development: a case study', *Journal of Workplace Learning*, 18:6, pp. 367–383.

Avis, J., Bloomer, M., Esland, G., Gleeson, D. and Hodkinson, P. (1996), *Knowledge and Nationhood*, London: Cassell.

Backman, J., Bowers, D. and Marcus, P. (1968), 'Bases of supervisory power: a comparative study in five organizational settings', in Tannenbaum, S. (ed.) *Control in organizations*, New York: McGraw Hill, pp. 229–239.

Barnes, B. (1988), *The Nature of Power*, Urbana and Chicago: University of IllinoisPress.

Billet, S. (2001), 'Knowing in practice: reconceptualising vocational education', *Learning and Instruction*, 11:1, pp. 431–457.

Billett, S. (2004), 'Learning through work: workplace participatory practices', in Rainbird, H., Fuller, A. and Munro, A. (eds), *Workplace Learning in Context*, London: Routledge, pp. 109–125.

Boud, D. (1990), 'Assessment and the promotion of academic values', *Studies in Higher Education*, 15:1, pp. 101–111.

Boud, D. and Solomon, N. (2001), 'Future directions for work based learning: reconfiguring higher education', in Boud, D. and Solomon, N. (eds) *Work Based Learning: A new Higher Education?*, Buckingham: Open University Press, pp. 215–226.

Bryson, J., Ward, R. and Mallon, M. (2006), 'Learning at work: organisational affordances and individual engagement', *Journal of Workplace Learning*, 18:5, pp 279–297.

Burns, T. and Stalker, G. (1961), *The Management of Innovation*. London: Tavistock.

Caley, L. (2001), 'The possibilities in a traditional university', in Boud, D. and Solomon, S. (eds) *Work Based Learning: A new Higher Education?*, Buckingham: Open University Press, pp. 113–125.

Callender, C. (1997), 'Full and part time students in higher education: their expressions and expectations', *National Committee of Inquiry into Higher Education, Report 2*, London: HMSO.

Campion, M. and Renner, W. (1992), 'The supposed demise of Fordism: implications for distance education and higher education', *Distance Education*, 13:1, pp. 7–28.

Charlton, B. and Andras, P. (2002), 'Auditing as a tool of public policy; the misuse of quality assurance techniques in the UK University expansion', *European Political Science*, 2:1, pp. 24–35.

CIHE (2006), *The Market for Work Based Learning: An input to the review by Professor Marilyn Wedgewood*, London: Council for Industry and Higher Education.

Conole, G. (2004), *The Empire Strikes Back – Organisational culture as a facilitator/inhibitor*, York: JISC Infonet conference, When worlds collide: changing cultures in twenty-first-century education.

Conole, G., Carusi, A., de Laat, M., Wilcox, P. and Darby, J. (2006), 'Managing differences in stakeholder relationships and organisational cultures in e-learning development: lessons from the UK eUniversity experience', *Studies in Continuing Education*, 28:2, pp. 135–50.

Costley, C. (2001), 'Organisational and employee interests in programmes of work based learning', *The Learning Organisation*, 8:2, pp. 58–63.

Costley, C. (2000), 'The boundaries and frontiers of work based knowledge', in Portwood, D. and Costley, C. *Work Based Learning and the University: New perspectives and practices*, Birmingham: SEDA (SEDA Paper 109).

Dahl, R. (1957), 'On the concept of power', *Behavoural Science*, 2, pp. 202–203.

Davenport, J. (1993), 'Is there any way out of the andragogy mess?', in Thorpe, M., Edwards, R. and Hanson, A. (eds) *Culture and Processes of Adult Learning*, London: Routledge, pp. 109–117.

Department for Education and Employment (DfEE) (1998), *The Learning Age: A new renaissance for a new Britain*, Norwich: HMSO.

Drennan, D. (1992), *Transforming Company Culture*, London: McGraw Hill.

Elliot, M. (2002), 'Blended learning; the magic is in the mix', in Rossett, A. (ed.) *The AJTD E Learning Handbook*, New York: McGraw Hill, pp. 58–63.

Eraut, M., Alderton, J., Cole, G. and Senker, P. (1998), *Development of Knowledge and Skills in Employment*, London: Final Report of a Research Project funded by 'The Learning Society' Programme of the Economic and Social Research Council: University of Sussex Institute of Education.

Evans, K., Hodkinson, P., Rainbird, H. and Unwin, L. (2006) *Improving Workplace Learning*, London: Routledge.

Field, J. (2006), *Lifelong Learning and the New Educational Order* (2nd edn), Stoke-on-Trent: Trentham Books.

Follet, M. P. (1924), *Creative Experience*, New York: Longman Green.

French, J. and Raven, B. (1960), 'The bases of social power', in Cartwright, D. and Zander, A. (eds) *Group Dynamics*, New York: Harper and Row, pp. 607–623.

Fuller, A. and Unwin, L. (2002), 'Developing pedagogies for the contemporary workplace', in Evans, K., Hodkinson, P. and Unwin, L. (eds) *Working to Learn*, London: Kogan Page, pp. 95–111.

Fuller, A. and Unwin, L. (2004), 'Expansive learning environments: integrating organizational and personal development', in Rainbird, H., Fuller, A., Munro, A. (eds), *Workplace Learning in Context*, London: Routledge, pp. 126–44.

Garnett, J. (2007), *Challenging the Structure Capital of the University to Support Work Based Learning*, Buxton – Work based learning futures conference. Bolton: UVAC.

Garrison, D. and Cleveland Innes, M. (2003), *E-learning in the Twenty First Century.* London: Routledge.

Garrison, D. and Kanuaka, H. (2004), 'Blended learning: uncovering its transformative potential in higher education', *The Internet and Higher Education*, 7:2, pp. 95–105.

Gibbs, G. (1998), *Learning by Doing: A guide to teaching and learning methods*, Oxford: Oxford Further Education Unit.

Gleeson, D. and Keep, E. (2004), 'Voice without accountability: the changing relationship between employers, the State and education in England', *Oxford Review of Education*, 30:1, pp. 37–63.

Handy, C. (1993), *Understanding Organisations*, Harmondsworth: Penguin.

Harris, S. (2005), 'Rethinking academic identities in neo-liberal times', *Teaching in Higher Education*, 10:4, pp. 412–433.

Harvey, M. (2007b), *The Changing Power Balance between Learners, Universities and Work Contexts*, Buxton: Work based learning futures conference. Bolton: UVAC..

Hughes, G. (2007), 'Using blended learning to increase learner support and improve retention', *Teaching in Higher Education*, 12:3, pp. 349–363.

Jackson, N. and Carter, P. (2007), *Rethinking Organisational Behaviour: A poststructuralist framework* (2nd edn), Harlow: Prentice Hall.

Jamieson, D. and Thomas, K. (1974), 'Power and conflict in the student–teacher relationship', *Journal of Applied Behavioral Science*, 10:3, pp. 321–336.

Jones, G. (2006), '"I wish to register a complaint": the growing complaints culture in higher education', *Perspectives*, 10:3, pp. 69–73.

Knowles, M., Holton, E. and Swanson, R. (1998), *The Adult Learner* (5th edn), Woburn, MA: Heinneman-Butterworth.

Lave, J. and Wenger, E. (1991), *Situated Learning: Legitimate peripheral participation.* Cambridge: Cambridge University Press.

Leonard, D. and Talbot, J. (2009), 'Developing new work based learning pathways for housing practitioners whilst participating peripherally and legitimately: the situated learning of work based learning tutors', UVAC conference, University of Derby, 30 April.

Liebbrandt, G. (1997), 'The Open Universiteit in the Netherlands', in Muggeridge, I. and Reddy G. (eds) *Founding the Open Universities: Essays in memory of G. Ram Reddy*, New Delhi: Sterling Publishers, pp. 101–121.

Lukes, S. (1986), *Power: A radical view*. Oxford: Blackwell.

Lukes, S. (1993), 'Three distinctive views of power compared' in Hill, M. (ed.) *The Policy Process: A reader*, Hemel Hempstead: Harvester Wheatsheaf, pp. 51–58.

Machiavelli, N. (1513), *The Prince*. Translated by Bondanella, P. and Musa, M. (1995), London: Oxford Paperbacks.

McNay, I. (1995), 'From the collegial academy to corporate enterprise: the changing cultures of universities', in Schuller T. (ed.) *The Changing University?*, Buckingham: Open University/SRHE, pp. 105–115.

McNay, I. (1999), 'Changing cultures in UK Higher Education: the state as corporate market bureaucracy and the emergent academic enterprise', in Braun D. and Merrien F.-X. (eds), *Towards a New Model of Governance for Universities: A comparative view*, London: Jessica Kingsley, pp. 34–58.

Minton, A. (2007), *Negotiation of Learning Contracts and Assessment in Work Based Learning*, Hendon: Work Based Learning Network annual conference, University of Middlesex.

Moon, J. (2000), *Reflection in Learning and Professional Development*, London: Kogan Page.

Morgan, G. (1989), *Creative Organisation Theory: A resource book*. London: Sage.

Murdoch, J. (2004), 'Developments in the evaluation of work based learning: a UK perspective', *Industry and Higher Education*, 18:2, pp. 121–124.

Nesler, M., Aguinas, H., Quigley, B. and Tedeschi, J. (1993), *Credibility and Perceived Power Ratings*, Arlington, VA: Eastern Psychological Association.

Nixon, I., Smith, K., Stafford, R. and Camm, S. (2006), *Work Based Learning: Illuminating the Higher Education landscape*, York: Higher Education Academy.

O'Neill, O. (2002), 'Called to account', Reith Lecture, 1 December, London: BBC. Available at: http://www.bbc.co.uk/radio4/reith2002/.

Onyx, J. (2001), 'Implementing work based learning for the first time', in Boud, D. and Solomon, N. (eds) *Work Based Learning: A new higher education?*, Buckingham: Open University Press, pp. 126–140.

Parsons, T. (1967), *Sociological Theory and Modern Society*. New York: Free Press.

Perrin, D., Weston, P., Thompson, P. and Brodie P. (2009), *Facilitating Employer Engagement through Negotiated Work Based Learning: A case study from the University of Chester*, London: Higher Education Funding Council for England/Department for Work and Pensions.

Perry, W. (1976), *Open University: A personal account by the first Vice Chancellor*, Milton Keynes: Open University Press.

Perry, W. and Rumble, G. (1987), *A Short Guide to Distance Education*, Cambridge: International Extension College.

Power, M. (2007), 'The theory of audit explosion', in Ferlie, E., Lynn, L. and Pollitt, C., *The Oxford Handbook of Public Management*, Oxford: Oxford University Press, pp. 326–346.

Raven, B. (1992), 'The bases of power: origins and recent developments', Washington, DC: American Psychological Association.

Raven, B. and Erchul, W. (1997), 'Social power in school consultation: a contemporary view of French and Raven's bases of power model', *Journal of Social Psychology*, 35:2, pp. 131–171.

Robbins, S. (1996), *Organisational Behaviour, Concepts, Controversies, Applications* (7th edn), Englewood Cliffs, NJ: Prentice Hall.

Rush, M. (1992), *Politics and Society: An introduction to political sociology*, London: Prentice Hall.

Russell, B. (1938), 'The forms of power', in Lukes, S. (1986) *Power*, New York: New York University Press, pp. 19–27.

Sharpe, B. (2005), 'Overcoming the cultural challenges', *The Think Tank: Making lifelong learning a reality*, London: JISC Infonet.

Shetty, Y. (1978), 'Managerial power and organisational effectiveness: a contingency analysis', *Journal of Management Studies*, 15:2, pp. 176–186.

Singh, B. (1979), 'Distance education in developing countries – with special reference to India', in Hakemulder, J. (ed.) *Distance Education for Development*, Bonn: German Foundation for International Development, pp. 234–241.

Singh, H. (2003), 'Building effective blended learning programs', *Educational Technology*, 43:6, pp. 51–54.

Slowey, M. (2000), 'The United Kingdom: redefining the non-traditional student: equity and lifelong learning in British higher education 1985–2000', in Scheutze, H. and Slowey, M. (eds) *Higher Education and Lifelong Learners: International perspectives on change*, London: Routledge, pp. 101–124.

Smith, A. and Webster, F. (2002), 'Changing ideas of a university', in Smith, A. and Webster, F. (eds) *The Post Modern University? Contested visions of higher education in society*, Buckingham: Open University Press/Society for Research into Higher Education, pp. 1–14.

Smith, J. and Spurling, A. (2003), *Understanding Motivation for Lifelong Learning*, London: Campaign for Learning/NIACE.

Sporn, B (1996), 'Managing university culture; an analysis of the relationship between institutional culture and management approaches', *Higher Education*, 32:1, pp. 41–61.

SQW and Taylor Nelson Sofres (2006), *Demand for Flexible and Innovative Types of Higher Education: Report to HEFCE*. Histon: SQW Ltd.

Sutherland, J. (1998), *Workplace learning for the Twenty First Century: Report of the Workplace Learning Task Group*, London: Unison.

Tauber, R. (1985), 'Power bases: their application to classroom and school management', *Journal of Education for Teaching*, 11:2, pp. 133–144.

Tauber, R. (1992), 'Those who can't teach: dispelling the myth', Reston, VA: *NASSP Bulletin*, 76:541, pp. 97–102.

Tauber, R. and Knouse, S. (1983), 'The perceived effectiveness of French and Raven's five power bases for vocational High School teachers and students', Lancaster, PA: Pennsylvania Vocational Education Conference.

Trow, M. (2005), 'The decline of diversity, autonomy and trust in post war British Higher Education; an American perspective', *Perspectives*, 9:1, pp. 7–11.

Unwin, A. (2007), 'The professionalism of the higher education teacher: what's ICT got to do with it?', *Teaching in Higher Education*, 12:3, pp. 295–308.

Walsh, E., Wanberg, C., Brown, K. and Simmering, M. (2003), 'E-learning: emerging uses, empirical results and future directions', *International Journal of Training and Development*, 7:4, pp. 245–258.

Weber, M. (1947), *The Theory of Social and Economic Organisation*, Chicago: Free Press.

Weinstein, K. (1995), *Action Learning* (2nd edn), Aldershot: Gower.

Wenger, E. (1998), *Communities of Practice: Learning, meaning and identity*, Cambridge: Cambridge University Press.

Wheeler, S. (2007), 'The influence of communication technologies and approaches to study on transactional distance in blended learning', *Alt-J, Research in Learning Technology*, 15:2, pp. 103–117.

Wrong, D. (1979), *Power: Its forms, bases and uses*, Oxford: Basil Blackwell.

Zeece, P. (1996), 'Power lines: the use and abuse of power in child care programmes', *Child Care Information Exchange* 112, pp. 23–28.

Chapter 11

Women of the Diaspora

Transnational identities at the intersection of work and learning

Mary V. Alfred

Introduction

These contested spaces that Butler (2000) speaks of come partly as a result of transnational immigration. In case of the US, every wave of migration has brought significant changes to the nation and its social systems. Most importantly, the Immigration and Naturalization Act of 1965 has had a profound impact on the ethnic and racial composition of the US population that continues to influence all aspects of American life (Portes and Rumbaut, 2006). Unlike past waves of migration that were drawn primarily from Europe, today's immigrant groups come mainly from the developing nations of Asia, Latin America and the Caribbean (Schmidley, 2003) with immigrants of colour representing about 80 per cent of US foreign-born population. Indeed, only 12 per cent of today's foreign-born population originates from Europe. This massive demographic shift makes the nation 'visibly mixed race, multiethnic, and multicultural' (Butler, 2000, p. 8). As a result, this wave of transnational migrants is, perhaps, more controversial than earlier waves of white European immigrant because it is dominated by people of colour who bring their cultures, values and mores to the new nation, some of which are in contrast to those of the receiving country. As with the US, other world nations are faced with similar demographic shifts as a result of migration and globalization.

This significant shift in the composition of many developed countries speaks to the need for workplace organizations, including institutions of higher education, to pay attention to the experiences of immigrant workers and learners to understand how they learn to negotiate and integrate elements of the old and the new cultures in their process of acculturation to the world of work. Since the majority of migrants seek to improve economic opportunities for themselves and for their families, many view higher education as a vehicle to fulfil that goal. Moreover, institutions of higher education have become the vehicle by which a select group of foreign-born individuals enters the United States as international students and eventually become immigrants (Alfred, 2004; Li and Beckett, 2006a, 2006b; Skachkova, 2007). That is particularly relevant for many of the international students from Asia, Latin America, Africa and the

Middle East who, upon receiving their doctorate or other professional degrees, choose to join the ranks of the professoriate and become workers in US higher education. Not all immigrant women working in higher education came through that route, but no matter how they came, the realities of their lives as workers and learners reveal the tensions and struggles they endure in the pursuit of their lifelong goals to acculturate and to be successful in the academic workplace (Alfred and Swaminathan, 2004; Li and Beckett, 2006a, 2006b; Sadeghi, 2006).

Since today's immigration to the US is dominated by people of colour, it is important to examine their perceptions of work and learning since traditional studies on migration have particularly focused on White Europeans and have neglected to include the experiences of ethnic minorities (Portes and Rumbaut, 2006). In more recent immigration studies, however, we are beginning to see an increased emphasis on issues of diversity and the structural, contextual and ethnic group factors that influence the transitional experiences of immigrants in the United States. These newer studies (Alfred, 2004; Li and Beckett, 2006a, 2006b; Sadeghi, 2006) have introduced a broad range of factors to explain transcultural adaptation among immigrant groups. Nonetheless, despite the diversity of contextual factors considered in newer immigration studies, not enough consideration has been given to the contexts of gender and race or the process of learning and change among immigrant adults in the host country. In addition, Grasmuck and Grosfoguel (1997) observe that women have dominated legal migration during the last half of the twentieth century, resulting in their increased participation in the US workforce; yet, there is a persistent tendency to portray and theorize immigrant behaviour and experiences from the male migrants' experience. As a result, there is a need for more exploration into the transnational experiences of immigrant women. Since the literature points to an ever-increasing number of immigrant women in higher education (Alfred and Swaminathan, 2004; Li and Beckett, 2006a, 2006b; Sadeghi, 2006), this chapter highlights how race, ethnicity, identity, and perceptions of place intersect to inform immigrant women's experiences as workers and learners in one workplace context, that is, the higher education institution. There is no doubt that higher education institutions represent powerful sites of work communities where identities, practices, structures and knowledge systems become interconnected to inform the realities of women of the Diaspora as they learn and work in geographical spaces away from the homeland.

Understandably, transnational migrants come to their new society with prior learning experiences, practices and worldviews that shape their behaviours, practices and learning in the workplace. As they navigate new cultures, they tend to hold on to some of their earlier concepts of learning and notions of work as shaped by prior socialization and other experiences in the home country. Workplace learning is now viewed as a complex phenomenon entwining identity, desire, cultural communities of practice, discourses of work and success, multiple knowledges and spheres of life activity and cognitive processes. For the immigrant woman, learning to learn and learning to work across borders must be understood within the broader concepts of Diaspora and migration, place and the politics of location, and the negotiation and reconceptualization of identity. To explore the experiences of work and learning among immigrant women in US higher education, a brief literature review is presented that explores how migration impacts identity and one's sense of belonging and the role of workplace communities in the acculturation of immigrant groups. The chapter concludes with a presentation of the experiences of immigrant women in higher education and their perspectives on identity and sense of place in a world of work away from their homeland.

Migration, identity and belonging

There is a general agreement among scholars regarding the salience of ethnicity for people of the Diaspora (Butterfield, 2004). Similarly, those who study ethnicity are in general agreement that racial and ethnic categories are only meaningful when viewed within social relations and the historical contexts in which they are embedded. According to Olnek (2001), 'Ethnic identities are not inheritances or preservations but are ongoing active constructions that emerge out of interactions among groups within socio-political and symbolic contexts' (p. 318). An emerging dimension of Olnek's assertion is the presence of individual agency in the creation of one's identities.

Noting the plurality of identities, I argue that identities are contextual and that one evokes the most fitting from multiple identities in the construction and negotiation of everyday life events. For ethnic minorities in majority organizations, the challenges of negotiating multiple identities are more critical. That is particularly true for immigrants of colour who are in a constant search for a safe place to work and to learn in a new country that is troubled with prejudice, racism, homophobia and hegemonic ideals. As members of a transnational population, they yearn for a sense of belonging and a sense of community. Having a sense of belonging in the workplace influences the interpretation one makes of one's experiences in such spaces. Therefore, the immigrant woman's perceptions of herself and her experiences within work organizations influence what she learns, how she learns and how she uses that knowledge to leverage her position in the workplace. Having a sense of belonging in the workplace community is aligned with what Fenwick and Hutton (2000) view as 'cultural communities of practice', an element they find necessary to consider in our understanding of the factors that can influence work and learning. However, one's positionality as defined by one's race, ethnicity, gender and national origin, to name a few factors, determines the extent to which she is welcomed to such communities of practice. Noting that such communal spaces provide a rich venue for formal and informal learning opportunities, alienation from such communities may create a barrier to full participation to learning at work.

Workplace communities as sites for learning

Within newer conceptualizations of lifelong learning, the workplace is viewed as a pivotal site for the construction and the sharing of knowledge. While the conceptualization of the workplace as a site for learning is not a new phenomenon, the process of workplace learning in today's institutions and organizations has become much more complex as a result of the cultural and ethnic diversity of the workforce. Despite its complexity, Lave (1993) posits that there is no separation between engaging in work activities and learning as the two are interdependent. Therefore, how learning through work takes place must be understood in terms of the personal and structural factors that support or hinder one's learning (Billet, 2001).

Lave and Wenger (1991) perceive learning as an integral dimension of social practice and suggest that activities that take place within communities of practice become fertile grounds for learning to occur. Such engagement, they note, can be viewed as a sign of belonging to the community and having full membership in the community. Fuller et al. (2005) note that it is the fact of becoming a member that allows participation and, hence, for learning to take place. The processes, relationships and experiences constitute the participant's sense of belonging, thus creating opportunities for future learning. Accordingly, Lave and Wenger (1991) agree that these three elements – relationships, processes and experiences – collectively shape the learning experience and should not be considered in isolation from each other. According to their thesis, to fully understand how learning occurs in the workplace, one must consider the learner's relationship with other members of the community, the experiences and identity capital she brings to the environment, and the processes or organizational structures that support or hinder learning for individuals and groups within the community of practice.

It must be acknowledged that communities of practice or learning communities are social structures where tensions exist as a result of power dynamics. Moreover, the way power is exercised and perceived can make membership within the community either empowering or marginalizing, causing instability and inequity within the work group and the organization at large. Despite that reality, communities of practice are often described 'as rather stable, cohesive, and even welcoming entities' (Fuller et al., 2005, p. 53). This benign representation of the workplace as a homogeneous community of learners denounces the diversity of cultures, ethnicities, and worldviews that make up today's work organizations. As Alfred (2002, p. 10) noted:

> The underlying values of a discourse community or community of practice shape how we think and produce knowledge and facilitate shared understanding and interaction. We must also understand that even as a discourse community facilitates learning, it may also work to constrain it as it sets up boundaries, parameters, and criteria for membership, thus engendering exclusionary practices.

What Alfred suggests is that a community with majority members of a dominant group, as found in predominantly White organizations, takes on the values and mores of that dominant group, regarding them as the norms by which all members should be judged. As a result, values and behaviours that do not mirror those of the majority are often viewed as deviant or wrong. This is worth noting because foreign-born workers bring their values and cultural practices about work and learning, creating possibilities for cultural clashes and for tensions to result from the differences in orientation. Therefore, it is important to view the workplace as a contested terrain where experiences are often shaped by group membership, and it is through membership interactions that the immigrant learner/worker garners the social capital resources necessary to capitalize on the funds of knowledge inherent in communities of practice. Oftentimes, minority workers are excluded from participating in such communities, thus denying them opportunities to partake in the resource and funds of knowledge (Hernandez-Leon and Zuniga, 2002) inherent in the community.

To make visible the challenges that women of the Diaspora face within the context of higher education, I drew from the narratives of those who occupied different roles and responsibilities as teachers, scholars and administrators to get a glimpse of their life in US academe as workers and learners and to gain insights into the ways by which they theorize and negotiate identity and a sense of belonging in institutions of higher education. For as Billett (2001) suggests, learning comes from engagement in a learning community; however, one must first make entry into that community to capitalize on the social capital resources inherent in that community. Since people of colour are most vulnerable to gaining access, examining Diaspora women will help dispel the myth of equity and democracy in social capital engagement within the workplace community of higher education.

Diaspora women in higher education: Working, learning and surviving

The cases presented here stem from the narratives of 14 immigrant women of colour who were participating in US higher education in various capacities. They consisted of nine faculty members, one department chair, one Associate Dean of a large urban technical college, one programme director from a teaching university and two doctoral students who were also working as teaching assistants. The participants migrated from Africa, Asia, the Caribbean and Latin America. The women were initially invited to contribute to a book that explored immigrant women's experiences with US institutions of higher education and how they were faring in the academy. The book, *Immigrant Women of the Academy: Negotiating borders, crossing boundaries in higher education* by Alfred and Swaminathan (2004) highlights their struggles, triumphs and transformations. The women whose narratives inform this chapter include Alicia, Helen, Janice, Ming-yeh, Nomsa, Otrude, Xae and Zandille. The narratives of the co-editors, one from the Caribbean and the other from India, also informed this project.

Drawing from the women's narratives, I explored the process of identity formation and transformation within the contexts of migration, learning, and working in US higher education. It was important to highlight the ways in which issues of race, gender, language, identity and nationality intersect to affect how women conceptualize their transnational experiences in workplace communities away from the homeland. Furthermore, it was important to examine immigrant women's concept of 'home' and how they define and negotiate the multiple constructions of 'homeplace' in and out of academe.

In analysing the women's narratives, three primary themes were highlighted. The first revealed recursive identity that shifted as one moved in and out of the workplace. The second theme emphasizes the struggles immigrant women face, the constant battles they fight, and it centralizes the various strategies and tools they use to craft a space in the academy. The third theme reveals a struggle to define 'home' and how they used their scholarship to validate home while creating new images of home in the world of work. Overall, their stories reveal a commitment to social justice and the necessity to carve out a political project that educates and, ultimately, dismantles ideologies of white supremacy, thus creating opportunities for cross cultural engagements in a workplace that is becoming increasingly diverse.

Negotiating and reconstructing identities in new work spaces

According to Bhabha (1990), the question of identity is 'always poised uncertainly, tenebrously, between shadow and substance' (p. 192). In thinking about issues of identity, a person's reflections of self and group identity come into play. As Darder (1995) notes: 'The yearning to remember who we are is a subject that is rarely discussed in the realms of traditional academic discourse' (p. 1). However, for transnational migrants who go through a process of acculturation in the new country and in a particular workplace, the question of self-identity and belonging becomes critical to their adjustment and must be made visible and understood. Yet, the yearning within is not easily measured or observed through quantitative enquiry or through the basic focus group or ethnographic approaches to qualitative inquiry (Darder, 1995) because identity is multi-layered with human experiences of life and living. Exploring identities is 'a complex and a messy endeavour' (p. 1) and calls for one to 'listen to the "whisper within" and giving voice to an unspoken, yet ever present memory of difference – "dominant areas of consciousness" that must be awakened' (p. 1). Therefore, exploring the concept of self in a world of work away from the homeland, is the focus of this section.

The women discussed the question of identity in both externally and internally-defined constructs. The external definition had to do with the ways others defined them, based on the multiple roles they play and societal images of them as immigrants. The internal conception, on the other hand, has to do with their internal definition of self and the identities they constructed along the way to manage their bicultural life structures. They all reflected on who they were before the migration experience and how they were later viewed as immigrants, both positively and negatively, in their new homeland. They lamented that members of the host country had certain expectations of them as foreigners, expectations that were often framed from the stereotypical images of their race, ethnicity and nationality. Zandille, for example, noted: 'There is a certain image that people are looking for when you say you are from Africa. You must act "African," whatever that means.' Omi and Winant (1986) point out that how one is categorized is far from a merely academic or even personal matter. They further note that being named is a political issue that has an impact on access to opportunities as well as both public and private goods.

The women understood the politics of naming in that the label can deny access to important networks and resources, and as a result, they resisted being named by others and chose names that they felt were safe. However, they soon discovered their idea of safety was an illusion as they could not escape the external definition imposed by others and the politics that determined their location. Otrude, an immigrant from Zimbabwe, shared the emotional tension she experienced as her sense of self was shattered by the stereotypical images that were used to define her as an alien from the African continent. She left her homeland with a strong sense of self to have it shattered upon entering the academic workplace. In her narrative, she noted:

> On the continent, most of us consider our own being, our families, relatives and perhaps our ethnic group as part of the collective that defines us. But when one steps outside the physical borders of Zimbabwe, my Africanness meets with an unwelcome host. As immigrants in the host country, we are regarded as strangers who occupy a marginal space with the presumed mainstream group. Our being is determined by the fact that as Africans, we have been denigrated to the lower status in the Euro-American society from the beginning. We are viewed as importing undesirable qualities . . . As Africans in racially-hegemonic universities, we are often relegated to a position as the other, the undesirable.

The externally defined self as inferior, marginal and alien is quite in contrast to the internalized self as a member of a welcoming community, consisting of friends, families and supporting members from one's ethnic and network group.

Like Otrude, the other participants described how, for the first time, they found themselves identified as minorities in the workplace and were expected to take their place as such. As Helen commented: 'The term minority means less than, inferior, second class. I never had to deal with the term "minority" until I came to the United States.' In their country of origin, they never had to question their identity or their place within community; however, here in the US, they were immigrant women of colour occupying multiple undesirable identity constructs as defined by Western standards. They initially resisted the external identification, but later came to terms with the contradictions of internal and external definitions of self. This excerpt from Janice's story exemplifies their dilemma:

> As a Black Caribbean immigrant female doctoral student, I was categorized as a minority and had become an alien resident. I had come from a society in which I did not know what it was to be considered a minority, and I resisted being placed into that category. I had never had to think about my ethnicity before, and now it seemed I had to define and redefine myself constantly as I struggled with the hyphens. It is within this sociohistorical cultural context that I began the educational journey that would put me in touch with diverse characters, texts, and a range of discourses that would contribute to my constructions and reconstructions of self.

Janice spoke of her annoyance at being identified as African American, for being categorized by virtue of the colour of her skin. She identifies as African; however, she understood the possibilities for racial profiling as a result of her black body. As she noted: 'I was filled with contradictions.' Of course, Janice had taken up residence in the US, a country that Waters (1999) describes as a 'contradictory place for immigrants – a land of greater opportunities than their homelands, but simultaneously, a place of racial stigma and discrimination' (p. 79). The racial stigma and discrimination that Walters spoke of are among the most pronounced barriers and challenges that confront minorities in the workplace.

Similarly, like Janice and Otrude, Ming-yeh struggled with the constructions and reconstructions of self upon inhabiting her new country. She, too, tried to resist the stigma of racism by positioning herself away from the 'minority' label and adopting a national identity that she assumed would protect her from the stigma of a racial identification. She explained:

> As an international student from a racially homogeneous society, I had just begun to grapple with the meaning of race and racism. When I first came to the US, I used to position myself as a Chinese student from Taiwan, or an international student, who did not self-identify with any one racial group. The label of being a Chinese student from Taiwan, an international student, a foreigner, I believed, suited me better than 'Asian-American' or a woman of colour, not only because I did not have American citizenship but also because these non-American labels seemed to create a comfort zone to distance myself from the racial politics and oppressions in the United States.

Over time, as a result of her mentoring relationship with Juanita, an African-American professor, while a graduate student, Ming-yeh began to reflect on her identity within her perceived place of safety. By witnessing the endless battles her mentor endured as a result of her dual position as a woman and a person of colour, she then began to question her own self-definition, recognizing that she could not escape the stereotypical images that the new society has of her as an Asian immigrant, a woman of colour. She wrote:

> The longer I worked with Juanita, the more similarities I could draw from our backgrounds, cultures and experiences. Eventually I decided to identify myself as an Asian American and a woman of colour, adding a new layer to my changing identities, and to form alliances with my respectable colleague and sisters like her.

From Ming-yeh's and the other women's narratives, there was a revealing confirmation that identities are multiple, fluid, contradictory and strategic. They are constructed and co-constructed in and out of workplace environments, and one often strategically evokes identities that help negotiate particular spaces and contexts. However, immigrant women often find it difficult to de-identify and at times, they are not always aware of how they are constructing themselves or how they are being constructed in and out of relations. However, the women of this study were very aware of how they were being constructed and the constructions were quite in contrast to their own construction and definition of self. These external definitions and the stereotypical images that they conjure have implications for forming bridging networks with US citizens, resulting in their lack of access to social capital resources inherent in workplace communities and other networks.

Navigating and negotiating the academic workplace

Several of the women evoked Du Bois' (1996) concept of double consciousness to describe their bicultural existence in and out of academe. They described the process of entering the new country and later accessing institutions of higher education, the culture shock they experienced, their struggles to make sense of the US classroom dynamics, their alienation and marginalization as students and later as professors, and the disheartening realities of an academic culture that encourages the subordination of ethnic cultures and worldviews for the more Eurocentric, elitist ways of knowing. As Alicia articulated:

> Academia is a context of alienation which has never been an open institution. It is an elitist system that scrutinizes participants, duplicating the divisions and categories of the larger society by reproducing, even enforcing, immigrant status and colonization. As newcomers, signs of our culture, class, and other distinguishing origins make us different than most professors and students and, consequently, we feel self-conscious as outsiders. Thus, we are pressured to assimilate to the culture of academe . . . Our success within the academic environment means losing much of our native power and grace.

This excerpt from Alicia's narrative highlights the tensions and contradictions that the immigrant woman of colour experiences as she crosses the border into

US higher education. Alicia sees the culture as alienating, hegemonizing and, thus, mirroring the traditions of the colonial past from which the majority of immigrants from those traditions aim to escape.

Similarly, Otrude talked about the politics of race, gender and nationality that compound the challenges of immigrant female faculty of colour in higher education. She noted:

> The position of an immigrant woman faculty of colour in the academy, though ambiguous, and often tenuous, is filled with challenge and hope . . . She is often an object of sexism and racism because of her gender, colour, and her immigrant status. She suffers the chill and oftentimes brutal animosity from minority colleagues who believe that her position has taken away one slot from among the few available. Students who harbour their own biases from their upbringings often treat her with disrespect . . . They frequently challenge her knowledge and competence because of their unwillingness to understand her accent. However, those who survive the onslaught, stand a chance to contribute to the depth and breadth of knowledge in the academy.

While Alicia's sentiments represented those of the women who view higher education as a place where cultural knowledge and nonwestern ways of knowing are subordinated with intent of extinction, Otrude, along with others, see opportunities, as immigrant women, to expand the discourse, thus creating new knowledge despite their marginal positions. hooks (1990) emphasized that sentiment, noting that one does not need to shed one's identity in order to make a contribution in the academy. Zandille agrees, noting that immigrant women intellectuals must insist on history and memory of their own heritage as the basis of their identity and their scholarship. The message, then, is that women of the Diaspora do not have to succumb to the process of assimilation, but to proceed through the acculturation process, learning and negotiating strategies for performing successfully in their chosen professions. One of the pronounced strategies that the women identified to navigate the academic workplace was the reconstruction of home away from the homeland.

Reconstructing home in the Diaspora

How the women named themselves and their place in the world changed as they better understood their own positions vis-à-vis local and global politics. Through all this came the awareness of their own privilege in the midst of their marginalization. They acknowledged the experience of being an 'Other' also provided new opportunities to build social and political agendas that would connect the traditional home with home as the place of work in the academy. Nomsa, in summarizing the experiences of the immigrant faculty of colour in higher education, speaks of her scholarship as a place of resistance, a place where she connects the old and the new. She writes:

> As a scholar who is Black, a woman, an immigrant from Africa, I, too, have contended with uneasy paradoxes in my life and work, which often marginalize me in the US academy. However, instead of being buried in this paradox, I have been conscious of it. Through my experiences, I have developed a 'knapsack of strategies' which allows me to engage my politics. Such an engagement begins from an understanding of practices and consequences of global regimes of domination, which are ever present in my day-to-day relations.

Understanding the politics allows Nomsa to reposition herself in the academy and to use her knapsack of strategies to negotiate a space within her workplace community. She also uses strategies from her knapsack that allow her to form both bonding and bridging networks where she can benefit from some of the social capital resource inherent in academic workplace culture. She further notes that through her research, she bridges issues from Africa with those of the US to create new forms of knowledge, thus broadening the discourse on diversity and globalization in higher education. Her political and social agendas for expanding the knowledge base in the academy were shared by many of the women engaged in this project. For example, Otrude noted:

> It matters to me to continue to strive to attain respect for all humanity, to expand my horizons, to propose new ideas, and to succeed in my endeavours, no matter how modest they may be. These are some of the motivations for engaging in the academic discourse as an African, as a woman, as a scholar, and as a transmigrant, straddling multiple borders, networks, and multiple roles in the country of my residence, the United States as I link experiences from the country of my origin, Zimbabwe, and the African continent.

Like Otrude, Xae draws from her bicultural experiences as a Puerto Rican to weave a professional agenda that encompasses the possibilities offered by her two cultures. She uses these possibilities as a platform for her research and for her teaching. As she said:

> The transnational nature of my Puerto Rican identity has allowed me to weave a professional life that draws from the possibilities offered by the two cultures. I see strength in nurturing the bicultural identity and overcoming the vestiges of colonialism of my island nation, while I reaffirm the characteristics and traditions that separate me from the mainstream in the United States as well as those that allow me to understand its dominant culture . . . Through my teaching, I help students reflect on the experiences of the 'Other' through dialogue. Reflecting on these practices is crucial for providing reliable information to shatter stereotypes about those of us who continue to be perceived as the 'Other.'

Drawing from the margins to inform the centre appeared to be the overall agenda of these women's activism. They use their scholarship and their teaching as platforms of resistance as well as avenues for learning about people and cultures from other nations. By so doing, they are validating home in the country of origin while creating new images of home in the host country. The notion of place and one's place in the world continues to be a powerful force that preoccupies immigrant women of colour in their quest to find home and the struggle to retain real or imagined images of home. Through their work, they attempt to connect 'home' from the homeland to 'home' in the Diaspora.

To Helen, an Anglophone Caribbean immigrant, home is not just as a physical space, but a place where one can live and work without having to succumb to external definitions or stereotypical expectations. In her narrative, she wrote:

> Lately, I have been thinking about 'place' and the idea of one's place in the world, in the academy, and in teaching . . . The term 'place' is used synonymously with 'home' as the physical place as well as a place you might call the geography of the soul, where I can be free, a place where I would always feel welcomed or taken in . . . It is a place where my African-American brothers and sisters would welcome me as a relative and not feel threatened by my presence as a 'new' hyphenated Black American. The result is finding one's own voice and one's own values, without having to oversubscribe to societal norm.

Similarly, Papastergiadis (1998) reminds us that the question of belonging in the new country requires a fundamental shift of our thinking in relation to place. Therefore, as Helen noted, in our search for 'home' in and out of the workplace, it may be appropriate to move beyond the physical space to a more spiritual place – a place that she calls the geography of the soul. Bell hooks (1990) sees 'homeplace' as a safe place – a place where the marginalized can retreat from an oppressive and dominating social reality. Indeed, the question of belonging in the new country and in our communities of practice requires a fundamental shift of our thinking in relation to self and place. Today, the notion of belonging is drawn from a perspective that suggests that transnational migration and globalization have resulted in more fluid social affiliations and more hybrid cultural formations (Papastergiadis, 1998). Papastergiadis also cautions that the questions 'Who am I?' and 'What am I?' can no longer be answered by identifying our place of origin and the time of living there. What he suggests is that we should move beyond 'home' as a geographical space to 'home' as a more fluid space, a space where self-definition and sense of belonging can coincide. Women of the Diaspora look to the workplace to provide the climate where they can work without the feeling of being the outsider.

Conclusion

As previously noted, the United States has seen several important demographic changes since the last Immigration Act of 1965. These changes, in turn, hold consequences that are highly relevant to the approach that institutions of higher education take in providing an environment where employees of diverse background can work and learn without sacrificing identity and cultural moorings. The challenges that immigrant women face in the new country and the resiliency they demonstrate in dealing with these challenges are indisputable. The women whose narratives informed this research revealed that their travels have been both geographic and intellectual, a movement motivated by the search for education and economic stability in countries away from the homeland. Through autobiography and life history approaches, they interpreted their experiences in the contexts of home, the academy, society and community. These stories illuminate their struggles to work and to learn within the context of US higher education and their quest for home in and out of academe. It was quite clear that their multiple identities of race, ethnicity, gender and nationality served as barriers to important networks within their workplace communities, thus, hindering them from fully benefitting from the funds of knowledge inherent in such communities. However, what is most telling is the women's resiliency and use of agency in navigating the terrain of the White academic workplace. Otrude used the metaphor of the 'knapsack of strategies' to represent agency in creating space for them to learn and to work in US higher education.

The women's stories reveal a need for a broadened understanding of workplace learning, one that is informed by the realities of people of the Diaspora in the world of work. With the movement of people across nations, today's workplace represents a tapestry of cultures, identities and ethnicities, all intersecting at various junctures to inform our experiences of work and learning. Therefore, it is important to move beyond the static notion of workplace learning to one that is informed by the subjective realities of a multicultural workforce.

References

Alfred, M. V. (2002). 'The promise of sociocultural theory in democratizing adult education', in Alfred, M. V. (ed.) (2002), *Learning and Sociocultural Contexts: Implications for adults, community, and workplace education*, San Francisco: Jossey Bass, pp. 3–14.

Alfred, M. V. (2004). 'Coming to America: The politics of migration and our realities as transnational migrants in US higher education', in Alfred, M. V. and Swaminathan, R. (eds) (2004), *Immigrant Women of the Academy: Negotiating boundaries, crossing borders in higher education*, New York: Nova Science Publishers, pp. 1–20.

Alfred, M. V. and Swaminathan, R. (eds) (2004). *Immigrant Women of the Academy: Negotiating boundaries, crossing borders in higher education*, New York: Nova Science Publishers.

Bhabha, H. (1990). 'Interrogating identity: The postcolonial prerogative,' in Goldberg, D. T. (ed) *The Anatomy of Racism*, Minneapolis, MN: University of Minnesota Press, pp. 183–209.

Billett, S. (2001). *Learning in the Workplace: Strategies for effective practice*, Sydney, Australia: Allen & Unwin.

Butler, J. E. (2000). 'Reflections on borderlands and the colour line', in Lim, S. G. and Herera-Sobek, M. (eds), *Power, Race, and Gender in Academe: Strangers in the tower?*, New York: Modern Language Association of America, pp. 8–31.

Butterfield, S. P. (2004). 'Challenging American conceptions of race and ethnicity: Second generation West Indian immigrants', *International Journal of Sociology and Social Policy*, 24:7/8, pp. 75–102.

Darder, A. (1995). 'The politics of biculturalism: Culture and difference in the formation of warriors for gringostroika and the new mestizas,' in Darder, A. (ed.), *Culture and Difference: Critical perspectives on the bicultural experience in the United States*, Westport, CT: Bergin & Garvey, pp. 1–20.

Du Bois, W. E. B. (1996). *The Souls of Black Folk*, New York: Vintage Books.

Fenwick, T. and Hutton, S. (2000). Women crafting new work: The learning of women entrepreneurs. In Sork, T. , Chapman, V. , St. Clair, R. (eds), *Proceedings of 41st Annual Adult Education Research Conference*, Vancouver, Canada: University of British Columbia, pp. 127–132.

Fuller, A., Hodkinson, H., Hodkinson, P. and Unwin, L. (2005). 'Learning as peripheral participation in communities of practice: A reassessment of key concepts in workplace learning', *British Educational Research Journal*, 31:1, pp. 49–68.

Grasmuck, S. and Grosfoguel, R. (1997). Geopolitics, economic niches, and gendered social capital among recent Caribbean immigrants in New York City, *Sociopolitical Perspectives*, 40:3, pp. 339–363.

Hernandez-Leon, R. and Zuniga, V. (2002) 'Mexican immigrant communities in the South and social capital: The case of Dalton, Georgia', University of California, San Diego: Center for Comparative Immigration Studies. Retrieved 28 June 2009 from http://www.ccis-ucsd.org/PUBLICATIONS/wrkg64.pdf.

hooks, b. (1990). *Yearnings: Race, gender, and cultural politics*, Boston: South End.

Lave, J. (1993). 'The practice of learning,' in Chaiklin, S. and Lave, J. (eds), *Understanding Practice: Perspectives on activity and context*, Cambridge: Cambridge University Press, pp. 3–32.

Lave, J., and Wenger, E. (1991). *Situated Learning: Legitimate peripheral participation*, Cambridge: Cambridge University Press.

Li, G. and Beckett, G. H. (2006a). *Strangers of the Academy: Asian women scholars in higher education*, Sterling, VA: Stylus Publishing.

Li, G., and Beckett, G. H. (2006b). 'Reconstructing culture and identity in the academy,' in Li, G. and Beckett, G. H. (eds), *Strangers of the Academy: Asian women scholars in higher education*, Sterling, VA: Stylus Publishing, pp. 1–14.

Olnek, M. (2001). 'Immigrants and education,' in Banks, J. A. and Banks, C. A. (eds), *Handbook of Research on Multicultural Education*, San Francisco: Jossey-Bas, pp. 310–330.

Omi, M. and Winant, H. (1986). *Racial Formation in the United States from 1960s to the 1980s*, New York, NY: Routledge

Papastergiadis, N. (1998). *Dialogues in the Diaspora*, New York: Rivers Orem Press.

Portes, A. and Rumbaut, R. G. (2006) *Immigrant America: A portrait* (3rd edn), Berkeley, CA: University of California Press.

Sadeghi, S. (2006). 'Gender, culture, and learning: Iranian immigrant women in Canadian higher education', *International Journal of Lifelong Education*, 27:2, pp. 217–234.

Schmidley, D., (2003). 'The foreign-born population in the United States', Current population reports, Washington, DC: US Census Bureau.

Skachkova, P. (2007). 'Academic careers of immigrant women professors in the U.S.', *Higher Education,* 53:6, pp. 697–738.

Waters, M. C. (1999). *Black Identities: West Indian immigrant dreams and American realities*, Cambridge, MA: Harvard University Press.

Chapter 12

Developing capacity in workers

A pre-condition for lifelong learning

Jacqueline McManus

Introduction

A new paradigm of lifelong education was introduced to the world in 1972 in the United Nations Educational, Scientific and Cultural Organisation (UNESCO) publication, *Learning to Be: The world of education today and tomorrow*. This new approach placed lifelong education in a humanistic framework, emphasising personal fulfilment. The general theme was education as a means of creating self-awareness. A key follow-up report released in 1996, *Learning: The treasure within*, identified four 'pillars' of learning for supporting lifelong learning in the twenty-first century: learning to know, learning to do, learning to live together and with each other and learning to be. In this report the focus on the role education plays in personal development and repeated reference to self-knowledge and self-understanding was again striking. Lifelong learning, according to the report, 'should enable people to develop awareness of themselves and their environment and encourage them to play their social roles at work and in the community' (UNESCO, 1996: 19).

Significant activity has taken place around this concept, and how it can be embraced (see Chapter 9, for example). Burns (2002: 44) describes this activity as a 'growing mandate from the late 1990s for lifelong education to integrate a constellation of individual, social and economic goals'. The implementation of this, however, has been somewhat problematic; for example, through the regulation, structure and formalisation of policies supporting lifelong learning, including competency-based training systems. That is, it has been the economic goals alone that have dominated and consequently there has been an apparent loss of focus on the individual and social goals and therefore the core theme of self-awareness. Indeed, Hager and Halliday (2006: 1) argue that: 'currently the balance within policies and practices of lifelong learning has shifted too far towards formal learning'. Rather than approach lifelong learning from a systematic, structured and formalised perspective, they suggest that what is needed is a 'different conception of rationalism which is much less deterministic than commonly supposed' (2006: 4).

In this chapter, I propose a different conception of learning. It is focused on learning for and at work, although it potentially has a broader more general application. This conception of learning takes a holistic approach and is much less deterministic. It provides a means for taking into account all factors at play in a person's life; that is, in accordance with UNESCO's position in 1972, centred in personal development, self-awareness and self-directed learning. This approach provides the basis for understanding how a person can prepare for lifelong learning, where individuals are capable of adapting and learning in different situations throughout their lives and more fully able to effectively apply or make better use of what they learn, including what is learned informally.

Capacity in this context might be thought of as a condition for lifelong learning (see below for a discussion of the concept) – a condition necessary for attracting a person's attention to learning, enabling them to learn, and benefiting from what they learn. This condition or capacity includes awareness and understanding of both oneself (including identity and reason for action) and their environment. Satisfaction of these conditions, for workers in particular, results in a person not only knowing how to learn and providing motivation for them to do so, but also enabling benefits to arise from what they learn (at a personal and a workplace or an organisational level). This concept of capacity, in principle, may not seem to be different to what has been advocated by UNESCO (for example, in learning to be). However, rather than imagine this will occur as a part of lifelong education, I suggest specific focus must be placed on first developing capacity as a precondition to lifelong learning, so that learning at work is lifelong. Furthermore, and perhaps more significantly, the departure or innovation in my proposal lies in the (holistic) approach that underpins this capacity.

This chapter first introduces the concept of capacity, specifically in relation to workers. In the following section, the connection between capacity and lifelong learning unfolds and the significance of the shift to an holistic approach to learning is highlighted. The holistic approach to learning proposed is an approach aligned with complexity thinking, bringing together a range of ideas from various perspectives that provide a different, more sustainable way of learning throughout life. This approach then is explained in more detail, with reference to its philosophical underpinnings, to highlight the implications that need to be taken into account when considering how capacity can be developed in practice. In particular, the drivers of individuals' learning and the role of agency and its connection to a person's identity are explored. Finally, suggestions for how the development of capacity in workers can be supported through work practices, processes and procedures and activities and events such as workplace-based capacity-developing programmes, are discussed.

Capacity

The term 'capacity' is specifically used to distinguish it from other similar terms used in the literature related to learning for and at work, such as competence and capability (McManus, forthcoming). One of the reasons for the need to distinguish these terms and the essence of their differences in the way they are used in this context is alluded to in the Introduction above with regards to the over-formalisation of learning, for example, in competency-based training. Additionally, the idea of capacity is different to competence or capability in that it is not about a capacity in or for a specific skill, activity or action. Capacity is broader than this, relating to a person's potential more generally. This is about a potential to be capable of specific activities or actions, as circumstances change. Individual who have capacity are: 'confident, capable, connected, curious and committed learners, who interact with their environments so that they are in dynamic balance between life and work and who take effective and appropriate actions at work' (Staron et al., 2006: 40).

Capacity defined in this way, being generally about the possibility of performance, is immeasurable. Although performance or the ability to do something can be assigned quantitative metrics this ability bears no direct or predictive relationship to the possibility of performance, which may be referred to as one's potential or capacity (Ericsson, 2003: 120). Ericsson also challenges the long-standing view in psychology that a person's capacity is stable and innate. Rather, Ericsson (2003: 120) claims that individuals gradually develop what potentially leads to 'elite levels of performance'. Passmore (1980: 40) also acknowledges this developmental aspect of capacity in his discussion of the concept in the context of teaching, and goes further to name two types of capacity: open (capacities that can always be improved upon, or undertaken better by someone else, for example, playing the piano), and closed (those capacities that allow for total mastery).

The concept of capacity is, perhaps for the reason of immeasurability, rarely referred to in the literature on workplace and lifelong learning. And when referred to in other literature, capacity is largely discussed in terms of organisations or groups rather than individuals, and typically in relation to achieving sustainable economic results through 'capacity-building' or 'capacity-development'. The United Nations and the World Bank, for example, typically refer to 'capacity-building' in the context of assisting national institutions to improve governance and economic management (UNDP, 1998; Picciotto and Wiesner, 1998). In non-governmental and voluntary service organisations, capacity-building is often associated with the empowerment of groups and grassroots organisations (Eade, 1997). And in management schools, capacity-building often means organisational development (Harrison, 1994). In the context of management, for example, Morgan (1997) defines 'capacity-development' as the process by which groups and organisations improve their ability to carry out their functions and achieve desired results over time.

The organisation-based definition of capacity provides valuable insights into the concept. The definition higlights two important points: that capacity-development is largely an internal process of growth and development, and that capacity-development efforts should be results-oriented – although a direct link between development and results is unlikely. Indeed, capacity-development is often considered necessary to raise the performance levels of a particular organisation. In this context the organisation's performance subject to such development will be monitored and measured with respect to its effectiveness, efficiency, and sustainability. It is recognised that an organisation's performance, however, also depends on its internal motivation and the external conditions of its operating environment (Lusthaus et al., 1995).

The notion of capacity-development in organisations considered in this way highlights the interelatedness of a whole range of relevant elements (resources and environments). I believe the same notion of capacity can be applied in terms of an individual worker and their learning since the same key issues apply to them; internal motivation is necessary, and external conditions impact on it. This is not a cause-and-effect relationship, but something more complex and generally missing in the literature on workplace and lifelong learning. The need for a different and more holistic approach has, however, been recognised more recently with emerging exploration and support for an holistic approach to learning and embodied learning (O'Loughlin, 2006), but has not yet been explored or applied. The following section provides an outline of an holistic approach to learning, which enables a foregrounding of relationality that exists in capacity, and consequently the connection between capacity and learning. This connection is paramount in the claim that capacity is a pre-condition for lifelong learning.

An holistic approach to learning: a complex matter

In this section, the dominant approach to lifelong learning based on economic drivers is challenged by presenting a case for an holistic approach learning underpinned by complexity thinking. The economic case for lifelong learning is based on a presumption that learning involves a cause and effect relationship where a direct correlation between learning and ability exists. This approach has manifested in the very formal, structured approach to lifelong learning directed by governments for workforce planning. However, it has been shown that a cause-and-effect relationship does not exist in the learning context. Learning skills, for example, do not necessarily improve performance in workers (Ashton and Sung, 2002). The holistic approach to learning presented here addresses these shortcomings by recognising the unpredictable, non-linear nature of our world.

Learning is a dynamic phenomenon, involving a range of variables, and therefore can only be truly understood by considering the whole and acknowledging associated complexities. The idea of an holistic approach to learning is something that has re-emerged more recently with respect to workplace learning. The essence of these ideas was the basis of Dewey's (1896) explanations of learning, which he described as 'organic' and 'environmentally embedded'. Dewey's 'organic learning' refers to a non-dualistic approach to learning, meaning it engages the whole person. Beckett and Hager (2002: 165) more specifically describe this organic-type learning as having an holistic, integrative emphasis on learning that

> aims to avoid other dualisms common in educational writing such as mind/body, thought/action, pure/applied, education/training, intrinsic/instrumental, internal/external, learner/world, knowing that/knowing how, and process/product.

Holistic learning involves the recognition that all the variables or elements associated with learning are relevant and important. This allows one to accept and acknowledge research resulting from a reductionist approach and based on 'false dualisms' (Hodkinson, 2005), but only such that they help advance an understanding of aspects of learning that are then considered as part of a whole. Indeed, '[h]olism accepts that a whole is constructed out of many smaller parts, but it considers that those smaller parts create, via interaction, more than the sum of the separate parts' (Baets, 2006: 20). An holistic approach to learning exposes and embraces the complexity of learning and indeed the 'risks' associated with it. The increasing support for an holistic, embodied approach to learning in the workplace is partially founded in the recognition of the weakness in isolating issues and promoting them as focal points of a general theory. When simplicity and equilibrium are emphasised in research, problems or phenomena are studied in isolation from their context and mostly ignore mutual interactions (Prigogine, 1997).

This central problem with a fragmented, segregationist approach to learning is rooted in the decreasing relevance and validity of the current view of learning (for example, as described by Beckett and Hager, 2002: 96–100). A segregationist and reductionist approach allows learning to be configured and reconfigured in temporary and unhelpful forms, always ignoring relationality; an holistic approach overcomes this problem, as it is a more integrated approach. However, one main risk in taking an holistic approach is that every situation is rendered unique, and it is therefore difficult to generalise or theorise. There is a danger that the whole becomes unwieldy and unmanageable, and that nothing will be gained but confusion. However, one cannot make sense of part of the picture or adequately address a small part without knowing and understanding the whole. Wheatley (2006: 5) suggests that: '[t]he layers of complexity, the sense of things being beyond our control and out of control, are but signals of our failure to understand a deeper reality of organizations, and of life in general'.

The traditional scientific view or 'reigning paradigm of observation' (Baets, 2006: 37) has been the basis of the belief that people's decision processes can be captured in rules. Baets (2006: 37) suggests this has been overstated and infers the paradigm of objectivity has been brought into question as a result. Complexity theory, he claims, affords us new insight to better understand the dynamic relation between subjectivity and knowledge, extending educational discourses to cultural and ecological levels. These new discoveries (founded in science) must be incorporated into our approach to lifelong learning. A very brief outline of complexity theory follows, to demonstrate how it supports and enables us to work within an holistic approach to learning.

Complexity theory is the study of complex systems. A complex system can at one time behave chaotically but on other occasions appear perfectly deterministic, a simpler behaviour. As a result, complex systems are described as unpredictable (Baets, 1998). Complexity theory fundamentally questions causality, as it provides an explanation of the non-linear. It applies where there are many uncontrolled, unobservable variables that undermine any attempt to claim a cause-and-effect relationship. A system, including organisations, can be referred to as complex in the sense that a great many independent agents are interacting with each other in many ways (Waldrop, 1992). The behaviour of the system as a whole is generated by its elements and their interaction. The individual components of a complex system adapt themselves in a process that is not centrally controlled and that ultimately leads to a whole of which the sum cannot be traced back to the behaviour of the individual parts. Observers are entirely outside the system, and therefore, perceive the system as well as the environment. Such a system is often referred to as self-organising.

This theory has also been applied to individuals (who are considered complex systems) and in this context is discussed in terms of 'enacted cognition' (Maturana and Varela, 1980). Enacted cognition refers to a process where knowledge will only be knowledge if it is combined with action and creation – otherwise it is information. That is, the world is created through activity. Maturana and Varela's (1980 and 1998) joint work: 'attempts to understand human cognition as the biologically grounded languaging process enacted by autonomous humans whose observations shape, and are shaped by, the physical and linguistic systems within which they are embedded' (Horn and Wilburn, 2005). As a result, they explain learning as an organic and embodied process based on the 'inseparability between a particular way of being and the way the world appears to us' (Maturana and Varela, 1998: 26).

Applying this theory to organisations and individuals creates a new perspective: under this scenario, organisations are a group of components (people) that are interacting with each other and pursuing their own individual goals (self-organising). That is, these systems create order by themselves, by apparently modifying know-what and know-how as a consequence of interaction with the environment and its effects on the actions and beliefs of the living system and others (Holland, 1995). Every process contributes to all other processes. The entire network is engaged together in producing itself (Capra, 1996: 99). And change is prompted only when someone decides that changing is the only way to maintain him/herself (Wheatley, 2006: 20).

Stacey (1996: 264) explains the implications of complexity theory:

> What the science of complexity adds is a different theory of causality, one in which creative systems are subject to radical unpredictability, to the loss of the connection between action and long-term outcome. The purpose of the theory and the research is then to indicate how conditions might be established within which spontaneous self-organisation might occur to produce emergent outcomes.

Based on the premise that an individual is a complex, self-organising system, I suggest that developing an individual's capacity is the conditioning that is necessary for lifelong learning (being the emergent outcome that Stacey refers to above). And though this understanding of complexity thinking, the need for foregrounding of the interrelatedness of internal and external factors highlighted in the definition of capacity (see section above) becomes clear. This capacity, or potential conditioning, is essentially about enabling individuals to understand themselves, their environment, and how they interact and interrelate, such that they can grow and adapt as circumstances change (self-organise effectively). This is explored further in the next section to provide a deeper understanding of how the development of capacity and thus lifelong learning can be supported in an organisation.

Understanding capacity through the lens of holistic learning

Acknowledging that people exist within complex systems, and that individuals themselves are a form of a complex, self-organising system, necessitates the acceptance of the assertion that there is not a direct causal link between learning and performance, as briefly outlined above. Instead, it is shown that individuals will set their own goals and operate in a self-organising way (through their actions) in order to achieve them. Given the unpredictable nature of many individuals each operating in this self-organising way and the complexity within organisations that results (since they are made up of a number of individuals) and the lack of control over this activity I argue that what is required is a means for encouraging, as far as possible, awareness and means for, and the benefits of, alignment of individual workers' values and goals and their employer organisations'. As a result, rather than trying to control an uncontrollable situation, the reality of self-organisation is recognised and capitalised upon. That is, by becoming aware of one's values and goals and attempting to find points of alignment between them and the organisations', the self-organising mechanism focussed on attainment of personal goals (self-realisation) is maximised.

The critical learning that must take place then, is about oneself, and how one can develop or grow to meet the challenges of organisational goals. The link between capacity and workplace learning is established through focus on enabling the learner (worker) to improve their self-awareness: an understanding of whom they are, how they learn, what motivates them, and why they do what they do (in the context of work, although this would necessarily also encompass personal issues). Furthermore, developing capacity draws the learners' awareness not only to themselves, but to their working environment (on various levels) and how it is interrelated with and impacts on who they are and encourages them to begin to rationalise how the two function together – and if they do not function well together, how the differences can be minimised or eradicated. This includes knowing how best to do this, or how to find out how to do it (how to learn).

Fundamentally then, the conditioning for workers' lifelong learning through the development of capacity is founded in a worker's action and centres around their identity. Understanding more about one's agency and how it is connected with a person's identity then, is critical to understanding capacity in workers.

A more recent focus on agency and its relevance has begun, which contributes to these ideas in practice. Beckett's work (2006; also see Beckett and McManus, 2006) has begun to enable a better understanding of agency in the context of work, a more 'holistic agency' theory, where the whole is presented in such a way as to understand context and *will-ful* action. Beckett (2006) presents five features of a richer conception of agency, which emphasise selfhood as embedded in the holistic, material, socially-located and decisional nature of human experience. So an ontological claim is made: self-determination is about *coming to be* in the world (one of the pillars of lifelong learning, UNESCO, 1972). In its intentional decisionality, action generates and re-generates workers' selfhoods or identities. Understanding this connection, which runs from the epistemological to the ontological, or from practices to identities, marks the transformation a worker goes through in undertaking workplace learning of the deeply reflective and broadly experiential kind, and provides insights into how to encourage it. Moreover, this infers an emergent nature of understanding.

Spinoza provides the philosophical underpinnings of Beckett's expanded theory of agency (Beckett and McManus, 2006). The link between the richer conception of agency, presented by Beckett (2006), and workplace learning, is 'freedom' in Spinoza's terms or 'free will' as Vygotsky (1997) referred to it. The key is to accept the possibility that will is 'inextricably linked to intellect' (Derry, 2004: 115) and that

> [t]o be educated is also *a process of which becoming free is intrinsically a part*, for to be educated is not to 'know' a range of propositions or perspectives but to understand the reason for holding particular beliefs and rejecting others [emphasis added].

This conception of freedom or free will is important yet difficult to understand as it is somewhat counterintuitive to commonsense beliefs (Derry, 2004: 114). But understanding this is critical, since '[t]o be guided by adequate rather than inadequate knowledge is to be free from external determinations' (Derry, 2004: 117). And according to Spinoza, it is self-preserving action that drives self-determinative action (Spinoza, 1675, Propn IX: 136). Moreover, Beckett and McManus (2006) note that it is the *decisional* nature of these experiences to which Spinoza draws attention, by re-casting thought as thinking, and constructing an holistic – materially, phenomenally rich – account of human action. And here the importance of understanding the self-determined and decisional nature of human action can be seen, supporting and complimenting the scientific claims explored above regarding the self-organising nature of individuals.

The benefits of understanding the role of agency in learning at and for work can be achieved through holistic and integrated enaction of relevant learning strategies promoted in the literature on workplace learning and related areas. This approach does not isolate one specific idea as key, but embraces the core of each of these ideas, reconnecting them in a situationally specific way to the whole – the whole person and the whole workplace/organisation. Thus, agency is shown to be inextricably linked to self-awareness and identity. Accordingly, workers will benefit where they can be inwardly focussed, and develop as individuals, within their outward workplace context, developing capacity in the workplace. This capacity is four-fold: capacity in the sense of potential, capacity to grow and adapt, capacity to be more attuned to one's environment, and capacity to better focus efforts on activities that will create positive outcomes for the worker and the employer.

The essence of the foremost argument in support of recognising the significance of agency in relation to capacity is that learning changes the learners. Notions of the self, especially as these revolve around self-efficacy, self-determination, and self-belief, are shaped by learning and potentially educative practices. In short, these practices are agentive; they imply and invoke identity construction and re-construction, not merely for the individual, but also inter-subjectively. And consequently, it is argued that agency shapes selfhood, or identity, in ways that have a direct bearing on certain educative practices in many adults' workplaces (Beckett and McManus, 2006).

Capacity-development in workers

The idea of capacity then, encapsulating agency and identity in an holistic way, shifts us closer to the goal of understanding how workers might develop capacity and become lifelong learners at work. The next crucial step is to find ways of applying these ideas in practice. In this section, I explore the link between capacity and learning (holistic learning) further to highlight the issues that should be understood and addressed in attempting to support the development of capacity in workers and to provide some suggestions for enacting that support.

Issues to consider in supporting workers' capacity-development in organisations

The connection between action and self-awareness or identity explored above can create various effects that organisations need to take into consideration before considering how they might support the development of capacity in its workers. These effects centre around: workers' willingness to engage in activities that identify them as learners; the degree to which workers identify directly with their job title/position; the impact work has on activities and personal goals outside of work and vice versa; and the power of one's internal drive for self-realisation and natural focus on achieving it. These are expanded on below.

Stacey (2003: 331) cautions that learning can give rise to anxiety because it challenges the learner and their identity; learning 'can only be understood in terms of self-organising communicative interaction and power relating where identities are potentially transformed'. The transformative nature of learning is threatening as it causes the learner (worker) to move into the unknown, which may be seen by others as incompetence. As a consequence, Stacey (2003) cautions and, as Boud (2003) found, that some learners might react defensively to learning events or activities and close down learning processes. Consequently, the way the support provided to develop capacity in workers is positioned, how participants are engaged and even the naming of it can play a critical role in its effectiveness. Activities designed around work and learning event or programs, for example that are described or entitled somehow with the 'learning' label may negatively impact on the numbers of workers who engage in these activities and events and/or their impact.

Another consideration relates to the importance of a wide perspective in the design and the context in which activities and events to support the development of capacity are created and provided. Senge (1990: 18–19) believes that workers who identify themselves with their position, or perhaps more precisely as their position description or title, can create what he describes as an organisational disability:

> When people in organizations focus only on their position, they have little sense of responsibility for the results produced when all positions interact. Moreover, when results are disappointing, it can be very difficult to know why. All you can do is assume that 'someone screwed up'.

According to Senge (1990) this situation arises because workers tend to see their responsibilities limited to their job and not the purpose of the organisation for which they work. Garvin (2000: 191) also supports this view in part, and provides another perspective, suggesting the learner identity may simply not reach a worker's radar. He explains from a workers' point of view that 'the urgent frequently drives out the important, and learning . . . becomes an unnecessary frill. It is easily postponed in the face of immediate demands'.

These narrow views that workers can hold in relation to their work and their impact need to be borne in mind so as not to potentially alienate them when providing support for their capacity-development but also so that the negative impact this attitude can have on achieving personal and work goals and the development of capacity can be reduced or eliminated as a result.

In stark contrast to the negative impact that identifying with one's job title or position can have, it is also important to bear in mind that other researchers have found that workers are able to use their work to play out their broader goals in developing their sense of self. For example, against Billett and Pavlova's (2005) predictions, they found that workers were able to enact their working lives in ways that broadly served their personal interests and goals, even to their detriment at work. The implications for the organisation are very important in these cases, as it cannot be assumed that workers are willing or able to contribute to the achievement of their employer organisation's goals. Baets (2006: 69) highlights this point and takes it further, suggesting: '[i]ndividuals determine their goals themselves . . . the false reasoning we often make with reference to this is to think that the individual will do their best so that the company attains its goals. But it doesn't work like that'. Baets' assertions affirm the importance of developing capacity in workers so that they are better placed to realise their goals, and those of the organisations. Some practical suggestions for this are briefly outlined below.

Practical suggestions for supporting the development of capacity in workers

There are various ways in which an organisation can support the development of capacity in workers. Each has pros and cons and needs to be considered in the context of the specific situation in which it is to be implemented and maintained. Ideally, a combination of approaches will be most effective. The two main approaches: either embed information and activities in work practices, processes and procedures; or design specific programmes for workers based on their workplace and particular work issues. Pros and cons for each of these approaches and some examples follow.

The most sustainable way of supporting the development of capacity in workers within an organisation or workplace involves a review and revision of work practices, procedures and processes. The embedding of information and activities within everyday practice not only provides a long term, sustainable approach to developing capacity in workers but also overcomes the potential stigma (referred to above regarding resistance to learning activities and events) and can minimise the cost that can be associated with designing and delivering learning events such as workshops or programmes. There are some less attractive consequences of taking this approach though, including the slower impact it may have and the possibility of not reaching all workers or at least not consistently. Tailored programmes designed to support the development of capacity in groups of workers has the advantage of being very targeted and so reduces these shortcomings.

Some examples of the types of work practices and procedures that might apply more generally to organisations of any size and type that can be introduced or modified to incorporate information and activities that can support the development of capacity in workers include:

- orientation and induction for new staff;
- performance management systems;
- promotion and salary review procedures.

The types of information and activities that would support workers' capacity development would focus on: the organisation's history, values, business intent, strategic goals, business context (for example, its place in the market, profession, service or industry, etc.), current pressures or drivers and so on; the expectations of the worker in their position; how the expectations are set and reviewed and why; recognition and rewarding workers' contributions; self-assessment and analysis of performance and career development; and how the workers' position/division/area in the organisation contributes to the organisation achieving its goals. Other activities might focus on building relationships between workers, divisions or areas of work in the organisation and the value of this.

More specific practices relating to the type of work undertaken can also incorporate and enforce capacity-development in workers where self-awareness, appreciation and understanding of the working environment and the inter-dependencies between work areas/divisions are highlighted and explored.

Some groups of workers, however, might need or benefit more quickly from a more targeted approach, for example a structured programme to support the development of capacity in workers. The remainder of this section focuses on how capacity might be developed in workers through a tailor designed workplace-based programme.

Designing programmes for the development of capacity in workers

Particularly in relation to current workers, but not excluding newcomers, developing capacity in workers might begin with a programme that acts as a catalyst for workers to begin their own personal journey of self-awareness and capacity-development in their work: a tailored capacity-development programme. And although such programmes in different organisations and/or for different groups of workers will differ, since they need to be designed for a specific situation at a particular time, certain key elements are likely to be common. This section outlines these key elements and provides some broad suggestions for designing for capacity-development and thus lifelong learning at work.

When designing for the development of capacity in workers, what is required is an appreciation of the intersection of complex systems and the consequences, directing the focus for designing for workplace learning to the individual – an 'interdependent individual' in a workplace. For workers, this is likely to be a process taken on by the organisation, at its cost, for a group of workers with similar duties and responsibilities within the organisation. The programme designer needs to enable the individual workers in this group then to be exposed to, and be able to deal with, a deeper understanding of themselves and their environment. In addition, and perhaps most significantly, designing a programme for capacity-development must also create an awareness of, and develop an ability to deal with, how the workers and their environments interact and impact on each other, that is, an awareness and understanding of self *within* their environment.

This approach necessitates a move away from focussing on a narrow conception of learning, training, and skills and the expectation that these will have a direct impact on performance, towards the concept of capacity and an approach that will attempt to develop and increase capacity. And so this approach can be described as holistic (see above). It is holistic in that it recognises the person as a whole, a whole person with capacities that can be expanded and developed. And part of being that whole person necessarily involves their existence within a range of environments – environments in which this person will use, adapt, and continue to develop their capacities, and ultimately their selfhood. Furthermore, the holistic approach, underpinned by complexity theory, acknowledges that any interaction, personal development, or growth will be self-organising.

The shift in approach to designing for learning at and for work required, as a result of an holistic approach to learning, is essentially about moving from a 'needs analysis' approach, where it is anticipated that individual workers can easily be categorised and grouped by a programme designer such that optimum learning strategies can be used to assist them, to a 'self-awareness/self-analysis' approach. The latter approach, accepts that every individual is different and that in many cases individual will not themselves have recognised this sufficiently to understand who they are, and how they are in their work environment, and why. Until this is established, change will be difficult at best, and haphazard if it occurs.

That is, self-realisation (knowing who you are and why you are that way) is the key to developing (growing), adapting and changing. But this can only be achieved by the individual. This is especially so in the case of informal learning, since the 'control of learning rests primarily in the hands of the learner' (Marsick and Watkins, 1991: 25). Only the individual worker will be able to 'know thyself': who s/he is, and who s/he becomes as a result of a self-organising process, influenced by their history and their current environments (that is, their perception and understanding of those environments based on their mental models, both individual and shared). This requires recognition of one's strengths and weaknesses, and the ability to learn to live with them. The literature on learning explores related ideas in the context of learning or knowing how to learn. For example, Burns (2002: 256) describes learning to learn as meaning

> that adults possess a self-conscious awareness of how it is they come to know what they know; an awareness of the reasoning, assumptions, evidence and justifications that underlie our beliefs that something is true.

Furthermore, the capacity-development programme designer must enable improvement and positive outcomes for an organisation through the opportunity for, and encouragement of, the alignment of an individual worker's goals, with their employer's goals (based on the recognition of the self-organising, self-preserving nature of people, as discussed above). That is, information and discussion regarding organisational goals will need to be included in a capacity-building programme to provide context for the specific type of work the participants are engaged in within the organisation. And the discussion during the programme will need to centre on the participants' role in the organisation, how they contribute to organisational goals, the skills and knowledge they require and how they can maintain currency in them. This intertwining of worker and organisation better recognises the relationality between the two; it enables greater awareness and ultimately encourages workers to self-organise in a way that satisfies the employer's goals.

There are various facilitation tools that can be used, the choice of which will depend on the circumstances. The programme designer will need to understand the programme participants' role in the organisation and their environment and design for capacity-development accordingly. For example, the programme designer will require an appreciation of the qualifications (if any) required of the participants, the organisational policies and practices relevant to them, their profession, industry, relevant laws and regulations, impact of the economy, and so on. Resource and time constraints may also play a part in these decisions, as such a programme will typically require some time away from productive activities.

In particular, it is anticipated that learning strategies will be used that allow learners to understand their learning styles, and how they differ from others' learning preferences; increase their awareness of self, for example using reflective activities such as keeping learning journals; understand the importance of learning for and at work; and enable application of what is learned. These strategies (and their value) are predominantly encapsulated in the literature on learning how to learn, also referred to as learning skills (for example, Smith, 1982; Hautamäki et al., 2002), self-directedness (for example, Zimmerman, 1998), and identity (for example, Solomon, 2003).

As noted above, the rich literature on learning skills, however, is currently disconnected from the whole picture of workplace leaning. In many ways, learning and other 'generic' skills, are still considered as 'add-ons', that can be learnt through participation in isolated 'generic'-type training, rather than integrated and situational elements of a worker's abilities. And although there is work on contextual issues and transferability of skills more recently in the literature, there is a lack of explicit discussion of the emergent and relational or interdependent characteristics of these learning and related skills.

To avoid this trap, developing skills with 'situational understanding' that is relational (Hager and Beckett, 1995; Hinchliffe, 2002) is required. To achieve this, the designer of a programme to support the development of capacity in workers will embed the learning skills activities and discussions within the work related programme content, that is, they will be contextual and situated. The programme designer must understand that: '[i]t is not just that each person learns in a context, rather, each person is a reciprocal part of the context, and vice versa' (Hodkinson et al., 2004: 7). People are both subject to, and subjects of, their circumstances. Role plays around relevant work situations that require the use of learning skills, including communication and open-mindedness towards others and different approaches (to work), for example, may be employed to help with this interwoven contextualisation of skills. And where possible, simulated work activities and other work-based learning strategies could be employed. The 'contextualised' (Perkins and Salomon, 1989), holistic approach to skills is essential, particularly in addressing non-routine tasks at work, which are increasingly common in the current working environment (Hager et al., 2007).

Organisational goals and history will be foundational in this contextualisation. In order to work towards a greater alignment between the worker and the employer's goals, not only must both parties' goals be apparent to the worker, but the worker also needs to recognise their significance and the potential gains from the alignment, through self-analysis. Further, they need to be capable of employing the self-analysing techniques regularly for and at work, in order to continually improve, adapt and grow as the work environment and they themselves change.

The holistic approach espoused causes the alignment of the worker and their environment through the coverage of issues across all aspects of learning (behavioural, emotional, cultural and social). The end result, in the form of a capacity-development programme, will not be a flat, disjointed number of activities directly correlating to a number of relevant items (according to a programme designer). The programme development will be dynamic and cause the issues to be covered in the programme to be drawn together and layered. Gathering information for a programme will be an iterative, complex process. There will be links between individual and organisational issues, and how the details of these unfold for the programme designer may impact on how they are addressed. The integration of the issues within the strategies employed in the resulting programme will begin to demonstrate the ways in which they can be aligned.

This alignment and integration of individual, environment and the learning outcome is one of the most important aspects of the programme for capacity-development as the individual worker needs to know what the organisational goals are, and how to align themselves with them, if they are to perform well – so simultaneous development of an individual's skills, in the context of work undertaken, and an understanding of the overall purposes of the organisation and reasons for the choice of methods used in achieving them is paramount. If the worker's and the organisation's goals cannot be aligned, there will be resistance, less than optimal performance, and dissatisfaction for both the worker and the employer.

Additionally, in accordance with an holistic, relational approach to learning, it must also be acknowledged that the self is not static, and thus the self-awareness and development must be continual. As a result, the design for learning cannot simply aim for a one-off 'enlightenment' event or a one-off 'alignment' of worker and employer goals. It must aim to skill workers sufficiently to regularly and naturally continually reflect, and analyse their own situation, and how that relates to their workplace. Indeed a programme of this kind would be one small aspect of the capacity-development an organisation should afford workers. Both in the design and delivery of a capacity-development programme, through participation in it and as a result of the workers' growth and shift in awareness after it, many paths for embedding opportunities for capacity-development in work practices will emerge or become apparent. The option to review and revise policy and systems and supporting procedures and thus practices, must be available to honour the holistic, relational approach to enhance and support the capacity-development. Organisations must be able to shift in their ways and adapt as workers develop, or in some cases in order for workers to develop.

As indicated above some organisations may choose to or be able to effectively encourage and support capacity-development through the design and implementation of policies, systems, procedures and ultimately work practices alone rather than a specially designed programme – this is more likely the case in smaller organisations or workplaces. And in some cases, after successful capacity-development programmes over a period of time, organisations may be able to replace them with appropriate policies, systems, procedures and work practices that support capacity-development. However, based on the limited experience within organisations now offering forms of capacity-development programmes, it is suggested that a combination of both a tailored programme and supporting policies, systems, procedures and the like, will result in the greatest capacity amongst workers and the most sustained and effective (or lifelong) learning.

Conclusion

The holistic approach to learning, presented in this chapter, as individualistically embodied, organic, and holistic is based on the premise that people are, and exist within, complex systems. On this basis it is argued that there is not a direct link or causality between learning and performance. Instead, it is shown that individuals set their own goals (based on an internal need for self-realisation) and operate or *act* in a self-organising way to achieve them. Furthermore, this approach suggests that it is the worker and their perceptions, based on who they are through their history, experiences and situations or context that is central to their being and *becoming*.

This analysis then reveals the importance of understanding oneself in order to achieve further and continual growth through learning, particularly for workers. The critical learning that must take place then, it is concluded, must be about oneself and how one can develop or grow to meet the challenges of one's (and hopefully, simultaneously, one's employer's) goals. I describe this process as capacity-development. So the link between learning and development is made, such that this learning about oneself (self-wareness) provides greater capacity for development, but equally capacity-development 'constitutes' *learning* based in actions and experiences. Thus, capacity-development is a precondition to lifelong learning.

Capacity-development, for ongoing and sustained learning, premised on a holistic model of learning, acknowledges the importance of all the dimensions of learning, and the relationality between them. In practice, workers can be encouraged and supported in developing capacity by focusing on enabling the learner (worker) to improve on their self-awareness: an understanding of who they are, how they learn, what motivates them, and why they do what they do in the context of work. Furthermore, attention should be drawn to not only the learners' awareness of themselves, but also to their working environment (on various levels), and they should be encouraged to begin to rationalise how the two function together – and if they do not function well together, how the differences can be decreased or removed. In sum, it is asserted that when a worker's capacity is increased, there is a greater chance their performance (in terms of meeting organisational goals) will too. This might occur within a programme where essentially the aim will be to align individual workers' goals and their employer organisations through this process of increasing awareness of self and one's environment – influencing 'will-fullness' in workers' agency, based on 'adequate knowledge' (Beckett and McManus, 2006).

The development may take time and will manifest itself differently in each worker. Some workers will feel 'enlightened'; others will be reluctant to admit any change even if they know something intangible, such as their perspective, has changed or that they have begun to question and think about their actions; and others may leave with barriers to learning firmly in place; there is no saying when or if this will change (McManus, 2006). Based on the understanding of the non-linear nature of complex systems related to organisations and individuals presented in this chapter, however, it is essential that it is understood that there is no claim that workers will automatically or instantaneously improve their learning and capacity or show signs of capacity-development as a result of engaging in work practices, activities or events designed to support the development of capacity on workers.

On the positive side, even though improvement is not guaranteed, based on the foregoing analysis, improvement will not occur in a sustained fashion unless workers have opportunity: that is, achieve the pre-condition for lifelong learning. And it may be, for example, through a successful capacity-development programme that draws on and highlights the interrelated nature of the worker and the organisation (their context) in an holistic way, as described above, that capacity can be developed. It is through the development of capacity in workers that they become more aware of themselves *within* their workplace, sufficiently well (that is, they understand the rationale) to know how to best apply their skills to achieve self-preservation and hopefully also perform more efficiently and effectively at work.

References

Ashton, D. and Sung, J. (2002), *Supporting Workplace Learning for High Performance Working*, Geneva: International Labor Office.

Baets, W. (1998), *Organisational Learning and Knowledge Technologies in a Dynamic Environment*, Dordrecht: Kluwer Academic Publishers.

Baets, W. (2006), *Complexity, Learning and Organisations: A quantum interpretation of business*, New York: Routledge.

Beckett, D. (2006), 'A useful theory of agency at work', paper presented at the 10th

International Network of Philosophers of Education Biennial Conference, University of Malta, 3–6 August.

Beckett, D. and Hager, P. (2002), *Life, Work and Learning: Practice in postmodernity*, London: Routledge.

Beckett, D. and McManus, J. (2006), 'Spinoza, selfhood and the Australian Taxation Office: "Where there's a will . . . there's a reason"', paper presented at Philosophy of Education Society of Australasia, University of Sydney, 23–26 November.

Billett, S. and Pavlova, M. (2005), 'Learning through working life: Self and individuals' agentic action', *International Journal of Lifelong Education*, 24:3, pp. 195–211.

Boud, D. (2003), 'Combining work and learning: The disturbing challenge of practice', keynote address to the International Conference on Experimental-Community-Workbased: Researching Learning Outside the Academy, Glasgow, 27–29 June.

Burns, R. (2002), *The Adult Learner at Work*, Sydney: Allen & Unwin.

Capra, F. (1996), *The Web of Life: A new scientific understanding of living systems*, New York: Anchor.

Derry, J. (2004), 'The unity of intellect and will: Vygotsky and Spinoza', *Educational Review*, 56:2, pp. 113–120.

Dewey, J. (1896), 'The reflex arc concept in psychology', *Psychological Review*, 3, pp. 357–370.

Eade, D. (1997), *Capacity Building: An approach to people centered development*, Oxford: Oxfam.

Ericsson, K. (2003), 'The search for general abilities and basic capacities', in Sternberg, R. and Grigorenko, E. (eds), *The Psychology of Abilities, Competencies and Expertise*, Cambridge: Cambridge University Press, pp. 93–125.

Garvin, D. (2000), *Learning in Action: A guide to putting the learning organisation to work*, Boston: Harvard Business School Press.

Hager, P. and Beckett, D. (1995), 'Philosophical underpinnings of the integrated conception of competence', *Educational Philosophy and Theory*, 27:1, pp. 1–24.

Hager, P. and Halliday, J. (2006), *Recovering Informal Learning: Wisdom, judgement and community*, Dordrecht: Springer.

Hager, P., Johnsson, M. and Halliday, J. (2007), 'Examining context in collective learning: A cross-case analysis' paper presented at the 5th International Conference on Researching Work and Learning, University of Cape Town, South Africa, 2–5 December.

Harrison, M. (1994), *Diagnosing Organizations: Models, methods and processes*, Thousand Oaks, CA: Sage Publications.

Hautamäki, J., Arinen, P., Eronen, S., Hautamäki, A., Kupiainen, S., Lindblom, B., Niemivirta, M., Pakaslahti, L., Rantanen, P. and Scheinin, P. (2002), *Assessing Learning-to-Learn: A framework*, Helsinki: Helsinki University Printing House.

Hinchliffe, G. (2002), 'Situating skills', *Journal of Philosophy of Education*, 36:2, pp. 187–205.

Hodkinson, P. (2005), 'Theoretical constructions of vocational learning: Troubling dualisms and problems of scale', paper presented at the 6th International Conference of the Journal of Vocational Education and Training, 13–15 July.

Hodkinson, P., Hodkinson, H., Evans, K., Kersh, N., Fuller, A., Unwin, L. and Senker, P. (2004), 'The significance of individual biography in workplace learning', *Studies in Education of Adults*, 36:1, pp. 6–24.

Holland, J. (1995), *Hidden Order: How adaptation builds complexity*, Cambridge, MA: Perseus Books.

Horn, J. and Wilburn, D. (2005), 'The embodiment of learning', *Educational Philosophy and Theory*, 37:5, pp. 745–759.

Lusthaus, C., Anderson, G. and Murphy, E. (1995), *Institutional Assessment: A framework for strengthening organizational capacity for IDRC's research partners*, Ottawa: International Development Research Center.

McManus, J. (forthcoming), 'Developing capacity for lifelong learning', *International Journal of Lifelong Education*.

McManus, J. (2006), 'Enhancing tax auditors' capability: tackling tax non-compliance head on', in McKerchar, M. and Walpole, M. (eds), *Further Global Challenges in Tax Administration*, Birmingham: Fiscal Publications, pp. 227–242.

Marsick, V. and Watkins, K. (1991), *Informal and Incidental Learning in the Workplace*, London: Routledge.

Maturana, H. and Varela, F. (1998), *The Tree of Knowledge: The biological roots of human understanding* (revised edn; original 1987), Boston: Shambhala Publications.

Maturana, H. and Varela, F. (1980), *Autopoiesis and Cognition: The realization of the living*, London: D. Reidel Publishing Company.

Morgan, P. (1997), 'The design and use of capacity development indicators', paper prepared for the Political and Social Policies Division, Policy Branch, Canadian International Development Agency (CIDA). Hull: CIDA.

O'Loughlin, M. (2006), *Embodiment and Education: Exploring creatural existence*, Dordrecht: Springer.

Passmore, J. (1980), *The Philosophy of Teaching*, London: Duckworth.

Perkins, David and Salomon, Gavriel (1989), 'Are cognitive skills context bound?', *Educational Researcher*, 18:1, pp. 16–25.

Picciotto, R. and Wiesner, E. (eds) (1998), *Evaluation and Development: The institutional dimension*, New Brunswick, NJ: Transaction Publishers.

Prigogine, I. (1997), *The End of Certainty*, New York: Free Press.

Senge, Peter (1990), *The Fifth Discipline: The art & practice of the learning organization*, Sydney: Random House.

Smith, R. (1982), *Learning How to Learn: Applied theory for adults*, Cambridge, New York: Adult Education Company.

Solomon, N. (2003), 'Changing pedagogy: The new learner-worker', OVAL Research Working Paper 03–20, The Australian Centre for Organisational, Vocational and Adult Learning, Sydney.

Spinoza, B. [*c*. 1675] (1949), in James Gutmann (ed.), *Ethics*, New York: Hafner Publishing Company (Hafner Library of Classics).

Stacey, R. (2003), 'Learning as an activity of interdependent people', *Learning Organization*, 10:6, pp. 325–331.

Stacey, R. (1996), *Complexity and Creativity in Organisations*, San Francisco: Berrett-Koelher Publications.

Staron, M., Jasinski, M. and Weatherley, R. (2006), *Life Based Learning: A strength based approach for capability development in vocational and technical education*, Australian Department of Education Science and Training.

United Nations Development Program (UNDP) (1998), 'Capacity assessment and development in a systems and strategic management context, Management Development and Governance Division', Technical Advisory Paper No. 3, New York: UNDP.

UNESCO (1972), *Learning to Be: The world of education today and tomorrow*, Paris: UNESCO Publications (Faure Report).

UNESCO (1996), *Learning: The treasure within*, Paris: UNESCO Publications (Delores Report).

Vygotsky, L. (1997), *The Collected Works of L. S. Vygotsky, Volume 4: The history and development of higher mental functions* (M. Hall, trans.; R. Reiber, ed.), New York: Plenum Press.

Waldrop, M. (1992), *Complexity: The emerging science at the edge of order and chaos*, New York: Simon & Schuster.

Wheatley, M. (2006), *Leadership and the New Science: Discovering order in a chaotic world*, San Francisco: Berrett-Koehler.

Zimmerman, B. (1998), 'Developing self-fulfilling cycles of academic regulation: An analysis of exemplary instructional models', in Schunk, D. and Zimmerman, B. (eds) *Self-regulated learning: From teaching to self-reflective practice*, New York: Guilford, pp. 1–19.

Part III: Conclusions

Sue Jackson

The chapters in the final Part of this book have continued to engage with developing greater understandings of innovative practices in lifelong learning, that move beyond the current global focus on skills based learning and training, to broader conceptualisations. Although the current context of neo-liberal discourses and policies concentrate on lifelong learning for work and the economic participation in the workplace of individuals, the chapter authors have shown how new communities of practice may develop in the work arena, in more diverse workplace terrains. Like the preceding chapters, the chapters in Part III has been concerned with issues of diversity, participation and non-participation, of power and resistances, and of challenges to hierarchical and dominant constructions of knowledge, this time through an exploration of work-based learning and learning through work.

The next chapter – the final one of the book – moves to draw some conclusions about innovations in lifelong learning.

Conclusions

So where are the innovations in lifelong learning?

Sue Jackson

Introduction

As I write this conclusion (May 2010), the general election in the United Kingdom has come and gone with no decisive result and a resultant coalition government concerned about the global financial situation; the financial downturn in Europe has left Greece in economic and social turmoil and created uncertainty for the euro; many countries across the world are showing high levels of political instability; and 2010 is likely to see 'increasing risks of non-payment of sovereign debt and rising political interference as a result of the growing fallout from the economic crisis' (Lloyds, 2010). The collapse of Lehman Brothers in the United States in September 2008 seems to have triggered, or at least exacerbated, a global recession, which has been named by some as the Great Depression (see e.g. Douglas, 2010).

If ever there was a demonstration of globalisation and its impact, this must be it. Ripples become waves; waves wax and wane; for some bringing catastrophic consequences, and for others a mere wetting of the toes. The effects of a global recession are not uniform, with differing consequences for nations and for their peoples. The poorest are hit hardest: the economically and socially deprived, migrants and asylum seekers, women and children, the unemployed. There are estimates that by the end of 2010 more than 57 million people will be unemployed in OECD (Organisation for Economic Co-operation and Development) countries alone (Fix et al., 2009). And if the effects are not uniform, then neither are the solutions to lessen the impact of economic crises. For some it is a time to impose severe and swingeing budget cuts, including to education; for others it is a time to recognise that an educated population can aid economic and social recovery.

Despite differing positions about the role of education and the management of educational institutions within nation states, in a globalised world, education itself has become globalised. In part this is a result of mass movements of peoples and the subsequent spread of globalised discourses (see Spring, 2009). Discourses, of course, are not neutral, and global discourses are dominated by the worldviews of primary groups. They are historically, socially and culturally defined ways of representing the world, specific ways of defining and producing knowledge, as though the representations and the definitions are 'truth'. The predominant flow of ideas comes from those countries with greater economic and social power, thus reinforcing and re-creating dominant ideologies.

Discourses have spread across the developed world about the role of education in enabling nation states to play a leading role in a globalised knowledge economy, There are global discourses about neo-liberalism; about human, social and other capitals; and about lifelong learning. Critical discussions of international perspectives on innovations in lifelong learning are set against such backdrops. In this concluding chapter, I will consider some of these perspectives by outlining the impact on lifelong learning of the global discourses of neo-liberalism and the knowledge economy, and returning to themes raised in the introductory chapter and throughout this book to summarise some transformative practices and innovations in lifelong learning, including cultural diversity, transformation and lifelong learning as a political act.

Critical perspectives I: neo-liberalism and global knowledge economies

The World Bank has frequently argued that lifelong learning *is* education for the knowledge economy (World Bank, 2003: xiii). Globalisation, and the increasing emphasis on global knowledge economies, has undoubtedly been a consistent driver in more recent developments of lifelong learning:

> The global knowledge economy is transforming the demands of the labor market throughout the world. It is also placing new demands on citizens, who need more skills and knowledge to be able to function in their day-to-day lives. Equipping people to deal with these demands requires a new model of education and training, a model of lifelong learning . . . Lifelong learning is crucial to preparing workers to compete in the global economy. But it is important for other reasons as well. By improving people's ability to function as members of their communities, education and training increase social cohesion, reduce crime, and improve income distribution. (World Bank, 2003: xvii)

Nevertheless, education is inadequate in most developing countries (World Bank, 2003: 7) and knowledge economies are differently experienced across the world:

> Developing countries and countries with transition economies risk being further marginalized in a competitive global knowledge economy because their education and training systems are not equipping learners with the skills they need.
>
> (World Bank, 2003: xvii)

Yet whatever the experience, whether there are stable, additional or decreasing funds in the education pot, lifelong learning has been viewed as an answer – at least in part – to global problems of recession. Policies across much of the world continue to emphasise a skills agenda linked to the economy, with individuals expected to make the most of the policy developments which have led to a growth in vocational education and training, to benefit themselves, their nation states and the global economy. As Yvonne Hillier shows (Chapter 8), there are some activities that equate to learning in and for participation in a knowledge economy, and others that do not, and individuals are expected to make considered and 'proper' choices about such participation. Patricia A. Gouthro argues (Chapter 5) that although structural conditions impact on what may be perceived as individual choice, 'increasingly our educational contexts are shaped by the discourses of neoliberalism that emphasise individualism, competition, and the value of the market place'.

Neo-liberalism emphasises a decreasing role for governments and states in determining economic (and therefore social) policies, emphasising instead the role of individual autonomy and responsibility. Their role has become one of organising the conditions by which individuals and educational institutions can ensure that they have the capacities to respond to the changing needs of employers, and thereby secure individuals' personal economic positions, and the prosperity of the nation (Brown and Lauder, 2001). Neo-liberalism's discourses of markets, individual autonomy and choice mask strucutural and discursive inequalities of, for example, gender, social class, 'race', sexuality and more, and rendered the perceptions of 'free and individual choice' mere illusion.

Freire describes neo-liberalism as the transference of knowledge for industrial productivity (Freire, 2004: 77). Education has come to be about technical knowledge, training learners in skills that enable them to adapt to economic globalisation, with neo-liberal constructions of individual and forever flexible worker/learners leaving little space for innovations in lifelong learning. Nevertheless, Gemma Piercy (Chapter 9) argues that although the (re-)emergence of neo-liberalism has challenged emancipatory visions, such visions can be resilient against neo-liberal dominant ideologies of labour force training. Indeed, whilst learners and teachers may struggle with dominant discourses of neo-liberalism, governments struggle with the competing challenges of the imperatives of individualised learning within neo-liberalism, learner and the global learner citizen (Arnot, 2009).

Discourses of education for global citizenship and debates about social inclusion, cohesion and participation litter debates about lifelong learning. Although the World Bank (2003) calls for increased social, but especially human, capital in order for the global knowledge economy to develop, Barry Golding (Chapter 4) is critical of any focus on education for human capital, which is limited to economics but not to other benefits. Like Golding, Jan Etienne and Sue Jackson (Chapter 3) demonstrate ways in which social capital and social networks develop for older people and marginalised groups outside workplace settings. However, Lisa Baumgartner and Juanita Johnson-Bailey (Chapter 6) show that the transmission of cultural capital of privileged norms and knowledges further oppress and reproduce inequalities and social capital can exclude as well as include. It may be helpful to move from a focus on human, social or cultural capital to the development of relational capital (Jackson, 2010), the capital that is acquired from the development of a relational understanding of different realities, of the relationship between things, of different ways of knowing and experiencing sometimes competing worlds, which can lead to innovative practices.

Critical perspectives 2: innovations in lifelong learning

Cultural diversity and intersected identities

In order for lifelong learning to be innovative, as several contributors to this book argue, it needs to encompass social equity and justice through enhancing engagement with cultural diversity. In Chapter 1, for example, Shibao Guo and Zenobia Jamal show how nurturing cultural diversity can enhance learning and teaching, with environments that support cultural diversity contributing towards an empowering environment for all learners. There is, they say, a need to understand and challenge the impact of hierarchies of power and privilege, and the impact of multiple oppressions on marginalised groups.

Too much of what is 'known' about lifelong learning, dominating its discourses, comes from the hierarchical valuing of Western thought (see Mejai B. M. Avoseh, Chapter 2) yet, as Gemma Piercy (Chapter 9) argues, lifelong learning needs to take account of the increasingly diverse and multi-cultural citizenry with whom and for whom it operates. What is needed is greater engagement with a critical multiculturalism, which like critical race theory for example (see e.g. Dixson and Rousseau, 2007) both recognises and critiques discourses of power and power relations, including the power of definitions of 'citizen'.

As can be seen in several of the chapters, but perhaps especially in Part I, identities are constructed and negotiated through such definitions, and through the intersections of gender, race, age, class and more. Mary V. Alfred (Chapter 11) shows how cultures, identities and ethnicities intersect to inform experiences of learning in complex ways, informed through diasporan experiences. As Stuart Hall (2000) states:

> Precisely because identities are constructed within, not outside, discourse, we need to understand them as produced in specific historical and institutional sites within specific discursive formations and practices, by specific enunciative strategies. Moreover, they emerge within the play of specific modulations of power, and thus are more the product of the marking of difference and exclusion . . . Above all . . . identities are constructed through, not outside, difference.
>
> (Hall, 2000: 17)

The multiple lenses of intersected identities, understood through cultural diversity, are essential to further innovations in lifelong learning, resisting the exclusionary discourses of 'difference'. In Chapter 11, Mary V. Alfred demonstrates the ways in which women and other minority groups use resilience and agency through a complex entwining of identities, desires, multiple knowledges and cultural communities of practices, arguing for a need for spaces to be opened where identities can be negotiated and reconceptualised.

Contestations and transformations

Baumgartner and Johnson-Bailey (Chapter 6) argue that resistances to the status quo must be deliberate in the efforts to make transformative changes. Resistances are

> counter-hegemonic practices that operate at the micro level of everyday experience and attempt either consciously or unconsciously to challenge and subvert hegemonic regimes of truth and privileged discourses and identities.
>
> (Burke and Jackson, 2007: 140)

They should be understood as grounded within relations of inequalities. They are not necessarily, or even usually, 'large and dramatic acts; they are often subtle and implicit and take place in everyday routine practices' (Burke and Jackson, 2007: 142).

Some of those small acts of contestations and resistances can be seen through otherwise marginalised and intersected identities, including gender, race and age (see for example Chapters 3, 4, 6, 7 and 11), as well as in the classroom (Chapters 7 and 8), beyond the classroom (Chapters 3 and 4), through the politics of participation (Chapters 5 and 9), and through re-membering histories, communities (Chapter 2) and the creativity of earlier practitioners (Chapter 8).

Lifelong learning should be understood, practiced and experienced as 'contested space', and learning developed through deliberative and transformative spaces. Some of these spaces come about through a valuing of the importance of life experiences. As Patricia A. Gouthro (Chapter 5) argues, working with life experiences is as important as imparting subject knowledge, including the enhanced understandings which can develop through working with the life experiences of marginalised and/or minority groups. Yvonne Hillier (Chapter 8) shows how long traditions of community writing foster innovative practices, developed through different lenses and different contexts. She argues that the transformative nature of learner centred approaches can act as an agent for change. Jon Talbot (Chapter 10) demonstrates the complexity and variability of the balance of power between participants in lifelong learning, including learners, teachers and employers, and argues that the current balance of that power needs to be explicitly contested. Keith Percy and Fiona Frank (Chapter 7) extend this to outline contestations and transformations that come about when the distinction between those who teach and those who learn are blurred, turning lifelong learning into a political act.

Lifelong learning as a political act

In this book we have seen many examples of and arguments for innovations in lifelong learning. However, Gemma Piercy (Chapter 9) argues that innovations in lifelong learning must be supported by governments for them to become real and embedded and, as Frank and Percy (Chapter 7) remind us, we should not forget the realpolitik of the moment. Lifelong learning does not always recognise people's non-linear learning trajectories (see for example Chapters 3, 4 and 5), and Baumgartner and Johnson-Bailey (Chapter 6) clearly demonstrate how racism and white privilege preserve the status quo. However, as the contributors to this volume have shown, innovations in lifelong learning are occurring across nations and across differing contexts of learning, sometimes unexpectedly, often working against the grain of discourses of neo-liberalism and global knowledge economies.

Shibao Guo and Zenobia Jamal (Chapter 1) call for the need to work against the grain of these discourses in developing lifelong learning, arguing that education is always contested, and educators cannot remain neutral. Jacqueline McManus (Chapter 12) calls for holistic approaches to lifelong learning that show the complexities of non-linearity and inter-relatedness. She calls for a move away from a focus on lifelong learning embedded in 'skills' although, as Hillier (Chapter 8) demonstrates, learning that is so often described, and described disparagingly as 'basic skills' can be both political and transformational.

In contributing to this book – in highlighting innovations in lifelong learning and exploring critical perspectives on diversity, participation and vocational learning – the chapter authors have been showing their own acts of resistances, demonstrating how innovative lifelong learning can be a political act. As bell hooks has so powerfully shown

> true speaking is not solely an expression of creative power; it is an act of resistance, a political gesture that challenges politics of domination that would render us nameless and voiceless. As such, it is a courageous act.
>
> (hooks, 1989: 8)

Such innovations, in such political times, are courageous. At the risk of being repetitive, I return in these conclusions to my opening words at the start of this book:

> It is the best of times, it is the worst of times; it is the age of wisdom, it is the age of foolishness; it is the epoch of belief, it is the epoch of incredulity; it is the season of light, it is the season of darkness, it is the spring of hope; we have everything before us, we have nothing before us; we are all going directly to Heaven, we are all going the other way. It is an age where, more than ever, the innovative policies and practices in lifelong learning described, experienced and lived by the contributors of this book can prevent our

learners and ourselves from 'going the other way' and bring about those springs of hope.

References

Arnot, M. (2009) *Educating the Gendered Citizen: Sociological engagements with national and global agendas*, London: Routledge.

Brown, P., and Lauder, H., (2001) *Capitalism and Social Progress: The future of society in a global economy*, Basingstoke: Palgrave.

Burke, P. and Jackson, S. (2007) *Reconceputalising Lifelong Learning: Feminist interventions*, London: Routledge.

Dixson, A. D. and Rousseau, C. (2007) *Critical Race Theory in Education: All God's children got a song*, New York: Routledge.

Douglas, J. A. (2010) 'Higher education budgets and the global recession: tracking varied national responses and their consequences', Research & Occasional Paper Series: CSHE.4.10, Berkeley, CA: University of California.

Fix, M., Papademetriou, G., Batalova, J., Terrazas, A., Yi-Ying Lin, S. and Michelle, M. (2009) *Migration and the Global Recession*, London: Migration Policy Institute.

Freire, P. (2004) *Pedagogy of Indignation*, Boulder, CO: Paradigm.

Hall, S. (2000) 'Who needs "identity"?', in du Gay, P., Evans, J. and Redman P. (eds), *Identity: A reader*: London: Sage.

hooks, b. (1989) *Talking Back: Thinking feminist, thinking black*, Toronto: Between the Lines.

Jackson, S. (2010) 'Learning through social spaces: migrant women and lifelong learning in post-colonial London', *International Journal of Lifelong Education* – Special issue: 'Lifelong Education in the Age of Transnational Migration', 29:2, pp. 237–254.

Lloyds Newscentre (2010) 'Global recession set to cause political instability in 2010', http://www.lloyds.com/News_Centre/Features_from_Lloyds/News_and_features_2009/360/Global_recession_set_to_cause_political_instability_in+2010.htm, accessed May 7 2010.

Spring, J. (2009) *Globalisation of Education*, New York: Routledge.

World Bank (2003) *Lifelong Learning in the Global Knowledge Economy: Challenges for developing countries*, Washington DC: World Bank.

Index

CPSIA information can be obtained at www.ICGtesting.com
Printed in the USA
LVOW101925070612

285166LV00001B/39/P